Also by George Thayer

THE BRITISH POLITICAL FRINGE
THE FARTHER SHORES OF POLITICS
THE WAR BUSINESS

Who Shakes the Money Tree?

AMERICAN CAMPAIGN
FINANCING PRACTICES
FROM 1789
TO THE PRESENT

by George Thayer

SIMON AND SCHUSTER
NEW YORK

SBN 671-21601-5
Library of Congress Catalog Card Number: 73-11830
Designed by Irving Perkins
Manufactured in the United States of America
by American Book–Stratford Press, Inc., New York, N.Y.

1   2   3   4   5   6   7   8   9   10

To
CAROL

Contents

Foreword

This is a book about the way we have raised and spent money in our political elections from 1789 to the present, with particular emphasis on developments since 1945. Throughout the book I have concentrated on Presidential, House, Senate and certain gubernatorial and mayoralty races, because it is most often these campaigns where relatively large amounts of money must be raised and spent, and where most of the difficulties and inequities exist. On occasion, however, I have strayed from these confines to comment upon less expensive state and local elections in order to put the entire subject into perspective.

The purpose of the book is not only to show who gives the money, who raises it and how it is spent, but to examine why people give, what they expect to get and what they actually get, the techniques of raising and spending money, the nature of campaign financing law and our attitude toward it, and the changing styles in and reaction to American campaign financing practices. More than anything, this book attempts to show things as they really are and the way they might be, not the way they are often portrayed and envisioned by purists, some reformers and apologists, so that a better perspective and understanding can be gained in our search for more dynamic, flexible, open and vital campaign financing practices.

Since disclosure of campaign financing information is in a relatively primitive state, all contribution and expenditure figures in the book have been rounded off, except where I believe a more precise figure is significant and can be proved. To my knowledge the range of understatement of dollar figures exceeds the range of overstatement. Campaign financing statistics are also in a relatively primitive state and have been limited to the absolute minimum to tell the story. Although all the dollar figures and statistics have been taken or extrapolated from acceptable sources (see Sources of Information, page 303), they have been viewed with considerable skepticism by me and should be so treated by the reader.

During the course of my research I interviewed several hundred individuals, most of whom volunteered information on the understanding that the source would remain confidential. To those who put their trust in me I wish to express my thanks.

Equally as valuable has been the help I have received from other sources, and I wish to thank them here in detail. I would first like to thank Dr. Herbert E. Alexander of the Citizens' Research Foundation for all the information and advice he offered me. I am also indebted to Senator Frank Church, Congressman Richard Bolling and former Senator Joseph S. Clark for all the insights and anecdotes they offered. Also most helpful in the search for information were Mr. Walter Kravitz, Mr. Robert L. Tienken, Mr. Frederick H. Pauls, Mrs. Margaret M. Kellogg, and Ms. Jean Allen of the Library of Congress. I am further indebted to the *Boston Globe, Chicago Daily News, Christian Science Monitor, Congressional Quarterly, Flint* (Michigan) *Journal, Milwaukee Journal, Philadelphia Evening Bulletin, Sacramento Bee, San Francisco Examiner, San Jose Mercury-News, Washington Post, Washington Star-News* and the House Committee on Standards of Official Conduct for allowing me access to their clipping files.

I am also most grateful to Mr. William R. Bechtel, Mr. and Mrs. Christopher Bird, Mr. David Bird, Mr. Sam Black, Mrs. Joan Braden, Mr. Thomas H. Crawford, Miss Cecelia Crean, Mr. George Crile, Mr. Oliver Cromwell, Mr. Tom Dawson, Mr. Delmer Dunn, Mr. and Mrs. Richard Edgerton, Mr. Warren Eisenberg, Mr. Gerald Elliott, Miss Susan Garber, Mr. Sven Groennings, Mr. Ward Just, Mr. Wayne Kelly, Mr. Joe LaSala, Professor Murray B. Levin, Mr. Martin Lobel, Miss Mary MacInnes, Mr. Neil MacNeil, Mr. James McCulla, Mr. Frederick T. Merrill, Jr., the Honorable Robert M. Morgenthau, Mr. Willie Morris, Mr. Neil R. Pierce, Mr. Walter Pincus, Ms. Sally Quinn, Miss Mary

Ann Riegelman, Mr. Charles H. Rogovin, Miss Ellen Schlafly, Mr. Franklin R. Silbey, Mr. Sumner Slichter, Mr. Stephen Small, Mr. Judd Sommer, Mr. Mark Talisman, Mr. Robert Walters, Mr. John Robinson West, Jr., and Mr. Anthony M. Zane for all the information and help they gave me.

I would like to give particular thanks to Miss Linda Glisson, who helped me with the paperwork, and my wife, Carol, who helped edit the manuscript.

To those who offered many valuable comments and suggestions on parts of the manuscript, I offer my sincerest thanks.

G. T.

Washington, D.C.
July 15, 1973

PART ONE

THE
PAST

I

Big Money at Work

The 1960 election was the first in which the general public came to understand the power of money in politics. It was not the first in which money was an issue, nor was it the last; but it marked the beginning of widespread public concern over American campaign financing practices which was to culminate a decade later in the passage of reform legislation, the Federal Election Campaign Act of 1971.

The specific issue that sparked the concern in 1960 was Kennedy money. Former Ambassador Joseph P. Kennedy, according to informed friends of the family, put up a minimum of $1.5 million beginning in 1958 for his son John's preconvention campaign for the Presidency. It was far more money than any of his rivals had to spend.

Spending lavishly to promote the careers of his sons was a Joseph Kennedy hallmark and predates the 1960 campaign. Some sources estimate that he spent $250,000 in 1946 to put his son John in Congress, although a more realistic figure would probably be $50,000. Even so, none of the other nine candidates in the race could match this sum. When John Kennedy ran against Henry Cabot Lodge for the U.S. Senate in 1952, Old Joe once again underwrote most of the costs of the campaign. Estimates of the total cost vary from $350,000 to over $500,000.

One contribution the elder Kennedy also made in 1952 was to the reelection campaign of Senator Joseph McCarthy in Wisconsin. McCarthy was an old family friend who had hired Robert F. Kennedy as counsel for his Senate Permanent Investigations Subcommittee. On occasion he had also played softball at the Kennedy compound in Hyannisport. The purpose of the contribution, while never admitted, was to keep McCarthy away from Massachusetts. Old Joe knew that his friend's appearance in the state would hurt his son's chances.

Several years after the election it was revealed that Joseph Kennedy had lent $500,000 to John Fox, editor of the *Boston Post,* shortly after the paper had switched its endorsement from Lodge to Kennedy. The elder Kennedy's Manhattan office claimed the loan was strictly business—"a purely commercial transaction, for 60 days only, with full collateral and full interest"—but there are those who doubt it.

The family money fielded an impressive political machine in 1952, a hint of things to come. There were squads of technicians, specialists and managers; the nucleus of the "Irish Mafia" had been formed in Kenneth O'Donnell and Dave Powers; and there were old pros James Landis, John Ford and Kennedy cousin Joe Kane. The John C. Dowd Agency was virtually the Kennedy family's personal advertising and public relations organization. Most of the campaign funds were channeled through it for distribution as needed.

This organization fielded 286 Kennedy "secretaries," backed up by over 20,000 volunteers around the state. They collected over 262,000 signatures for Kennedy's nomination papers, and each signer received a thank-you letter—a mark of the kind of money spent by the family.

Most valuable of all was the family itself—the brothers, sisters, in-laws and cousins who worked zealously for no pay. Their value to the campaign was incalculable. One Lodge worker moaned, "I don't worry about Kennedy's money. It's that family of his. . . . They're all over the state."

The skills of this team, maintained exclusively with Kennedy funds, were further honed in the 1956 Democratic Convention during the futile fight for the Vice-Presidential nomination, and in 1958 when JFK swept to easy victory in his reelection campaign for the Senate.

By 1960 the Kennedy financial apparatus was in top form. Headquarters for the operation were located in the Kennedy-owned building at 230 Park Avenue in New York City. Virtually all money matters were under the control of the Ambassador himself.

The family set up the Ken-Air Corporation and purchased, for $300,000, a specially fitted Convair airplane which it then leased to the campaign for $1.75 a mile, or approximately $15,000 to $19,000 per month. John Kennedy pointed out, characteristically, that such an arrangement was cheaper than flying by commercial carrier. The family's equity in the plane, however, was not considered a campaign contribution and, indeed, was not reported as such.

In the Wisconsin primary, the first major test of the campaign, both Kennedy and Humphrey spent approximately $150,000. To the Kennedys it was not considered a particularly large sum, but to Humphrey it meant he left the state not only a loser but $17,000 in debt. Throughout the primary Humphrey complained bitterly of the difficulties of competing with "Jack's jack."

In the West Virginia primary four weeks later, Humphrey ended up spending only $25,000, most of the money coming from Stevensonian liberals. The money dried up because Old Joe passed the word around the political money circuit that if any Stevensonians continued to finance Humphrey, Stevenson would not even be considered for Secretary of State. Connecticut boss John Bailey told Senator William Benton, publisher of the *Encyclopaedia Britannica,* that if he continued to support Humphrey he would never hold another elective office in Connecticut as long as Bailey had anything to say. Benton took the hint and put away his checkbook.

How much the Kennedys spent in West Virginia has never been revealed, but it was a tidy sum from all indications. Joseph Kennedy's unofficial biographer, Richard J. Whalen, refers to Humphrey as being "flattened by the brute force of massed dollars." Humphrey himself complained further: "I don't have any daddy who can pay the bills for me. I can't afford to run around this state with a little black bag and a checkbook." Kennedy's television expenditures alone across West Virginia were $34,000, more than Humphrey's total expenditures in the state.

While Hubert Humphrey had been eliminated from consideration in the West Virginia primary, there were still other contenders for Kennedy to beat. Lyndon Johnson's campaign for the Democratic nomination centered on winning delegate votes. His brain trust, made up of old guard liberals—Dean Acheson, Oscar Chapman, Thomas ("Tommy the Cork") Corcoran, William O. Douglas and Eliot Janeway—raised $135,000 to be used for the Senate Majority Leader's bid. Part of Johnson's plan of attack against JFK involved questioning the youthful senator's liberal credentials by noting that he, Johnson, had never contributed to the archenemy of liberalism, Senator Joseph McCarthy.

Spontaneous enthusiasm for Adlai Stevenson produced a sizable campaign kitty. One Stevensonian told a group of California volunteers not to use the money they collected in West Virginia because it would tag Stevenson supporters as anti-Catholic. "But what can we do?" they pleaded. "We have $100,000 and they keep shoving more money at us!" Some of the money was spent to promote an emotional demonstration at the convention. While the Stevenson campaign hardly left the ground, the demonstration notwithstanding, it still managed to end up $20,000 in debt.

The prenomination campaign of Stuart Symington cost approximately $320,000, most of the money being spent to create a favorable climate for the senator in the event of a convention stalemate. Wayne Morse ran an ad hoc campaign that appears to have cost about $50,000. He complained that Kennedy was "wallpapering" his home state of Oregon with money.

On the Republican side, Vice-President Nixon did not campaign actively for the nomination since he had no announced opposition. Financing was under the control of J. Clifford Folger, who later became Chairman of the Republican National Finance Committee. Approximately half a million dollars was spent on ten primaries, only two of which—Indiana and Oregon—were considered important.

Nelson Rockefeller was officially a noncandidate, but nevertheless maintained an extensive staff in the event Nixon faltered. He began making soundings back in 1959 to find out if the financial and business community and party regulars would support him. After spending many millions of dollars—the exact amount has never been revealed—he found that Wall Street and industry were cool to him, and that the party regulars had been sewed up by the Vice-President.

The entire 1960 Presidential election cost approximately $25 million, up 46 percent over the estimated $17.2 million spent in 1956. Of the $25 million, the Republicans and Democrats each spent close to $11 million. Labor groups spent another $2 million, and the remainder was spent by minor parties and nonparty pressure groups. From September through election day both parties spent at the rate of $100,000 a day. Both also ended up spending more than they had.

The total cost of all campaigns for all elective offices in 1960— from President to county clerk—is estimated to have been $175 million, up from $144 million in 1952 and $155 million in 1956.

The Republican and Democratic Presidential campaigns both received their funds from traditional sources: the GOP from Fat Cats and party faithful, the Democrats from Fat Cats, the party faithful and labor. Fifty-eight percent of all contributions to Republican committees at the national level came from individuals giving $500 or more. The Democrats did even better with 59 percent.

All the traditional names are there. Giving $10,000 or more to the Republicans were Mrs. Vincent Astor, Douglas Dillion, John Dorrance (of Campbell Soups), financier Jack Dreyfus, several Du Ponts, a Firestone, Amory Houghton of Corning Glass, New York lawyer John Humes, Thomas McCabe, Sr., of Scott Paper, a clutch of Mellons, several Olins and Pews, many Rockefellers, investment banker John Schiff, *Herald-Tribune* owner John Hay Whitney and racehorse owner George Widener.

Those giving similar amounts to the Democrats included Washington banker True Davis, ex-underworld figure John ("Jake the Barber") Factor, Bernard Gimbel, realtor Albert M. Greenfield, mining tycoon Joseph Hirshhorn, Arthur Krim of the Music Corporation of America, philanthropist Mrs. Albert Lasker, former New York governor and senator Herbert Lehman, bankers Harold Linder and Bart Lytton, Broadway producer Roger Stevens, and Thomas J. Watson, Jr., of IBM. The Somoza family, through a lobbyist, supposedly contributed $10,000 to swing sentiment in favor of a Nicaraguan canal linking the Atlantic and Pacific Oceans.

The amount contributed by the Kennedys themselves in 1960 has never been made public, although estimates run as high as $4 million. During the campaign John Kennedy once said jokingly: "On the matter of experience, I had announced earlier this year that, if successful, I would not consider campaign contributions as a substitute for experience in appointing ambassadors. Ever since I made that statement," he concluded, "I have not received one single cent from my father."

Other big contributors, however, had more faith in tradition. David Bruce and his wife contributed $3,500 and the former was appointed Ambassador to the Court of St. James's. Angier Biddle Duke (who contributed $4,420) was appointed Chief of Protocol at the State Department, Henry Fowler ($2,359) eventually became Secretary of the Treasury, John Kenneth Galbraith ($500) became Ambassador to India, Arthur Goldberg ($750) became Secretary of Labor, Harold Linder ($12,600) became head of the Export-Import Bank, John Rice ($5,000) became Ambassador to The Netherlands, Mrs. Marietta Tree ($3,500) was appointed to the United Nations Human Rights Commission, and Eugene Zuchert ($1,750) became Secretary of the Air Force.

Nearly twoscore individuals saw fit to contribute $500 or more to *both* Presidential candidates, among them Henry Crown of General Dynamics, Ralph Evinrude of Milwaukee, silk merchant Paolino Gerli, cosmetics manufacturer Martin Revson, and real estate speculator William Zeckendorf. None of them were given positions in the new administration.

Kennedy, however, did give a few jobs to Republican contributors. Douglas Dillon ($26,550 to Nixon, including his wife's contribution) was appointed Secretary of the Treasury, Lucius Clay ($4,000, along with his wife) became the President's representative in Berlin, John J. McCloy ($500) became a special assistant for disarmament and atomic energy, and physicist-businessman James H. Wakelin, Jr. ($500), became Assistant Secretary of the Navy for Research and Development.

Fund-raising dinners continued to prove to be a lucrative source of funds. The national GOP held nearly 150 such dinners in 1960, half of which were "Dinners with Ike." The average cost to the subscriber was $100, although there were a few $15 dinners. The Ike dinners plus the campaign dinners grossed $7.7 million, only $3 million of which ended up in the national campaign. The rest went to local, state and congressional races. The last-minute Nixon telethon put a strain on Republican fund-raising capabilities, but the necessary $200,000 (some say the true cost was closer to $600,000) was raised in four days.

From the beginning the Democrats were hampered by friction in their fund-raising efforts. Stephen Smith, Kennedy's brother-in-law, was in overall charge of raising the money, but the Democratic National Committee, under treasurer McCloskey, and the short-lived Democratic National Finance Committee each had jurisdictions it felt were being invaded by the others. Despite such haggles, over 70 dinners were held which grossed $1.4 million, although only a small percentage of this went into the Kennedy-Johnson effort. The bulk helped finance state and congressional races. On one occasion trading stamps were offered for contributions, and on another it was suggested that the party faithful eat frugally at home and contribute what they saved in food, baby-sitters and parking.

The Democrats benefited most from the $2 million in labor contributions. In conjunction with Kennedy's massive registration drive, labor's Committee on Political Education ran its own campaign to sign up new voters and to elect pro-labor candidates. The Teamsters reputedly spent $1.5 million to defeat antilabor legislators such as Congressmen Phil Landrum and (later Senator) Robert Griffin. As a gimmick to raise money for the effort, Teamster boss James Hoffa offered free perfume to anyone contributing $3 or more.

The manner in which unions chose to spend their funds shifted emphasis in 1960. There were fewer transfers of funds to national, congressional and state races than in 1956, and more direct expenditures by the unions themselves. This reflected an increased willingness of unions to become more directly involved in campaigns with their money. Almost half of all money for Democratic candidates at the congressional and state levels originated in labor committees.

Other fund-raising efforts were either insignificant, a failure or not undertaken for lack of enthusiasm. Both national parties, for instance, set contribution quotas for their respective state committees. As had happened repeatedly in the past, the 1960 quotas were undersubscribed, partly because state committees resent the national committee telling them what to do, partly because they have trouble enough raising money for their own needs without sending some of it to Washington, and partly because they do not believe they get a good return for filling their quotas.

Funds raised through the "Dollars for Democrats" effort bordered on failure, although receipts were up from 1958. A previously mildly successful Republican effort to suck up the $1, $5 and $10 contributions, called the "Neighbor-to-Neighbor" campaign, was not even undertaken at the national level in 1960 for lack of interest. The GOP did profit somewhat from purportedly nonpartisan efforts by corporations such as Ford and Kimberly-Clark to raise campaign funds, but one local Republican group was taken to the cleaners to the tune of $40,000 to $50,000 when it hired a private company to raise funds and then found out that the contract called for them to receive only 25 percent of all money raised.

Where was the money spent? Continuing the trend begun in 1952, the largest single expenditure by both parties was for television time, programs, advertisements and agency fees. The Republicans at the national level reported spending $2.3 million on television, or 23 percent of all their direct expenditures. However, Carroll Newton of Campaign Associates, the firm hired to run the Nixon-Lodge media campaign, admitted spending up to $4 million, or nearly 36 percent of the whole. The Kennedy-Johnson ticket reported spending $2.4 million, or 40 percent of all direct expenditures.

Total costs at all levels for political broadcasting, which would include both television and FM and AM radio, rose 150 percent over 1956, which was faster than other costs. The real growth, however, was not at the Presidential level, but at the state, senatorial and congressional level. By 1960, big costs had finally come to the grass roots.

Section 315 of the Communications Act, known as the "Equal Time Provision," was suspended in 1960 so that Nixon and Kennedy could debate each other without the public being forced to listen to the views of sixteen other candidates for the office. It is estimated that the free time offered by the networks for the four debates was worth over $2 million. This free time, however, did not save money for the parties: it simply allowed them to use what money they had for more paid television advertisements.

The purchase and distribution of campaign materials had become so immense and complicated by 1960 that the Democratic party was forced to set up a Materials Distribution Center. Altogether the Democrats spent $800,000 to buy approximately 90 million giveaway promotional items such as buttons, lapel tabs, bumper stickers, window decals, cards, posters, brochures and tabloids. And that did not even include the cost of handling or mailing. The Republican effort was of a similar scale. Put another way, it meant that the two major parties churned out one campaign promotional item for nearly every man, woman and child in the country. The Democrats purchased more buttons and lapel tabs (42.8 million) than there were voters for the Democratic ticket (34.2 million). There were three promotional items at the national level for everyone who voted for President.

Although the manner in which campaign funds were raised and spent in 1960, and the sums involved, caused concern among many thoughtful citizens, such behavior was not unique to the American political experience. Indeed, what happened in 1960 was simply the result of forces present in our society which can be traced back to the early years of the Republic. More than anything, our past behavior in matters of political finance explains why we behave the way we do today.

II

The Early Years

It began with no money being spent at all.

There were no primaries, conventions, caucuses, parades, bands, consultants, polls, advertising blitzes, or traveling and election day costs in the 1789 contest. In fact, there was hardly a campaign. George Washington had no competition and refused to promote either his candidacy or programs among the electors and voters.

To vote in the early days of the Republic one had to own property, which meant for the most part being a freehold farmer or a small business entrepreneur. Of the 4 million citizens in the United States at the time of its birth, less than 800,000 were qualified to vote. These individuals were scattered thinly along the eastern seaboard, from Massachusetts to Georgia, and as far inland as the Appalachian Mountains. Considering the primitive means of communications in existence at the time, organized campaigning, had it been necessary, would have been exceedingly difficult.

Furthermore, of the eleven states taking part in the first election (North Carolina and Rhode Island had not yet ratified the Constitution), only four—Maryland, New Hampshire, Pennsylvania and Virginia—with a total of 35 electoral votes, allowed property owners to vote directly for electors. The other states, with 46 electoral votes, either named electors through their local legislatures or had different, more complicated systems of restricted voting. The pattern continued over the following eight years when, of the five states to join the Union, only two allowed popular elections. Thus, at the beginning, the system favored candidates spending little or no money seeking votes among a few key legislators rather than those spending a great deal of money seeking support among the widely scattered populace.

In the century preceding the Revolution, most of the offices in the Colonies were appointive. The few elective offices were usually filled by candidates selected in secret conclave by the local aristocracy. Their choices, often fellow aristocrats, were then ratified with little dissent at town meetings through the use of the open (as opposed to the secret) ballot. This elective procedure involved the spending of almost no money.

It was not always this austere. Money could become a factor when competition arose for a particular Colonial office. The customary and most effective manner of winning votes then was to soften up the electorate with liquor shortly before and during election day. The voters in a particular district were usually small enough in number so that the candidates knew most of them; hence an offering of liquor was considered more a friendly gesture than a bribe.

One master of this form of campaigning was none other than George Washington. When he ran for the Virginia House of Burgesses from Fairfax County in 1757, he provided his friends with the "customary means of winning votes": namely 28 gallons of rum, 50 gallons of rum punch, 34 gallons of wine, 46 gallons of beer, and 2 gallons of cider royal. Even in those days this was considered a large campaign expenditure, because there were only 391 voters in his district, for an average outlay of more than a quart and a half per person.

The success of this system and its entrenchment in the public heart could be gauged two decades later when James Madison was defeated for reelection to the Virginia legislature because he refused to distribute whiskey to the voters. A committee reviewing his case refused to interpret gifts of liquor to the voters as bribery or corruption.

This manner of campaigning was not unique to Colonial America but dates back at least to ancient Greek and Roman times. The Greek ecclesia, the popular deliberating body to which all adult male citizens were eligible, experienced widespread vote buying and bribery. Wealthy candidates for office in ancient Rome were expected to entertain the voter with gladiatorial contests, games and acts of conspicuous generosity. The first election law dates back to about 432 B.C. when candidates for office in Republican Rome were forbidden to whiten their togas with chalk in order to attract attention.

Such corruption and large campaign expenditures as did exist in the Colonies were a reflection of English habits. English parliamentary campaign practices in the seventeenth and eighteenth centuries were particularly corrupt. "Rotten boroughs," in which voters were either bribed or told how to vote by their masters, were a common political phenomenon. So was the buying of appointive office. By contrast, the relative austerity of American election spending during the first years of the Republic was, in part, a reaction to the debasement of the English system. However, it was not to last long.

In 1791, anti-Hamilton Republicans organized themselves to underwrite the costs of the *National Gazette,* edited by poet Philip Freneau. Freneau's writings the following year against Hamiltonian "monarchists" were sufficiently effective to swing the Vice-Presidential electoral votes of Virginia, North Carolina and New York from John Adams to George Clinton. The Federalists, in turn, subsidized the pro-Hamilton and apparently more influential *Gazette of the United States,* edited by John Fenno, an ex-Boston schoolteacher. It is from these efforts that American campaign financing can be dated.

In the election of 1796 more funds were spent on newspaper campaigns for the votes of electors. In 1799, Thomas Jefferson sought to establish newspapers as organs of party propaganda. He collected a small sum for this purpose from a group of Philadelphians. The following year he spent $50—a considerable sum for those days—of his own money to publish partisan tracts.

In the late 1790's, Aaron Burr, then the leader of Tammany Hall, found that most workers in New York City were tenants and thus unable to vote. Federalist banks refused loans to known Democrats and, indeed, converted many anti-Federalist merchants to the cause by refusing credit unless they backed Federalist candidates.

At first Burr called upon wealthy Democrats to finance fellow Democrats in the purchase of land. But even these benefactors did not have the money Burr thought he needed, so the wily politician, through a complicated maneuver, had a bill passed in the State Assembly creating an anti-Federalist state bank which would loan the needed funds to Democrats.

Thus armed with dollars and new voters, the New York City Democratic organization grew quickly. These new voters were well furnished with leaflets, posters and speakers, and eventually were to become a formidable force on behalf of Burr's candidacy for President in 1800.

When the Jefferson-Burr Electoral College deadlock went to Congress, Alexander Hamilton, who hated both Jefferson and Burr, decided that the moral fervor of the former was less dangerous than the political skills of the latter, and he flooded the mails with anti-Burr tracts. Burr, wrote Hamilton, was immoral, corrupt, promiscuous, unprincipled, dangerous, and unfit to be President. His words undoubtedly influenced the outcome of the congressional vote in favor of Jefferson.

In the first quarter of the nineteenth century, campaign costs remained minimal. There was a general prejudice against what John Quincy Adams called "electioneering." All candidates played coy, which in those days cost no money. Campaigns were conducted almost exclusively through newspapers, at partisan rallies and public meetings. Costs were underwritten by the candidate and his friends, usually at no financial hardship to any of them.

While it is well known that Thomas Jefferson, James Monroe and other officeholders found themselves near bankruptcy at the end of their long public careers, it was not caused, as is commonly thought, by the costs of running for office, but resulted from the heavy expense of pursuing their duties properly while in office.

The 1828 election, which brought Jackson to the White House, was the first in which the popular vote played a significant role in the selection of electors. By now only 2 of the 24 states of the Union still chose electors in their legislatures; the others had either originally selected or switched to the popular vote route.

To engineer a popular majority out of more than one million eligible voters required organization and money. Although no precise figures are available, it is known that sums of $5,000 to

$10,000 were being sought that year on behalf of a gubernatorial candidate in Kentucky, which may give some idea of what was spent by both sides in quest of the Presidency.

Jackson's supporters tended to be frontiersmen rather than planters, newly arrived rather than established, employees rather than owners, states-righters rather than abolishionists. The Adams-Clay ticket drew much of its support from officeholders, entrepreneurs and the aristocracy. No single group stands out as having contributed a significant amount to either campaign.

During the Jacksonian era, many changes in government practices took place which tended to boost the costs of running for office. Political parties, for instance, became fixed and began to operate at the federal, state and municipal levels. Religious and property qualifications had been swept away, thus vastly increasing the number of voters to whom a candidate had to appeal. As the urban movement gathered strength, new towns with elected officials and councils were established. Partisanship ran from top to bottom of the political spectrum; it no longer was fashionable to sneer at "electioneering." In addition, the newer state constitutions, beginning with Mississippi's in 1832, transferred many offices from the appointive to the elective class. A few years later, in 1840, the convention method of electing candidates was to be established.

Spoils, or patronage, first became a significant factor in the 1828 election. There were charges by Democrats of corruption in the civil service, but incompetence was nearer the truth. The federal agencies were full of aged functionaries appointed years before, and soon after he became President, Jackson replaced 40 percent of the entire bureaucracy with his own men. One of his appointees was a bounder named Samuel Swartwout, a fellow conspirator of Burr's, who managed to steal more than one million dollars as Collector of the Port of New York before he was caught.

With mass participation in the franchise came the requirement for the organizational talents of professionals, men who had to be paid in money or patronage, or both. The 1828 election witnessed the first appearance of the middle-level technician—individuals who, win or lose, took money for their political skills, resulting in increasing the costs of campaigning. Some also sought patronage jobs as further reward for their work. It was expected of them, if they were given jobs, to kick back a certain percentage of their yearly salaries into the party war chest. New York City employees, for instance, were required to contribute 6 percent of their weekly pay to the Tammany campaign fund. Federal employees, who numbered less than 700 in those more frugal times, were expected to do the same.

The printing press was still the chief means of reaching the voters, and most money collected went to support the cost of partisan propaganda. Both Henry Clay and Daniel Webster were most adept at securing funds to support the *Whig* newspaper, often in exchange for vague promises of future favors returned.

The United States Bank under Nicholas Biddle had for years subsidized propaganda against Andrew Jackson. In 1832 Jackson vetoed the bank's recharter, and the bank, thinking itself a popular institution, spent $580 for printing, wrapping and distributing 30,000 copies of the veto message, thereby inadvertently financing Jackson the enemy. In a two-year period, 1830 to 1832, the bank spent $42,000 on literature favorable to itself, a sum equivalent in purchasing power to many more dollars than that today. At that time, Senator Webster was so heavily in debt to the bank for loans extended to him that in effect it "owned" him.

The vastly enlarged franchise also brought with it a marked increase in corruption. Getting out the vote now meant, in many instances, buying it. The price of an uncommitted vote in New York City in 1832 was approximately five dollars, which was two or three days' wages for an ordinary laborer. In the 1838 mayoralty race, both Whigs and Democrats imported paid "floaters" to vote early and often. The Whig bid of $22 for the first vote and $18 for each additional vote was sufficiently high to ensure the reelection of the Whig incumbent.

Contributions often came in the form of cash packed in satchels or carpetbags, no questions asked. In 1839, Whig lobbyist Thurlow Weed raised $8,000 from New York merchants, and the money was delivered in a bandana handkerchief. No one appeared to think it unusual.

These and other costs encouraged money raisers to devise new ways to fill the political coffers. One method developed by the early Whigs sought to bring in a steady influx of funds by assessing each member of the party one cent per week. The party hoped to raise $2,000 a week. This is the first recorded attempt by a political party to raise money from the ordinary voter, and like many subsequent efforts, the plan failed for lack of any consistent support.

In 1840, the electorate had expanded to approximately two and a half million people, most of whom expected to be courted for their votes. William Henry Harrison's workers handed out thousands of banners, badges, Harrison pictures, Tippecanoe handkerchiefs, log cabin songbooks, newspapers and mugs of cider. Torchlight parades and rallies abounded. The Whigs found financial support among people hard-pressed by the Panic of 1837 and the subsequent depression, old-fashioned states-righters offended by Jackson's stand on nullification, many New England and Middle States Yankees, pro-Clay Westerners and protectionist factory owners.

The unsuccessful campaign of Martin Van Buren spent its time in similar pursuits, and was backed financially almost entirely by loyal Jacksonites. Although no figures are available, campaign costs had risen sufficiently so that neither candidate had the personal financial means to underwrite his own efforts to win the Presidency.

Competition for spoils continued to be fierce. Harrison is supposed to have contracted his fatal illness shortly after becoming President as the result of stress brought on by the press of contributors and workers seeking appointments to office.

The rising costs of campaigning in the 1840's and 1850's forced many aspirants for high office to turn to men of wealth for funds. It was in this period of American history that the bonds between political and economic interests were first forged. They are bonds that have not weakened at all over the following 130 years.

Many self-made men, beneficiaries of the Industrial Revolution and America's natural bounty, recognized that numerous decisions of government on such issues as taxes, trade, tariffs and slavery directly or indirectly influenced the independence of their own enterprises. They realized it was in their own interests to exert whatever influence they could over the legislative and bureaucratic processes of government. The easiest way to exert influence was with cash at campaign time. Business had the money and the desire, candidates had the need and, if elected, the power: it was a natural alliance.

The Du Pont family of Delaware was the first group of wealthy individuals to back candidates for office with direct cash. Its members were the chief prop and support of the Whigs from the party's inception in 1839. The Du Ponts had grown rich in every war since 1812 by supplying the government with black powder. Many of them recognized that such a profitable relationship could be enhanced with a well-placed sum of money during elections. Their largesse extended down the political ladder to lesser offices than the Presidency, in one instance saving Delaware from a terrible fate: ". . . [B]ut for their powerful influence," wrote Senator John M. Clayton to U.S. Attorney General John J. Crittenden, "we should have sent two Locofoco senators to Congress for the last twenty years."

The Democrats in these years were backed heavily by August Belmont, the American representative of the Rothschild banking interests. He was President Buchanan's principal financial backer. The campaign of 1856, which brought Buchanan to the Presidency, was so close that Thurlow Weed later confessed that he thought $50,000 was the margin of Democratic victory, which is instructive since most scholars on the subject believe Buchanan's total campaign costs were $25,000. Belmont also underwrote most of the start-up costs of the Democratic National Committee in 1852 and, in fact, was its chairman for twelve years.

The financial travails of Abraham Lincoln from 1840 to his death in 1865 best illustrate the nature of campaign funding at midcentury.

Lincoln was a Presidential Elector in 1840, 1844, 1852 and 1856, which in those days required extensive stump speaking. In each instance he paid for all his own expenses and could not count on any income from his law practice to lighten the load.

In 1846 he was supposedly given $200 by friends in Illinois to pay for his expenses while running for Congress as a Whig. Lincoln claimed his total expenses were 75 cents for a barrel of cider, and that he returned the remaining $199.25 with thanks. The story is disputed by several authorities and is probably not true, but the tale is still widely circulated as an example of how inexpensive campaigning used to be. No doubt costs were less crushing then, but candidate Lincoln, as was the custom, still had to finance all of his traveling, living and publishing costs out of his own pocket. If the 75-cents story is true, it stems from Lincoln's believing that buying cider represented an extraordinary campaign expense.

After two years in Congress, Lincoln renounced any interest in a second term. He stayed in Washington to work for the election of Zachary Taylor for President. During the campaign he spent $132.30 of his own money publishing 7,580 copies of a speech on the origins of the Mexican War. This practice was common enough but the sum spent was considered quite large, since only 6 of the 232 members of Congress spent more than $100 on speeches in the 30th Congress. For a full month prior to election day he campaigned at his own expense throughout the state of Illinois for the Whig ticket.

Like many other contributors in the 1848 election, Lincoln sought his reward in the form of a $3,000-a-year federal patronage job that was then available. President Taylor, however, chose another man for the job; thus, Lincoln was forced to return to the practice of law to improve his financial position.

In his unsuccessful try for the Senate in 1856, Lincoln was forced to call upon his former Illinois backers for financial aid. Most of the several thousand dollars he was able to raise went to pay for publishing speeches and defraying the costs of a 4,200-mile campaign trip around the state. The candidate was so busy campaigning that, again, he neglected his law practice, his usual source of income. Following his defeat he was asked by the Republican state chairman to raise some money to pay party bills, but begged off. Lincoln pointed out that he had already contributed $500 to the party and that currently he was "the poorest hand living to get others to pay" and "absolutely without money now for even household expenses."

Once again he returned to his law practice.

The following year Lincoln undertook to campaign on behalf of various GOP candidates in the Midwest. Some of his expenses were paid for by the party. In Cincinnati, however, he received a bill for service from the Burnet House for $37.50. This seemed a "little steep" to Lincoln, who complained further that he was not responsible for the $16 listed for wines and cigars. "I can and will pay it if it is right," wrote Lincoln, but, he concluded, like many subsequent candidates of similarly limited means, "I do not wish to be 'diddled.' "

When he ran for President in 1860, Lincoln was once more dependent on others to provide him with the necessary campaign funds. His prenomination expenses were carried by personal friends from Illinois, and the money went mainly to entertain wavering committeemen with cigars, wine, whiskey and brandy. Author William Dean Howells wrote a flattering campaign biography of Lincoln and was subsequently rewarded by being appointed consul to Venice.

Two of Lincoln's serious primary rivals, William H. Seward of New York and Simon Cameron of Pennsylvania, were also dependent on others for funds. Cameron controlled his state's delegation and had the financial backing of Pennsylvania industrialists. When it became apparent that his Favorite Son candidacy was flagging, the Keystone State delegates were approached by Thurlow Weed and various out-of-state streetcar interests with immense amounts of cash in hand to persuade them to switch their votes to Seward. When, in turn, Seward's campaign for the nomination collapsed, his backers, including Weed, switched again to Lincoln.

Pennsylvania was a crucial state for Lincoln in the 1860 election. To his concern, he found that the usually wealthy sources in Philadelphia refused to contribute for fear they would lose their profitable trade with the South if he won. Only two leading Philadelphia businesses were supposed to have contributed to the Lincoln campaign that year.

Indiana was another pivotal state for the Republicans, but as was the case, state party officials complained to the Republican National Committee that they were not getting enough funds to carry on a creditable campaign. John D. Defrees, a veteran Hoosier Republican, wrote to Weed in New York and pleaded: "We need money very much." The $2,000 sent by the RNC, he continued, "has been exhausted in the payment of Carl Schurz and other speakers and on a few German Republican papers." Could he not, he asked, "influence the Committee to send a few thousand more?"

Lincoln's friend, Judge David Davis, following a visit to Indiana, also wrote to Weed begging funds: "I hope the National Committee will do all they can for the state. The whole money they asked for (and more if it can be raised) should be sent at once. *Men work better with money in hand."*

The Republican Presidential campaign of 1860, according to scholars, cost $100,000. This figure is probably low, considering the tens of thousands of other dollars that flowed into key states like Indiana, Pennsylvania and New York for the benefit of candidates running for lesser offices but which indirectly helped to elect Lincoln. The purchasing power of that $100,000 then would be at least five times as great as today.

Because there was never much doubt about the outcome, Lincoln's opponents had difficulty raising funds. The Breckinridge forces, or southern Democrats, were supported mainly by federal officeholders, and while never short of funds they were never able to equal the amounts raised and spent by the Republicans.

The northern Democrats, led by Stephen A. Douglas, found it nearly impossible to raise money because the usually reliable New York merchants believed there was no chance of winning. "My efforts to collect money in the City," wrote Belmont to Douglas in late July, "have met with but little success, and unless we give to our merchants and politicians some *assurance of success* I fear that it will be impossible to raise the necessary funds for our campaign.

"My opinion," he continued, underlining each word, *"is that if we could only demonstrate to all those lukewarm and selfish money-bags, that we have a strong probability to carry the State of New York, we might get from them the necessary sinews of war."*

Belmont suggested that more money might be pried loose if Douglas came to New York and spoke personally to his followers. But it was to no avail. Republican money carried the day.

Funds for Lincoln's reelection campaign four years later, in 1864, came from his friends, federal officeholders and government contractors. His biggest backer that year was Jay Cooke, the immensely rich Philadelphia banker who was a fiscal agent of the

Treasury in the sale of government bonds. Cooke originally gave money to Chief Justice Salmon P. Chase to further Chase's Presidential ambitions, but when Lincoln was renominated Cooke quickly contributed $1,000 to the Railsplitter's campaign.

The Civil War marks another major turning point in American campaign financing practices. Prior to the conflict, costs were relatively moderate, corruption—particularly the buying of votes, legislation and office—was the exception rather than the rule, fund raising was conducted in an amateur fashion, and the alliance between economic interests and politicians, though growing, was loose and flexible. Following the war, however, costs began to rise sharply, corruption grew widespread and obvious, the extraction of partisan money became the full-time, or near full-time, occupation of specialists, and the business-political alliance became fixed and permanent.

The Grant campaigns of 1868 and 1872 each cost approximately $200,000, far more than the Democrats spent in those years and double what the Republicans themselves reportedly had spent in 1860. Money was contributed by John Jacob Astor II, who was then worth between $75 and $100 million, various Vanderbilts, department-store magnate A. T. Stewart, land-grant railroad promoters, contractors with the Interior and War Departments, Indian traders and men who had grown rich from the war. Jay Cooke contributed $20,000 in 1868, or 10 percent of the total, but threatened to withdraw his financial support if the Republicans waged a campaign to repudiate the national debt. He contributed at least $50,000 in 1872, or about one quarter of the total. It has subsequently been said of Grant that seldom has a President labored under such heavy obligations to so few men of wealth.

Seymour and Blair, the Democratic nominees in 1868, also received the bulk of their funds from a wealthy few. The largest contributor, at $40,000, was an advertiser of patent medicines. Eight other monied men—among them August Belmont, inventor Cyrus H. McCormick, and lawyers Samuel J. Tilden and Charles O'Conor—agreed to come up with $10,000 apiece. O'Conor himself was a candidate for President in 1872 as a "Straight-Out" Democrat, and Tilden was the party's nominee in 1876, thus beginning a long Democratic party tradition of running rich men for office, a practice the Republicans did not take up with any gusto until the midtwentieth century.

The disputed Hayes-Tilden election of 1876 cost the Republican party a minimum of $200,000. Funds came principally from federal officeholders and businessmen. Rutherford B. Hayes's managers concentrated on channeling their funds into the key states of New York and Indiana and on buying votes in the South.

Tilden, on the other hand, who personally put up two thirds of the $150,000 Democratic party war chest, kept a tight rein on finances. In several pivotal states he refused to parcel out more than what he considered the minimum, and the South was told, in effect, to shift for itself. It was a costly error.

When the electoral votes were counted, Tilden was one shy of victory. The electoral votes of Florida, South Carolina and Louisiana were claimed by both parties and were eventually awarded to Hayes by the Electoral Commission. By that time, Tilden's campaign had been weakened, perhaps irreparably, by the discovery of coded telegrams during the electoral squabble which implicated leading Democrats, including Tilden's nephew, in schemes to buy fraudulently the needed electoral vote. While a cause célèbre in its day, the scandal paled in comparison to the day-to-day excessive behavior of some public figures in matters of political finance during the next fifty years.

III

The Golden Age of Boodle

The half century following the 1876 election, from the end of Reconstruction to the Great Depression, marks America's Golden Age of Boodle. Never has the American political process been so corrupt. No office was too high to purchase, no man too pure to bribe, no principle too sacred to destroy, no law too fundamental to break. The old Anglo-Saxon belief that public duty required certain personal and financial sacrifices was giving way to the conviction among certain men that politics, at least in part, was a lucrative source of personal enrichment. In Henry Adams's words, "The moral law had expired."

Boodling, of course, predates this era. In the 1860's, for instance, Boss William Marcy Tweed of Tammany, then a state senator, ran the "Black Horse Cavalry," a group of legislators in Albany who sold their votes for cash. Once, when the New York legislature was wrangling over whether Jay Gould or Commodore Vanderbilt would control the Erie Railroad, votes were being sold for as much as $5,000. When the two competitors called a truce, however, the price fell to $100.

Tweed openly looted the New York City treasury for political and personal financial gain. He was a master of extracting contributions from public works contractors; the money, in turn, was used to bribe legislators to pass or defeat certain bills. The flow of money into Tammany vaults during Tweed's reign was never accurately assessed but was once described modestly by The Boss himself as "a continuous dribble."

Edgar Allan Poe was one victim of this corruption. He died on

October 7, 1849, four days after an election in Baltimore. He appears to have died of alcoholism brought on by liquor he purchased with money received for selling his vote.

By 1876, federal officeholders were routinely being assessed for contributions. In 1880, James Garfield wrote to his national chairman asking how much money certain bureaucrats were contributing, with the implied threat of dismissal if they refused to ante up. "Honest John" Kelly, Tweed's successor at Tammany, instituted a procedure whereby all candidates contributed a fixed sum to a general campaign committee, and officeholders owing their jobs to Kelly were assessed a percentage of their salaries. He then defended exorbitant salaries for City Hall bureaucrats on the grounds that large demands for political contributions were made upon them.

In 1882, every state employee in Pennsylvania· received the following form letter:

> Two percent of your salary is ————. Please remit promptly. At the close of the campaign we shall place a list of those who have not paid in the hands of the head of the department you are in.

In Philadelphia by the turn of the century a regular schedule of required donations from all city employees was in force, ranging from 3 percent for salaries of $600 to $1,200, to 12 percent for those of $10,000 and above. In Louisiana, state employees contributed a flat 10 percent of their pay into the ruling party's campaign chest.

At one time an assessment was levied upon each Democratic member of the House of Representatives as a campaign contribution to the Democratic National Congressional Committee. The practice has since been discontinued, although to this day many congressmen from both major parties are still assessed a percentage of their salaries by local organizations.

Business became a prime source of campaign funds after the passage of the Pendleton Act of 1883, a law that banned contributions from civil servants. Some large corporations gave regularly to both parties in order to buy protection and favors and to be free of "annoyances."

At the national level, oil and mining companies, railroads and

SUMMIT
BANK

A2973 (4/98)

**CUSTOMER
RECEIPT**

banks paid heaviest. In the 1880 election, for instance, Garfield covertly sought and obtained the support of a "Mr. Rockafeller" and his agents in the crucial state of Indiana. Large shareholders in several steel companies, the New York Central and Pennsylvania Railroads also contributed to the Republican party.

In the campaign of 1884, Republican money, most of it from business interests, was used secretly to finance the Anti-Monopoly–Greenback candidate, Ben Butler, in an effort to draw Democratic votes away from Grover Cleveland. It was an unsuccessful attempt to offset the danger of Republicans who had bolted the party that year for the Prohibitionist candidate, John Pierce St. John, and who sought to punish James G. Blaine for what they thought was his contemptuous treatment of the temperance issue.

During the same campaign, Blaine attended a dinner at Delmonico's in New York given by some wealthy business friends, among them John Jacob Astor II, Jay Gould, Cyrus W. Field, Russell Sage and Levi Parsons Morton. After dinner, the candidate and his guests retired to a room to discuss campaign finances. All reporters present were excluded. The next day Blaine was vilified in the press as "Belshazzar Blaine" who dined on "Monopoly Soup," "Lobby Pudding" and "Gould Pie." Coming at a time when most citizens were feeling an economic pinch, the adverse publicity played a large part in Blaine's defeat.

Cleveland's antiprotectionist campaign in 1888 resulted in a large outpouring of corporate money to defeat it. It was the first campaign in which business participated in a significant way. John Wanamaker, the Philadelphia department-store magnate, and later Postmaster General in Harrison's Cabinet, convinced ten of his business peers to pledge $10,000 apiece to defeat Cleveland. Altogether Wanamaker raised between $200,000 and $400,000. Railroad tycoon James J. Hill supposedly offered a large sum of money to Matthew Quay, chairman of the Republican National Committee and corrupt political boss of Pennsylvania, for the Harrison campaign if one of three men were appointed Secretary of the Interior. Harrison not only refused but directed that no money from Hill should be accepted even without conditions.

Harrison believed his victory was the result of Providence, but Quay put it more realistically: "He ought to know," he said, "that Providence hadn't a damn thing to do with it."

The Democrats in these years also had their corporate money-bags. William C. Whitney, a streetcar pioneer, financed Cleveland in 1884 (and was to be rewarded by being appointed Secretary of the Navy) and William Jennings Bryan in 1896. Marcus Daly, owner of the Anaconda mines, publisher William Randolph Hearst and August Belmont also underwrote much of the Democratic party's costs.

At the state and municipal levels, raising funds was far less sophisticated. A particularly lucrative source of campaign money was companies or groups seeking to retain or obtain licenses or "concessions" such as utilities, racetracks, saloons, houses of prostitution, and gambling establishments. Some of the earlier state and big-city political machines—like those run by Quay and Boies Penrose of Pennsylvania, Kelly and "Squire" Croker of Tammany, "Bathhouse John" Coughlin and Carter Henry Harrison of Chicago, the "Old Regulars" in New Orleans, and A. A. ("Doc") Ames's machine in Minneapolis—could more than elect or defeat candidates for political office. They could make or break a business through the granting or withholding of licenses, franchises, building permits and special favors. Practical businessmen realized this and did not try to fight the system; whenever a call came for campaign contributions they kicked in, if for no other reason than to be free to go about making money.

Streetcar magnates Charles Tyson Yerkes of Chicago, William Elkins and A. B. Widener of Philadelphia and William C. Whitney of New York, for example, all contributed heavily and regularly for the privilege of running their tracks down certain city streets. Some aldermen were so greedy for money that they sold the same rights simultaneously to competing interests. None of the rights to a particular street were permanent: every time a company up-graded its equipment it would have to repurchase the same rights over again. All this activity brought in large quantities of campaign cash.

"Bathhouse John" Coughlin, long-time boss of Chicago's "Levee," for years received his major financial support from the operators of the Garfield Park racetrack. Carter Henry Harrison's reelection campaign for mayor of Chicago in 1892 was financed in large part—some say to the tune of $500,000—by gamblers. Such revelations today would hardly raise an eyebrow, but at the turn of the century they were considered quite unusual.

Business money in this period was so pervasive that it was sometimes able to control entire legislatures. It was often said, for instance, that Standard Oil did everything to the Pennsylvania legislature except refine it. Mark Twain once commented: "I think I can say, and say with pride, that we have legislatures that bring higher prices than any in the world." Samuel Huntington, the president of the Union Pacific, admitted under oath that in an eleven-year period his Washington lobbyist had handed out more than $6 million for what he called "legal" and "miscellaneous" purposes, but which were in reality bribes in the form of campaign contributions.

Illegal and quasi-legal businesses were also a rich vein of campaign funds. It was during the Golden Age of Boodle that the ties between politicians and the underworld became fixed. Both have since come to depend on each other: one for campaign funds (and some personal income, too), and the other for protection.

By the end of the century protection became the accepted rationale among these businesses for contributing to campaigns. Two chroniclers of Chicago's past vices, Lloyd Wendt and Herman Kogan, noted that by then "everybody paid":

> No longer were the collectors thrown into the street. They no longer needed even to make calls; the pimps and madames brought their payments in. They paid to [local bosses] Jim Colosimo, to Andy Craig, to Jakey Adler, to Hank Hopkins. They even paid to Bathhouse John personally. Minna Everleigh [a well-known madam] in . . . nine years had contributed $65,000, not including special assessments. Once Bathhouse John himself called for such an extra payment. "We're tryin' to get a bill stalled down in Springfield that wants to make you stop selling booze or wine in this place," was his excuse. Minna paid Bathhouse by check, the appropriate arrangements were made with the legislative pirates, and the bill was defeated.

How the money, once collected, was spent was another matter. For most candidates it was spent on the printed word, travel or rallies. The campaign routine in the late nineteenth century included stump speaking tours, where the candidate went to the people, or front porch campaigns, where the people came to the candidate; efforts to line up local editorial support; organizing ox roasts, bean feeds, dances and rallies (which were sometimes combined with efforts to raise money); and publishing and distributing considerable quantities of partisan literature.

But campaign funds were also earmarked for less noble causes during the Golden Age of Boodle, one of which was buying votes. In 1880, for instance, Republican election day money "flowed like water" in Indiana. Eight years later, Republican state treasurer, W. W. Dudley, instructed his Hoosier lieutenants: "Divide the floaters into blocks of five, put a trusted man with the necessary funds in charge of these five and make him responsible that none get away and that all vote our ticket." The letter created a sensation in the campaign. Republicans called it a forgery and Dudley threatened to sue. But, regardless of the truth in the matter, floaters were as prevalent, if not more so, than they were in the days of Thurlow Weed. Harrison won Indiana in 1888 by a scant 2,348 popular votes, so Dudley's floaters paid off.

In St. Louis, Colonel Ed Butler, the corrupt boss of the city, was once reported to have shouted across a police line to a crowd on election day: "Are there any more repeaters out there that want to vote again?"

In 1895, "Hinky Dink" Kenna, Bathhouse John's ally in Chicago's first ward, was defeated for alderman because his $100,000 campaign fund was stolen. He was outraged because he planned to use the money to buy votes.

During the municipal elections the following year, Bathhouse John was observed touring his precincts in a large overcoat that dragged on the ground. It was so overloaded with coins to pay off the voters that it made him appear round-shouldered.

Be that as it may, it occurred to the more sophisticated political boodlers that, as the electorate expanded and the cost of votes increased, better leverage could be achieved at less cost by paying off a few election officials rather than a horde of illegal voters. Senator Boies Penrose put it best when he observed:

> The fraud of an election does not really begin til night; then in
> dozens of precincts where the judges and election clerks of both

big parties have been "fixed" we put down just what returns we want, or may need to insure us a majority. John Smith may have 500 votes in a given precinct, but if John Smith is the man we want to defeat, we knock off two ciphers and credit him with five votes. This is cheaper than hiring 500 "Indians" to cast illegal ballots. With a five-cent pencil we can in five minutes cast more votes on paper than 5,000 citizens can cast in a ballot box in a whole day.

Money was also spent on the purchase of office itself. United States Senate seats were the most likely to be bought because, prior to the passage of the Seventeenth Amendment in 1913, senators were elected by their respective state legislatures. At the height of the Golden Age, winning office often meant turning the selection process into a blatant money auction between contenders. A majority of state legislators in both parties could be, and frequently were, bought or swayed by the use of money or promises of contracts and jobs. The only choice they faced was which of the candidates could pay more in cash or concessions.

Simon Guggenheim, a rich mining tycoon, bought his senate seat from the Colorado legislature. Two wealthy Montanans spent large sums in the late nineteenth century bribing the state legislature— one to get elected, the other to prevent him from being elected. Three senators from West Virginia—Henry Gassaway Davis (the Democratic Vice-Presidential candidate in 1904), Stephen B. Elkins and Clarence W. Watkins—all bought their seats from the state legislature.

Other offices were often purchased from the local or state boss. George Washington Plunkitt, the Tammany sage, once described how it should not be done:

A few years ago, he explained, a Republican district leader controlled the nomination for Congress in his Congressional district. Four men wanted it. At first the leader asked for bids privately, but decided at last that the best thing to do was to get the four men together in the back room of a certain saloon and have an open auction. When he had his men lined up, he got on a chair, told about the value of the goods for sale, and asked for bids in regular auctioneer style. The highest bidder got the nomination for $5,000. Now, that wasn't right at all. These things ought to be always fixed up nice and quiet.

There could be no better way to describe the moral temper of the age than to give brief sketches of three extraordinary politicians: Simon Cameron, Matthew Stanley Quay and Boies Penrose, all of whom at one time or another were senators from Pennsylvania. They were also corrupt, conniving and ruthless, the products of a politically feudal state. None left any permanent mark on the American scene save a new and cynical chapter in American campaign financing practices.

Cameron, for instance, bribed the Pennsylvania legislature no less than four times, in 1857, 1862, 1868 and 1874. It took no less than $20,000 to bribe one key legislator in 1862. Six years later, 21 legislators, by now wise, pledged themselves not to vote for Cameron, but the ante was raised and they fell into line.

Cameron's political machine developed what came to be known as the "Pennsylvania Idea," a belief that big business should use its funds to help the Republican party buy votes, if necessary, to stay in power. This machine, wrote Henry Adams, "worked by coarse means on coarse interests; but its practical success had been the most curious subject of study in American history." Cameron himself described his machine as "a regularly constituted agency for purchasing votes and the other vehicles of political power."

Despite the longevity of his service in the U.S. Senate, and as Lincoln's Secretary of War and Minister to Russia, Cameron left no notable speech, no compelling philosophy, and is known for no great effort. He is remembered primarily for his remark: "An honest politician is one who, when he is bought, stays bought."

Cameron's true political heir was Matt Quay who held one political office or another in Pennsylvania or Washington, D.C., from the 1850's until his death in 1904, and for fifteen years was the state's absolute boss. He was a suave, scholarly and sometimes gentle man, but also ruthless, cunning, cold-blooded and completely untrustworthy.

Quay's method of raising campaign funds were unique for those days: for thirty years he controlled the office of state treasurer, and through it he regularly and thoroughly looted the exchequer for his own use. Much of it stuck to his fingers, for he died a very wealthy man. Like Cameron, he believed that campaign funds were good for only one purpose: to bribe the necessary legislators and officials to get what he wanted.

Quay also developed the technique of "shaking the plum tree," or making deposits of state money in certain banks in return for advantageous loans or good investment tips. It was an inexpensive way to raise campaign funds and, at the same time, to line one's own pocket.

Perhaps the most infamous incident of Quay's political career took place during one of his reelection campaigns. The Pennsylvania legislature was unable to produce the necessary votes for his reelection, so the senator took the offensive by bribing four Democrats and five of John Wanamaker's insurgent Republicans. This, he believed, would be sufficient, but a later count showed that, despite the bribes, the votes were evenly divided between those for and against him. Quay then had several of his men round up a stray legislator who happened to be ill in the hospital. The man was carried into the chamber on a stretcher and he raised his hand weakly in favor of Quay's reelection. Quay's supporters whooped with joy and trooped out to celebrate their leader's victory. The ailing legislator, however, was forgotten in the ensuing commotion and was left to lie on his pallet in a cold hall outside the chamber. He contracted pneumonia and died soon afterward.

Quay's political heir, in turn, was the extraordinary Boies Penrose, a power in Pennsylvania from 1886 until his death in 1922, and undoubtedly the most influential Republican boss of his day in the country.

Penrose has been described by one observer as a "gutter Nietzschean" who had "fought his way down rather than up in the world." He was the product of a wealthy, Colonial Philadelphia family and had been educated at Episcopal Academy and Harvard University. Brilliant, insolent, lazy and an acknowledged authority on warblers, he was personally incorruptible but delighted in corrupting others.

He was physically enormous—six feet six inches tall, with a great girth and a neck that was indistinguishable from his chin. While a U.S. senator he ballooned to 350 pounds and could not fit into an ordinary Senate chair, so a large leather divan was installed for him in the rear of the Chamber where he sat toadlike for many hours during Senate sessions directing his affairs.

His appetites were similarly gargantuan. He could begin a meal with three or four dozen oysters, pique his hunger with a whole duck, slake his thirst with a quart of good liquor, and then call for the main course. He reveled in low-life associations and nonstop debauchery, and his framed, autographed picture graced the best brothels in the state.

Penrose developed several money-raising techniques which later became standard. One was known as "frying the fat," that is, inducing large corporations through fear to contribute regularly to the party. The phrase is ascribed to the president of a high-tariff organization who proposed putting Pennsylvania manufacturers on the fire and "frying the fat out of them." The practice became common with Penrose after 1883 when the Pendleton Act closed off civil servants as a source of funds. Penrose always established a quid pro quo when frying the fat: in return for large contributions, he promised that no hostile legislation would remain on the books or be passed into law.

Penrose also raised money by introducing "squeeze bills." Every year while he was a state legislator he would introduce, for instance, the Loan Shark Bill, which sought to limit interest charged by certain businesses to 6 percent. The sharks and pawnbrokers, because they wished to see the bill die in committee, contributed heavily to the Republican organization. Once a Loan Shark Bill was passed when the moneylenders balked at the ante demanded of them, but it was later vetoed after the insurgents had backed down and sent in the money. Squeeze bills hostile to utilities and heavy industry such as steel and locomotive companies were also common and produced the same results. This type of contribution, incidentally, replaced in large measure lobbyist bribes which were then so common in most state capitals.

Loyalty to the Republican party in Pennsylvania, Penrose believed, depended on manipulating the state's purse strings. If, for instance, someone in charge of a state-supported institution criticized the party, the annual appropriation was automatically held up until the miscreant recanted. Businesses dependent on state franchises were also systematically assessed. When he was a United States senator, he schemed with a manufacturer to underpay taxes due on imported raw materials. When the manufacturer later balked at contributing, Penrose threatened to expose him to the Treasury. As a result, the businessman promptly contributed $10,000 to Penrose's "war fund."

When he ran successfully for the U.S. Senate in 1896, he was able to raise $250,000 in New York City in 48 hours for his campaign. All told, he spent half a million dollars to bribe the necessary 254 members of the Pennsylvania legislature. His opponent was John Wanamaker, who was told mistakenly that he could win with only $400,000.

While Penrose was a genius at raising money, one of his biographers claims "he never really knew at any one given time the exact standing of the exchequer, for a thousand-dollar campaign contribution might be pushed into his pocket, there to circulate indiscriminately with his own funds." The policies of the Republican party, continues his biographer, "made billions in profits for his clients, the corporations. They in turn gave him millions for party support any time he asked them to give. He used these millions, many millions, for the continuance in power of the party he loved and served, but never a cent went to enrich himself."

Penrose's major source of funds came from wealthy men such as Charles M. Schwab of Bethlehem Steel, Samuel Vauclain of Baldwin Locomotive, Joe Grundy of the Pennsylvania Manufacturers' Association and industrialists Henry Clay Frick and Andrew Carnegie. "I'll take money [for campaign purposes] from any man," Penrose was quoted as saying. "You can't run a party on nothing and when you need money the place to get it is from them that have it."

To do the bidding of business was known around the turn of the century as "rope jumping," and no politician had more spring in his feet than Boies Penrose. Consistently throughout his career he voted the way business interests wanted him to. Once, for instance, Samuel Gompers sat down with Penrose and began to argue brilliantly in favor of some hoped-for anti-child-labor legislation. Penrose listened quietly and then remarked that he had seldom heard a cause more logically and forcefully advocated.

"But, Sam," he said, "you know as damn well as I do that I can't stand for a bill like that. Why those fellows this bill is aimed at—those mill owners—are good for $200,000 a year to the party. You can't afford to monkey with business that friendly."

Putting his hand on the famed labor leader's shoulder, he concluded, "Drop in anytime, Sam. It's always a pleasure to listen to you."

The behavior of such men as Penrose, Quay and Cameron, which was imitated time and time again by thousands of lesser politicians of all parties at all political levels, eventually produced a reaction among the voters. Their behavior had much to do with the passage of the Pendleton Act in 1883, and was responsible, at least in part, for the growth in electoral strength of both the Populists and the Progressives.

The 1896 Presidential election established several campaign financing firsts: it was the first campaign in which the telephone was used extensively, the first in which the candidate was promoted like soap, and the first to produce a modern technician in political finance, namely Mark Hanna.

Marcus Alonzo Hanna was a wealthy and successful Ohio businessman who first became involved in politics in 1880 when he started a "Business Man's Republican Campaign Club" in support of Garfield. He contributed heavily to "Fire Engine Joe" Foraker's campaign for governor of Ohio in 1885 and to the aged John Sherman's campaign for the Republican Presidential nomination three years later. He was seen openly handing out money to southern delegates in return for votes for Sherman. After Harrison won the nomination, Hanna joined the bandwagon and took on the duties of raising money for the campaign. The 1888 election was fought over the question of tariffs—the Democrats being in favor of revision, the Republicans in favor of protection. Thus, because he was a businessman, Hanna had a personal reason for becoming involved, and he managed to raise $100,000 for the Republican National Committee. His full involvement as a money raiser dates from this time.

Hanna was the first to recognize the Presidential potential of William McKinley, a fellow Ohioan and protectionist. On occasion he lent money to his protégé and contributed to his campaigns. When McKinley went bankrupt in 1893 while he was governor of Ohio, Hanna and some of his rich friends—among them Myron T. Herrick, H. H. Kohlsaat, Samuel Mather, John Hay, Charles Taft, Andrew Carnegie, Henry Clay Frick and Philander Knox—raised more than $100,000 to meet McKinley's obligations. They were to back him again financially in 1896.

Virtually all of McKinley's nomination campaign expenses in

1896, well over $100,000, were borne by Mark Hanna himself. At first, Hanna seriously considered setting up a campaign fund into which his rich friends could contribute, but then he decided to wait until the election campaign itself. He realized that, in the nominating process, a relatively small amount of funds flows to a candidate primarily for reasons of personal friendship, while in the election campaign itself a far greater amount of money flows to a candidate for reasons of party loyalty. To tap his friends in the early stages, he knew, would strain his fund-raising abilities in the last months of the campaign.

McKinley's only serious rival for the nomination was Thomas B. Reed, Speaker of the House of Representatives. Reed, however, lacked funds and was hostile to large contributions, and thus his chances for the nomination were diminished.

Hanna's claim to campaign-finance fame rests on the development of his businesslike methods of collecting money from corporations. He did not invent any new techniques, he simply used the old ones in a more orderly fashion. Nor did he forge the business-political tie; it had existed for over half a century prior to 1896. But he did systematize the collection of funds and, for better or for worse, raised the level of the entire financial operation of campaigns out of the trough of blackmail and bribery.

Generally, American businesses at the turn of the century were jittery. Most believed that the free coinage of silver would prove to be financial insanity, that any reduction in protective tariffs would wipe out economic prosperity, and that the stirrings of blue-collar workers were un-American and "socialist." They recognized that corporations had undergone radical transformation over the last two decades through the process of combination, and that they themselves, quite rightly, were vulnerable to both state and federal antitrust actions and to the rising tide of public criticism. Thus businessmen flocked enthusiastically to McKinley because he was one of them. Hanna, therefore, did not have to twist any arms for funds; he only had to ask for them.

Hanna, in his capacity as chairman of the RNC, levied regular assessments on all businesses of consequence throughout the country. No distinction was made between "big business" and "business." Assessments were apportioned according to each company's "stake in the general prosperity" and to its special interest in a region. Banks, for instance, were assessed one quarter of one percent of their capital; Standard Oil contributed about a quarter of a million dollars, and the large insurance companies slightly less. If a company sent in a check Hanna believed to be too small, it was returned; if a company paid too much, a refund was sent out.

Hanna accepted no contributions in return for promises of any kind. In one instance he returned a $10,000 check to a group of Wall Street bankers because a quid pro quo was implied in the contribution. Most companies, however, paid up willingly because they believed such contributions "bought" prosperity and safety from attack. It was understood by them that, if elected, the Republicans would conduct the affairs of government to the benefit of business.

Hanna also kept a close account of the money raised, and none of it lined his own pockets along the way. He did not believe in payoffs, graft or vote-buying, and in most cases he refused to pay campaign bills until results had been produced. The Quays and Penroses of American politics ridiculed Hanna's openhanded behavior, claiming he lacked true understanding of the American political process. But history was to prove Hanna the more prescient.

McKinley's 1896 campaign cost between $6 and $7 million, the most expensive campaign until after World War I. Hanna was personally responsible for raising most of the money. Three million dollars alone came from New York City Republicans, thanks largely to railroad magnate James J. Hill, who dispelled the reservations of fellow financiers by introducing Hanna, a midwesterner with few eastern contacts, around Wall Street.

Hanna conducted what can be considered the first modern advertising campaign. Like patent medicine ads, he had McKinley's face plastered on millions of posters, billboards, pamphlets, inscriptions, cartoons and buttons. He dispatched 1,400 trained speakers around the country to beat the McKinley drum, and he delivered each week to local newspapers prewritten squibs about his candidate. Over 300 million campaign documents, including some in German, French, Spanish, Italian, Swedish, Danish, Dutch and Yiddish, were sent out by the National Committee. This paper blizzard represented more than twenty pieces of literature for every eligible voter in the country.

Poet Vachel Lindsay best caught the mood of the election, and Hanna's part in it, in his poem "Bryan, Bryan, Bryan, Bryan," in which he wrote:

> Then Hanna to the rescue,
> Hanna of Ohio,
> Rallying the roller-tops,
> Rallying the bucket-shops.
> Threatening drouth and death,
> Promising manna,
> Rallying the trusts against the bawling flannelmouth;
> Invading misers' cellars,
> Tin-cans, socks,
> Melting down the rocks,
> Pouring out the long green to a million workers,
> Spondulix by the mountain-load, to stop each new tornado,
> And beat the cheapskate, blatherskite,
> Populistic, anarchistic,
> Deacon—desperado.

Bryan did not have a chance against McKinley and his money, but he did manage to spend $650,000 traveling 18,000 miles around the country making 600 speeches to a total of 5 million people. His campaign was financed in large part by western silver miners, principally by Marcus Daly of the Anaconda Company. Bryan was approached by a friend who told him that an aspirant for Vice-President would like to be on the ticket because "Bryan is poor and I can finance his campaign." Bryan indignantly turned his friend down.

Compounding Bryan's woes, the Republican National Committee also spent a large sum of money supporting Democrats who had bolted the party that year to support the splinter "National Democrats" of John M. Palmer and General Simon Bolivar Buckner.

The 1900 election was a repeat of 1896 except that far less money was needed to defeat Bryan. With his customary efficiency, Hanna shook down the business world for $2.5 million. All major corporations were assessed and most paid with no argument. Standard Oil contributed $250,000, but was refunded $50,000 when Hanna decided that the company's share in the general prosperity, while large, was still less than had previously been determined.

But by 1904, only four years later, many businessmen had lost their enthusiasm for the Republican party. Theodore Roosevelt's energetic trust-busting activities, the reform activities of such people as Hiram Johnson (who once ran for governor of California on the slogan "Kick the Corporations Out of Politics"), Ida M. Tarbell, Lincoln Steffens and Upton Sinclair, and the growing antibusiness sentiment throughout the country had taken their toll of many regular and potential givers to the party.

Recognizing this, Roosevelt disarmed his business opposition, led by Mark Hanna, by declaring early and unequivocally for his own reelection. Thus, any business-inspired financial boycott was hobbled from the start.

Roosevelt spurned raising money from small contributors as unworkable, and rejected the suggestion that he return funds from "tainted" sources, although he did refuse a $10,000 contribution from Standard Oil. Instead, he turned to some of the country's wealthiest individuals for the money he needed. RNC treasurer Cornelius N. Bliss, Sr., J. P. Morgan and one of his partners, George W. Perkins, contributed large sums. So did James Stillman of the National City Bank, James H. Hyde of Equitable Life, the Gould family and Philadelphia financier E. T. Stotesbury. For reasons best known to himself, Andrew Carnegie offered to contribute the *last* $50,000.

For the first time the Jewish community supported the GOP in a big way. Broker Jules S. Bache of J. S. Bache & Company, investment bankers Jacob H. Schiff of Kuhn, Loeb & Company, James Speyer of Speyer & Company, Isaac Seligman of J. & W. Seligman & Company, and copper magnate Adolph Lewisohn all contributed, none less than $10,000.

Edward H. Harriman personally raised $250,000 and claimed that Roosevelt offered him a quid pro quo in return for the money by offering to appoint Senator Chauncey Depew ambassador to France. The story is reinforced by Henry Clay Frick, who, years later, when referring to a visit he made to the White House with Harriman, supposedly remarked: "He [Roosevelt] got down on his knees to us. We bought the son of a bitch and then he did not stay bought." Perhaps because Depew was never appointed ambassador.

The Democrats in 1904 were in such poor shape financially that they nominated for Vice-President 80-year-old former Senator Henry Gassaway Davis of West Virginia. Davis's only qualification for the office was his immense wealth; it was hoped he would be the party's prime financial angel. In spite of all Davis could do, and it was not enough, the Democratic National Committee ended the campaign $900,000 in debt. When Urey Woodson, secretary to the DNC, told Thomas Fortune Ryan and August Belmont the sum of the debt, Ryan turned to Belmont and said, "That's very reasonable. Gussie, you send your check for $450,000 and I'll send mine for $450,000. We'll pay these bills and let Mr. Woodson and the boys go home." Belmont protested that he had already contributed $200,000 to the campaign. "Yes, Gussie, I know that," replied Ryan, "but remember, [Alton B.] Parker was your candidate."

In 1905 and 1906, the Legislative Insurance Investigating Committee, or Armstrong Committee, uncovered evidence from a series of reluctant witnesses that a number of large insurance companies had donated sizable sums to several campaigns as far back as 1896, and that such funds were concealed on their books as "legal expenses." Such firms as Aetna, Mutual, New York Life, Equitable and The Prudential, it was revealed, had long used funds belonging to policyholders for a variety of political purposes. Findings indicated that New York Life, for instance, had paid a lobbyist nearly half a million dollars, $75,000 of which was given in turn to the Republican National Committee.

Did not such contributions, asked counsel Charles Evans Hughes of Senator Thomas Platt, boss of the New York state Republican organization, put a candidate under moral obligation not to attack the financial interests backing him? "That is naturally what is involved," answered Platt matter-of-factly.

These revelations led to New York State passing legislation prohibiting insurance companies and other corporations from contributing to political campaigns. Coupled with the general antibusiness sentiment, it also led in 1907 to the passage in Congress of the Tillman Act, which prohibited national banks and corporations from making a contribution or expenditure in connection with any election to any political office. The same year, Congress passed amendments to the Civil Service Reform Act of 1883 (the Pendleton Act), strengthening the law prohibiting civil servants from taking an active part in political management or campaigns. It was also in 1907 that Theodore Roosevelt proposed that the government subsidize campaign expenses, that limits be placed on the amount a person could contribute, and that there be full financial disclosure of campaign funds.

The Presidential race of 1908 produced more grist for the reform mill. Bryan said that he would not accept more than $10,000 from any one person, but somehow loyal Democratic givers Ryan and Belmont ended up giving $80,000 and $250,000, respectively. Taft said that he would not take money from trusts or people identified with them. Outwardly he was so antagonistic toward Wall Street that in correspondence he referred to it as "a narrow strip of street in New York." Yet his campaign still managed to accept large donations from men with names like Bliss, Herrick, Morgan, Schiff, Stotesbury, Perkins, Frick, Gould and Harriman—men all closely associated with either trusts or Wall Street.

Both Bryan and Taft promised to publish lists of contributors and amounts, which they eventually did, although Taft refused to list his prenomination backers. Thus the 1908 election marks the first time in American history that campaign income and expenditures were voluntarily disclosed. The documents showed that the Taft campaign spent $1.7 million, the Bryan campaign $629,000.

In 1910 Congress passed a law, known as the Publicity Bill, requiring the treasurer of a political committee to file receipts and expenditures within thirty days after an election with the clerk of the House of Representatives. The major loophole in the bill was its failure to require anyone else to file. It also did not require preelection publicity of receipts and expenditures.

The following year amendments to the Tillman Act were passed providing for preelection publicity, and covering as well both primaries and conventions. It also required both senators and representatives to file statements, and limited their total contributions and expenditures to $10,000 and $5,000, respectively.

The Senate was particularly desirous of including senatorial candidates in the new law because of charges that two senators had secured their seats by corrupt methods. In the September, 1908, Wisconsin primary, a candidate for the U.S. Senate was charged with spending $250,000 to buy enough votes in the state legislature to win. Three years later, just prior to the passage of the 1911 amendment, the Illinois Senate adopted a resolution declaring that U.S. Senator William Lorimer had secured his election through bribery and corruption, and the seat was subsequently declared vacant.

One historian, writing in 1926, commented as follows on the reforms of 1907 and 1911: "The day of secret party funds had passed and thereafter [1911] the parties were to be held in strict accountability for the money raised and expended by them."

Republican money in the 1912 race was, like the party itself, split between the Old Guard Taftites and the Progressives of LaFollette and Roosevelt. The liberal Republican money committed to progressivism was largely withheld from LaFollette and given to Roosevelt, thus playing a significant part in securing the nomination for the latter.

In the general election itself Roosevelt was underwritten by Morgan partner George W. Perkins, journalist Medill McCormick (who was married to Mark Hanna's daughter), T. Coleman Du Pont, roller-bearing manufacturer Henry H. Timken, Jewish philanthropist Oscar Straus (who led the New York Bull Moose Convention delegates down the aisle singing "Onward, Christian Soldiers"), Mark Hanna's son, Dan, and two wealthy Roosevelt relatives.

More than 80 percent of LaFollette's campaign funds came from three people: plumbing manufacturer Charles R. Crane, Congressman William Kent, who had made a fortune in California real estate and livestock, and Gifford Pinchot, a wealthy conservationist who was later governor of Pennsylvania.

Taft could count only on the more conservative J. P. Morgan, E. T. Stotesbury, Boston stock speculator Thomas W. Lawson and powerful New York banker C. H. Kelsey. John D. Archbold of Standard Oil sent $25,000 to the Republican National Committee via Boies Penrose in fulfillment of an "understanding" between them—presumably the negotiated Standard Oil contribution quota for the year (which was by now against the law). Charles P. Taft paid his brother's entire prenomination costs of $200,000.

Woodrow Wilson, a relatively poor man unable to finance his own political career, was financed by his rich Princeton classmate, Cleveland H. Dodge, by financier Bernard M. Baruch, Charles R. Crane, James J. Hill, Henry Morgenthau, Sr., Jacob Schiff and William Jennings Bryan's brother. Early in the campaign Wilson tried to raise the bulk of his money from small contributions of $100 or less, but the effort was a failure and he returned to a few leading businessmen for his cash. However, he did write to Morgenthau, chairman of the Democratic Finance Committee, that there were "three rich men in the Democratic party whose political affiliations are so unworthy that I shall depend upon you to see that none of their money is used in my campaign." He was referring to Belmont, Ryan and Morgan.

Four years later Wilson was once again underwritten by wealthy friends. This time he willingly accepted funds from Belmont and Ryan. Between them and Baruch, Crane and Dodge, they raised nearly $800,000. One of Wilson's largest contributors was E. L. Doheny, who later won notoriety in the Teapot Dome scandal. Henry Ford also contributed and received a quid pro quo: he and his cars would be advertised during the campaign, and he would have the privilege of calling on the President in return for his sizable contribution.

Several developments during the years around World War I were to influence further the course of campaign financing. One was the ratification of the Seventeenth Amendment in 1913 requiring that senators be elected directly by the people. Another was the widespread adoption by states of the direct primary (as opposed to state and district conventions) as a means of selecting party candidates. Both increased the costs of running for office. In 1920, the Nineteenth Amendment was ratified, granting suffrage to women; it nearly doubled the general costs of campaigning.

The passage of the Underwood Tariff Act, the income tax law and the establishment of the Federal Reserve System in 1913, and the passage of the Clayton Anti-Trust Act of 1914, were other developments that clearly affected the course of campaign funding. As the government moved to intervene more deeply in the economic affairs of the country, it became necessary for businessmen, in order to protect themselves and their investments, to take a more active role in the political arena. The trend accelerated during Franklin D. Roosevelt's administration and has not slackened since. Labor unions were later to move in a similar manner when the government sought to control their activities. Thus, what began around the Civil War as an alliance of convenience was by the 1920's fast hardening into an alliance of necessity.

The 1920 election was unique in several respects. It was the first campaign in which a large-scale attempt was made to poll the electorate. Early in the year the *Literary Digest* sent out eleven million postcards testing the popularity of various candidates among middle-class voters. It was also a year in which unusually large sums were invested by Republican hopefuls in the Presidential nomination, with the prize going to the man who spent the least.

Maneuvering for the Republican nomination were Senator Hiram Johnson of California, General Leonard Wood and Illinois governor Frank Lowden. Johnson, Theodore Roosevelt's running mate in 1912, was financed by William Wrigley, Jr., of the chewing gum company, and Albert Lasker, the advertising genius and assistant chairman of the Republican National Committee. They raised approximately $200,000, which in this particular election was not enough to make Johnson a serious threat to Wood or Lowden.

Wood, on the other hand, was lavishly financed. His campaign manager, Colonel William C. Procter, a Cincinnati soap manufacturer, headed the Leonard Wood League, organized solely to push Wood's candidacy. The League pledged to raise $500,000, and Procter himself contributed $250,000 in cash and $750,000 in unsecured loans. Ambrose Monell, a steel executive, and two Wood friends, George A. Whalen and Rufus Patterson, each pledged $250,000. Dan Hanna pledged to raise $600,000, and Standard Oil executive H. H. Rogers and tobacco czar James B. Duke also promised large sums.

Procter spent a third of a million dollars in vain to win the Illinois delegation—even by today's standards a large sum. A vast amount of money was spent with more success for the ten delegate votes from sparsely settled South Dakota. One of Wood's lieu-

tenants told Samuel Hopkins Adams that the going rate for a
single southern GOP delegate was as high as $5,000.

Lowden underwrote most of his expenses out of his own pocket.
His father-in-law was a Pullman, which, even in those extraordinary times, tagged him with the taint of money. (Such considera-
tions were of less concern to the Democrats, who eventually chose
two very wealthy men to head their ticket.)

Lowden was further hurt by the revelation, shortly before the
convention, that one supporter had paid the Lowden manager in
Missouri $32,000 "to create Lowden sentiment." Over half the
money went to a Missouri national committeeman, who in turn
paid two uncommitted St. Louis delegates $2,500 each "for noth-
ing in particular but to create sentiment for Governor Lowden."
The two were sufficiently moved to declare publicly for Lowden.
When it was revealed how they were moved, Lowden's effort
began to flag.

So much money was being spent to win the nomination that
many believed there was a plot afoot to buy the Presidency.
Colonel Procter had spent so much promoting Wood, in fact, that
it backfired. In February, 1920, Hearst's *New York American* ran
an exposé of Wood's rich backers. Later in the spring Johnson
accused Wood of spending vast and improper sums that gave him
undue advantage. Senator William Borah, one of the major proponents of the plot theory, loudly condemned Wood's "saturnalia
of corruption."

In late May the Senate Committee on Privileges and Elections,
known as the Kenyon Committee after its chairman, Senator
William Kenyon of Iowa, appointed a subcommittee "to inquire
into the campaign expenditures of various political candidates of
both parties and any related facts that would be of public concern." The subcommittee found that there was no plot to buy the
Presidency but that the Wood forces had spent over $1.7 million
before the convention and probably three times that amount off the
record. This revelation branded Wood the rich man's candidate
and doomed his chances. The Lowden campaign, the subcommittee found, had recorded over $410,000 in expenses, the Johnson
forces $194,000 and the Harding camp only $113,000.

These disclosures played a significant part in creating a stale-
mate at the convention and led the bosses to select Warren Hard-

ing as a compromise choice. The dying Boies Penrose was supposed to have asked Harding: "Warren, how would you like to be President?" Harding was not particularly enthusiastic, claiming that he had no money and problems back in Ohio. Imperiously, Penrose said that money would be no problem. "I will look after that," he said. "You will make the McKinley type of candidate. You look the part. You can make a front-porch campaign like McKinley's and we'll do the rest."

Early in the 1920 campaign, Harry Daugherty, Harding's campaign manager and later Attorney General, set up a bootleg bank account in his brother Mally's Midland National Bank in Washington Court House, Ohio, ostensibly for the purpose of financing Harding's nomination effort. The account was known as the "Jess Smith Extra No. 3," after a Harding lieutenant. Not much was ever learned of this account, since Daugherty burned the bank records prior to the first of his two trials for malfeasance, of which he was acquitted in both instances. It is known, however, that at least $50,000 in Liberty Bonds was deposited in the account after Harding became President. This money was supposedly part payment from a German national who sought unsuccessfully to retrieve his American company that had been seized and sold during World War I.

GOP chairman Will H. Hays tried to limit contributions in the campaign to small amounts, nothing over $1,000. A third of the Republicans' $3 million budget was contributed by 12,000 individuals who gave an average of less than $90 each. The rest of the funds came from Wall Street and industrial leaders. One of Harding's most effective fund raisers was John W. Weeks, a Massachusetts stockbroker-turned-politician who was rewarded for his labors by being appointed Secretary of War. At the other end of the scale was Bill Orr, who also raised funds for Harding. Orr was a former secretary to the governor of New York but during Prohibition was to become a wholesale bootlegger.

In all, the Republicans reported spending $6 million and the Democrats $1.4 million on the 1920 Presidential race. Both parties ended up with deficits. Hays testified in 1928 before the Walsh Committee that he had appealed to oilman Harry Sinclair, a central figure in the Teapot Dome scandal, to make up the $1.2 million GOP deficit. Sinclair, according to Hays, "loaned" him

$260,000 in Liberty Bonds which Sinclair had acquired through a complicated maneuver resulting in stockholders being robbed of their dividends. Hays, in turn, tried to peddle these "hot" bonds to prominent Republican contributors in return for a subscription to the party deficit. It was at best an unethical move. He sent $50,000 in bonds to Andrew Mellon, the Secretary of the Treasury, who returned them, saying rather testily that he preferred to contribute an equal sum from his own funds. Senator T. H. Caraway of Arkansas called Hays a "fence" who "knew that certain goods were stolen goods and was trying to help the thief find a market for them." Mellon, he added, "although he declined to aid in the marketing of the goods . . . handed them back so that the fence could find somebody else who would act for him."

The distinguishing characteristic of both the 1924 and 1928 elections was the large contributions from very conservative and reactionary sources used to oppose the ambitions of various politicians. Singled out for special attention were Robert LaFollette, who headed the Progressive party in 1924, and Al Smith, a Catholic governor of New York, who sought the Democratic nomination for President in 1924 and 1928.

In the 1924 contest, a fund of $437,000 was used for the sole purpose of slandering and libeling LaFollette. Some of the money was spent on advertisements in the *Saturday Evening Post,* one of which called LaFollette the candidate of "the Reds, the Pinks, the Blues and the Yellows." LaFollette was also charged with having been financed by Soviet funds that had entered the country via Mexico. Altogether, LaFollette spent less than $250,000 and received close to 5 million votes.

The Democratic party that year was dominated by the Ku Klux Klan. An estimated 350 delegates to the national convention, or one third the whole, were Klansmen, and it was their money and votes that denied the nomination to Smith. Four years later the power of the Klan had waned sufficiently for Smith to win the nomination.

But Smith could still not overcome the national sentiment for Hoover in 1928. Smith appointed John J. Raskob chairman of the Democratic National Committee. Raskob, who previously had been chairman of the General Motors finance committee, appointed five millionaires to run the party's campaign activities:

broker M. J. Meehan, Herbert H. Lehman, Pierre S. Du Pont, New York contractor William Kenny, and Raskob himself. In spite of their efforts, the Democrats ran up a deficit of $1.5 million over the $7.2 million collected. The victorious Republicans spent $9.4 million, the largest sums coming from six Fisher brothers (of the Fisher Body Company) and Julius Rosenwald (of Sears, Roebuck).

Two developments in the 1920's were to affect further the course of political finance: one was Prohibition and the other was a general decline throughout the country in the demand for reform.

Prohibition affected campaign financing because it created an alliance between the underworld and politicians which most of the public encouraged. Anyone who wanted a drink usually overlooked the fact that it was available only because payoffs had been made up and down the political ladder. Al Capone, the country's leading bootlegger, was one of the biggest contributors to political campaigns during the 1920's, although his name does not show up in the records. He is supposed to have contributed $200,000 to the first campaign of Chicago Mayor William Hale ("Big Bill") Thompson, and $175,000 to James J. Walker in his campaign for mayor of New York in 1925. This was only the tip of the iceberg. These "campaign funds," in turn, went to pay off judges, policemen, businessmen and politicians at all levels so that everyone from the still operator to the drinking customer would be free of any harassment by the forces of the law.

Many political offices in a state like Louisiana, for instance, came to be financed in large part by bootlegger and mob money. A parish sheriff in those days might have all his campaign bills paid by bootleggers, in return for his overlooking the existence of roadside speakeasies. Frank Costello, a powerful New York mobster, was supposed to have made a deal with Huey Long toward the end of Prohibition for the gambling rights in the state, presumably in return for an annual contribution to the state Democratic party. One of Long's biographers, however, disputes the story.

The amount of money spent by the pro- and anti-liquor forces just prior to and during Prohibition was large. For instance, the Pennsylvania Brewers Association *alone* spent $922,000 between 1912 and 1916 fighting the "drys." Much of this money went to political candidates as contributions. Between 1920 and 1925, the Anti-Saloon League spent an average of $1.8 million yearly fighting the "wets." In the 1928 election the League spent $1.5 million to defeat Smith.

The lack of zeal for reform during the 1920's took its toll on campaign finance law. The Newberry case was the first setback. In 1918, Truman H. Newberry was a candidate for the U.S. Senate on the Republican primary ticket in Michigan. Henry Ford was a candidate on both the Republican and Democratic primary tickets for the same office. On primary day Newberry won the Republican nomination and Ford the Democratic endorsement. In the general election Newberry beat Ford and, several months later, took his seat in the Senate. But Ford protested that Newberry had spent far in excess of the $10,000 limit to secure the Republican nomination. Newberry was subsequently indicted on charges of conspiracy and violating the Tillman Act, as amended in 1911, and was convicted. But the case was reversed in 1921 on appeal to the Supreme Court which divided five to four, ruling that a primary was not an "election" as construed in the law. This decision cast doubt on the right of Congress to regulate nominations.

The true importance of Newberry's victory in 1918, however, lay in the fact that it gave the GOP a crucial one-vote margin in the Senate. Thus, Henry Cabot Lodge became chairman of the Senate Foreign Relations Committee, and he used his position to oppose successfully the United States' entry into the League of Nations. Had Newberry lost, or had the Newberry-Ford dispute been resolved immediately after the election rather than three years later, history might have taken another course.

Pressure for additional legislation to curb campaign financing excesses led to the passage in 1925 of the Corrupt Practices Act. The essential provisions of the act limited expenditures for a candidate for the House of Representatives to $5,000 and a candidate for the Senate to $25,000. All candidates for federal office were required to file periodic statements itemizing each contribution and expenditure received or made by him or by any person for him with his knowledge and consent. The law also reinforced the ban on contributions from national banks and corporations.

In keeping with the temper of the times, the law was more show than substance, for it was riddled with loopholes. The $5,000 and $25,000 expenditure limitations, for instance, could be evaded simply by claiming that certain expenses were made without the candidate's "knowledge and consent." Furthermore, no audits were required. The reports, filed in Washington, were generally unavailable to the public and were on file for only two years. The law also exempted certain costs such as stationery, postage, printing and telephone bills from the official tally. And in keeping with the Newberry decision, no primary election receipts and expenditures had to be reported at all. Thus, in states where a primary victory was tantamount to election, the law was next to useless. Finally, the ban on bank and corporate contributions was evaded either by having the money donated in the name of a corporate officer or by setting up "educational" or "nonpartisan" organizations through which the money could be channeled.

"The fact is," wrote political commentator Frank Kent in 1923, "that nowhere in the country has there been devised a legal method of effectively limiting the amount of money that may be spent in political fights. No law has been enacted through which the politicians cannot drive a four-horse team." This was just as true two years later following the passage of the Corrupt Practices Act.

In 1926 the Senate investigated allegations of excessive expenditures in the Pennsylvania senatorial primary. The contest between Willian S. Vare, a member of Congress and Republican boss of Philadelphia, and George Wharton Pepper, the incumbent Republican senator, was a factional fight between coalition tickets for political control of the state. Vare won both the primary and general election contests.

In December of that year, a special Senate committee, created in the spring to investigate campaign expenditures for senatorial candidates for the six-year term beginning March 4, 1927, found that in the primaries the victorious Vare team had spent $785,000, the Pepper coalition $1.8 million, and the Democratic candidate $10,000.

It was alleged that Albert M. Greenfield, representing utility and real estate interests, contributed $125,000 to the Vare campaign and that Thomas W. Cunningham, a party worker of no great wealth, had contributed another $50,000. Pepper's campaign, on the other hand, received over $600,000 from Joseph Grundy and several other wealthy industrialists, and $173,000 from three members of the Mellon family. Election-day workers were so numerous in both camps that it took over three days to pay them all.

The Senate Committee on Privileges and Elections, having reviewed the evidence, decided not to allow Vare to take his seat. But they declared that the Democratic candidate, whose listed expenses were within the legal limit, had not won either. The Corrupt Practices Act was weakened when Pennsylvania's governor appointed Grundy, a party to the original violation, to fill the vacancy, and the Senate did nothing to stop it. It was further weakened when Vare was not prosecuted for his illegal actions, as was required under the provisions of the act.

In the same year there were also allegations of excessive contributions in the Illinois senatorial primary elections. The same special Senate committee found that incumbent Republican Senator William B. McKinley had spent more than $500,000 in his renomination effort and that Frank L. Smith, chairman of the Illinois Commerce Commission, had invested over $450,000 in his successful challenge. By contrast, the Democratic candidate, who lost in the general election, did not exceed the $25,000 limit.

The committee also found that Samuel Insull, representing $650 million worth of Illinois public utilities (subject to regulation by the Illinois Commerce Commission), contributed $125,000 to the Smith campaign, and that Clement Studebaker, Jr., of Indiana, also an officer in Illinois utility corporations, contributed $20,000. In all, Illinois public service institutions contributed over $200,000 to the Smith campaign. Insull had further hedged his bets by donating $15,000 to the Democratic candidate.

The Senate, following the recommendations of the committee, refused to seat Smith or his Democratic opponent. (McKinley had died shortly after the general election.) Again, the law was weakened because there was no prosecution of Smith.

In 1928, Methodist-Episcopal Bishop James Cannon of Virginia was active in an organization called the "Southern Anti-Smith Democrats," into which large amounts of anti-Catholic funds flowed. One wealthy New Yorker contributed $65,000, of which $10,000 was in cash. A congressional investigating committee found that Bishop Cannon had received at least $130,000, much of which was not subsequently accounted for, and that he had not filed a report as required by the Corrupt Practices Act. Cannon and his secretary were eventually tried for conspiracy to violate the act but were acquitted when both defendants denied knowledge of such funds, making a conspiracy conviction impossible. The result further undermined the effectiveness of the Corrupt Practices Act.

Thus, the stage was set for widespread evasions of the spirit, if not the letter, of the law in the years ahead.

IV

The Age of Media

The Great Depression marks a point in American history when our attitudes and endeavors regarding campaign financing practices shifted perceptibly. On the one hand, while boodling had been widely accepted by the public prior to the stock-market crash, its most blatant manifestations were no longer tolerated afterward. While corruption of the process previously had been open and direct, following 1929 it became more devious and difficult to spot.

On the other hand, if there had been some effort to comply with the funding laws prior to the Depression, there were widespread evasions of them afterward. If there were a few fainthearted attempts to discipline violators before, there were none in the years to follow (except in the past few years, and most of those from an unexpected quarter). If, prior to the crash, there had been endeavors to build an ever-improving body of law designed to control campaign-financing practices, later efforts, at least until the passage of the Federal Election Campaign Act of 1971, were negative in that they did not strengthen that body by providing better machinery for enforcement, or encouraging compliance, or closing any loopholes.

Perhaps the most obvious change since the twenties has been the growing hypocrisy with which we have come to treat the subject. It has been most manifest in our speech. For example, while we previously called a bribe what it was—a payoff, a fix, or money for favors—we are now using euphemisms such as "speaker's fees," "convention book advertising," "testimonial dinners" and, on occasion, even "campaign contributions" itself.

By the time the Great Depression was upon us, the blunt language of a frontier society appears to have given way to the indirect idiom of a consumer-oriented middle-class society. Through the use of words we have come to sanitize the unsavory practice of bribery, the same way we have subsequently sanitized sewage by calling it "waste water." But the point should not be lost: these words may sound better to the ear, but it is still bribery and is no less corrupt.

Our actions have also reflected this hypocrisy. Year after year, as our campaign financing laws became increasingly unrealistic and difficult to police, otherwise honest and conscientious men felt compelled to perjure themselves in order to survive in the political arena. By the time the 1971 Federal Election Campaign Act was passed, nearly everyone involved in political finance was a willing hyprocrite, winking at the laws they broke as a universally acceptable practice. However, despite the existence of this new law, there is reason to suspect that we have not seen the last of this hyprocrisy.

But we are getting ahead of ourselves; the story should tell itself.

The Democratic party found itself in very poor shape financially following Hoover's 1928 victory. Raskob, in an extraordinary act of faith, came up with at least $30,000 a month between the years 1929 and 1932 to keep the Democratic National Committee afloat—all this at a time when he was "losing millions a day" in the stock market slide. He also contributed $148,000 to the 1932 Democratic campaign.

Two of the reasons national and state Democratic party leaders were so well disposed toward Franklin D. Roosevelt were his financial independence coupled with his ability to flush out large contributors. It was an important consideration in his selection as Democratic candidate for governor of New York in 1928, when the state party was deeply in debt, and it was also a factor in his winning the Democratic nomination for President in 1932.

The first of Roosevelt's alphabet agencies was the FRBC, composed of individuals who had committed themselves financially For Roosevelt Before Chicago. It was a small group first drawn together in 1930 by Edward J. Flynn, the long-time Democratic boss of The Bronx, to promote FDR's candidacy. Each member promised to contribute $2,000 or more; some gave as much as $50,000.

Its original members included Jesse Straus of Macy's, American Car & Foundry president and ex-Republican contributor William H. Woodin, Judge Robert Worth Bingham of the *Louisville Courier-Journal,* financier and movie producer Joseph P. Kennedy, Congressman (and wealthy banker) Guy Helvering, Senator Cordell Hull, former ambassador Henry Morgenthau, Sr., actor Eddie Dowling, New York lieutenant governor Herbert Lehman, Dutchess County neighbor Vincent Astor, and lawyers Frank C. Walker, James W. Gerard (whose father-in-law was Marcus Daly of the Anaconda Company), Lawrence Steinhardt, Joseph E. Davies and David Hennen Morris.

So important did Roosevelt and his advisers consider their financial help that nearly all of them were rewarded with prestigious jobs. Straus, for instance, became ambassador to France, Woodin became Secretary of the Treasury, Bingham was appointed ambassador to the Court of St. James's, Kennedy became the head of the Securities and Exchange Commission and later ambassador to London, and Helvering served as commissioner of the Internal Revenue Service. Hull became Secretary of State, Morgenthau's son was appointed Secretary of the Treasury, Lehman became Director General of the United Nations Relief and Rehabilitation Administration, Walker was appointed Postmaster General, Gerard represented the United States at the coronation of King George VI, Steinhardt served in a series of ambassadorial posts, Davies became our second ambassador to the Soviet Union, and Morris was appointed ambassador to Belgium.

Only Eddie Dowling and Vincent Astor refused appointments. Interestingly enough, FDR never appointed Bernard Baruch to anything, even though Baruch contributed at least $60,000 to the 1932 campaign (and never less than $12,500 to every Democratic Presidential candidate since 1912), because Baruch, like Astor, was not a "political" friend.

All these wealthy men, however, could not overcome the financial poverty of the party during the general election itself. "The great trouble with the Democrats," said Huey Long at one point, "is that we have all the votes and no money. In the present situation I believe the best thing we could do is to sell President Hoover a million votes for half what he is going to pay to try to get them. We can spare the votes and we could use the money."

Joseph Kennedy tapped William Randolph Hearst for $30,000, which was given with no publicity since Hearst had been for John Garner at the Chicago convention and strongly opposed to Roosevelt. John Nicholas Brown of Rhode Island also contributed, as did a Biddle from Philadelphia and a Guggenheim from New York.

At the end of their successful 1932 campaign, the Democratic National Committee had spent $2.2 million and found itself $600,000 in debt, which took five years to pay back. In fact, during Roosevelt's long administration there were few elections that did not produce a heavy party debt. "When the hunger became acute," wrote Charles Michelson, the DNC's publicity director, "you might hear [DNC Secretary] Chip Robert on the transatlantic telephone calling on Ambassador Tony Biddle for a hurry-up check for a few thousand to tide us over."

The Republican National Committee spent nearly $3 million during 1932, and nearly all of it came from a relatively few hardcore party faithful. Various Mellons gave $45,000, the Pratt (Standard Oil) family gave at least $36,500, Ogden Mills (Hoover's Secretary of the Treasury) gave over $30,000, and the Milbanks (of the Commercial Solvents Corporation) gave over $25,000. One report lists the Chase National Bank, J. P. Morgan & Company, and Kuhn, Loeb & Company as contributing $36,000, $13,500 and $28,500, respectively. On its face, the Chase contribution was against the law.

By 1936 some businessmen had become so hostile to FDR and his New Deal policies that they were willing to go to extraordinary lengths to see him defeated. The best-known anti-Roosevelt organization was the American Liberty League, made up mostly of diehard reactionaries and those disillusioned by Roosevelt's pragmatism. Among those who contributed to the League were the Bankers Trust Company ($20,000) and none other than John J. Raskob ($10,000).

Several months before his death in 1936, Huey Long was approached by several members of the League and offered $2 million in campaign funds from big business and banks if he would work to remove FDR from office. When Long replied that he was more radical than the President, one member of the group shot back: "Well, we're not for you, either!"

After four years of the New Deal, money was easier to collect for the Republican party. Frank Altschul, a member of a wealthy and aristocratic New York Jewish family, crossed parties and gave $20,000. Hugh D. Auchincloss and his wife contributed $24,300. The list of contributors giving more than $10,000 also included such familiar GOP names as Baker, Du Pont, Elkins, Frick, Guggenheim, Mellon, Milbank, Mills, Morgan, Pew, Rockefeller, Stotesbury, Vanderbilt, Warburg, Whitney and Widener. Between them, the Pews and Du Ponts gave $1 million. In all, the Republicans raised and spent nearly $9 million.

The Democrats, on the other hand, had to rely essentially on the same benefactors who had contributed in 1932. Pittsburgh oilman Walter A. Jones was a new contributor, giving over $100,000. C. V. Whitney, the Kentucky horse-breeder, gave $10,000. (His mother, Mrs. Payne Whitney, gave $25,000 to the GOP.) Jesse Jones gave $16,000 and was rewarded by being appointed Secretary of Commerce. Stock speculator and bear raider B. E. ("Sell 'em Ben") Smith came up with $10,000. White House speechwriter Charles Michelson claimed FDR turned down one $200,000 contribution because the donor believed it would secure him an ambassador's post. Altogether, the Democrats spent $5.2 million and ended up several hundred thousand dollars in debt. The bulk of the funds appears to have come from contributors giving $500 or more.

Labor unions first began to contribute to national campaigns in a significant way in 1936. In prior elections union contributions had been channeled through the National Non-Partisan Political Campaign Committee and were distributed in an erratic and ineffective manner. Some of the money went to Socialist party and Farmer-Labor party candidates. By 1936 labor money went principally to the Democratic National Committee, labor's Non-Partisan League for its registration and get-out-the vote drives, and the American Labor party, all of which helped Roosevelt.

Historian James MacGregor Burns tells the story of United Mine Workers president John L. Lewis, in his capacity as head of the Congress of Industrial Organizations, coming to the White House with a photographer and a union contribution of $250,000.

Roosevelt and his advisers realized, however, that unions were still held in sufficiently low regard by enough of the public that to be closely associated with one or all of them would be a political liability. So Roosevelt was cordial to Lewis but refused the check, saying he would be pleased to call on the labor leader in the future if money were needed. Lewis then left, knowing that he had been outsmarted. In the following weeks, Roosevelt's money raisers quietly requested small contributions from the CIO. By election day, nearly $500,000 had been siphoned from the union treasury for the Democratic campaign, and not a word of it made the press.

The Democrats also reaped $250,000 from advertisements in their "Book of the Democratic Convention of 1936." Most of the advertisers were companies doing business with, or regulated by, the federal government. A full-page ad cost $2,500, deductible as a business expense. The Republicans issued a similar, if somewhat less profitable, convention book that year.

Historically, the two parties had always sold programs at their conventions. They usually cost no more than twenty-five cents, were limited to essential information and carried no local or national advertising. But with the passage of the Corrupt Practices Act and subsequent restrictive legislation, this manner of fund raising grew in popularity as a way to attract corporate funds.

In 1939, Senator Carl A. Hatch of New Mexico introduced legislation to extend the Pendleton Act's prohibition of political activities by civil servants to virtually all government employees. Pressure for such an extension had been building since 1932 when the size of the federal bureaucracy began to expand enormously under the New Deal programs. But it was a charge, never disproved, that government employees in the Works Progress Administration were being coerced into working for the reelection of the Senate's majority leader, Alben W. Barkley, which actually tipped sentiment in favor of having the legislation passed. Neither party was enthusiastic for passage, and FDR, according to Harold Ickes, seriously considered vetoing the bill on the grounds that "a much more comprehensive bill should be passed."

The following year amendments were passed to the act extending prohibitions to employees of state agencies financed all or in part by loans or grants made by the federal government. Included in the bill was a spending limit of $3 million per campaign committee and a maximum contribution limit of $5,000 per person.

This legislation, like others in the field, was violated repeatedly after its passage. Career bureaucrats, if they bothered at all to be subtle, contributed through nominees when they were not being dunned privately at the office by their superiors. The $3 million limitation was set on the assumption that every campaign naturally would have only one committee handling a candidate's finances. From the start this restriction was evaded simply through the creation of additional committees. Furthermore, state and local committees were exempt from the law. The $5,000 restriction also came to be interpreted conveniently as the limit a person could give to one committee, not all committees.

The two Hatch Acts subsequently produced results not originally anticipated. For instance, they drove some large contributors partially underground and encouraged others to devise elaborate ruses to hide the names of big givers. The passage of these two laws, wrote Charles Michelson, "was to make constructive criminals of all the officials of the two great parties."

In addition, by ostensibly removing federal employees from the political process, the law shifted power in the states from senators to governors, whose patronage employees—the backbone of most vote-getting machines—were not covered by the acts. Thus, where senators such as Hanna and Penrose, twenty to thirty years before, might be crucial in the selection of Presidential candidates, now the power shifted to governors such as Thomas E. Dewey in New York and Earl Warren in California.

Wendell Willkie interpreted the acts as Senator Hatch meant them to be, and vowed to keep his total campaign expenses in 1940 within the $3 million limit. But it was evaded by his managers, who routed the money through state and local organizations—as much as $2.5 million in Pennsylvania alone.

Willkie's fund raising was run by Tom Girdler of Republic Steel. He drew on traditional Republican sources for funds, such as Ogden Mills, E. T. Stotesbury, Joseph Widener, Henry Clay Frick and George F. Baker. The Mellon family came through with over $130,000, and Lammot Du Pont, who had supported FDR in

1936, contributed $49,000. John L. Lewis and the CIO leadership also supported the GOP nominee in 1940. Lewis had broken with the President partly over the latter's condemnation of business and labor ("A plague on both your houses"), and partly over his long-held pique over the treatment he received at the White House in 1936.

The Willkie campaign was lavishly financed. Nearly $15 million was reported spent, and the actual figure was quite a bit higher. Edward J. Flynn, a biased source but nevertheless one who would know, claims he saw five Willkie headquarters on the main street of Phoenix, Arizona, alone.

The unrestricted flow of labor funds into political campaigns began to alarm Republicans and rural and southern Democrats by the early 1940's. Their congressional representatives, allied with anti-Roosevelt Democrats, moved to bring union contributions under the same restrictions as corporate and bank funds. In 1943, the Smith-Connally Anti-Strike Act was passed over the President's veto. Among other things, the law temporarily prohibited unions from contributing directly to national political organizations from their general funds. Four years later the Labor-Management Relations Act (better known as Taft-Hartley, and also passed over the President's veto) placed the temporary Smith-Connally restrictions on a permanent basis, extended the prohibitions on both union and corporate spending to include "expenditures" as well as "contributions" on behalf of a candidate or party, and broadened the restrictions by including primaries, conventions and caucuses.

Since businesses and unions as such were now prohibited from contributing directly from their respective treasuries to political campaigns, money raisers were limited to collecting funds either from individuals or from pro-business or -labor committees technically independent of a particular business or union. As a result, the fund-raising dinner and the political action committee were devised to cope with the problem of raising adequate political funds. The modern fund-raising dinner was supposed to have been invented by Matthew McCloskey, for years the Democratic party's treasurer, as far back as 1934, but it did not become a major fund-raising vehicle until after the passage of the Smith-Connally and Taft-Hartley bills. Political action committees, or PAC's, had their origin in a committee of that name established by the CIO in the early 1940's. It was a forerunner of the AFL-CIO's powerful Committee on Political Education.

During the 1944 election, when speculation arose as to who might be the Democratic Vice-Presidential choice, President Roosevelt was reported to have replied, "Clear everything with Sidney," referring to Sidney Hillman of CIO-PAC. The remark has subsequently been interpreted to indicate the extent of union influence in the election, thus justifying in many opponents' minds the passage of the Smith-Connally Act. Hillman's organization spent approximately $1.3 million in that election, and was to play a leading role in later elections, none more than the 1952 campaign when it denied the Democratic Presidential nomination to Alben Barkley.

The 1944 election also witnessed the first development of legal stratagems to evade the law. J. Howard Pew, of Sun Oil, for instance, contributed tens of thousands of dollars to the GOP by spreading his money among at least fourteen interstate committees. Both parties also began to set up independent, nonparty organizations to which a person could give more than $5,000. FDR had his One Thousand Club (which was almost a shadow DNC) and the Servicemen's Wives to Re-Elect Roosevelt. Dewey had his Democrats for Dewey, the National Association of Pro America, and the People's Committee to Defend Life Insurance and Savings. It was a portent of things to come.

The 1948 election is of special interest because of the drought of money available to the party in power. Ordinarily an incumbent President, seeking reelection, controls enough levers of power to pry loose as much campaign money as he needs. But in that year many Democrats were tired and dispirited after sixteen years in power and were convinced they would lose. Most Republicans believed that their loss in 1944 was a fluke due to the war, and they were in a bullish (overconfident, as it developed) mood.

Traditional GOP money flowed in with no hesitation. There was a scramble among some givers to climb onto the Dewey bandwagon early. Automobile dealers were squeezed for large sums by management and party officials working in concert. If a demand were not met, a dealer's quota of cars—very difficult to get in those days—was cut off the following month. Most dealers, as a result, paid up promptly.

Loyal Truman Democrats were also convinced that the Dixiecrats were being financed in part by northern business interests with southern connections. There is also some indication that some GOP money was diverted to the Dixiecrats and Progressives in order to help widen the Democratic split.

President Truman eventually persuaded Louis Johnson, an Assistant Secretary of War in the second Roosevelt administration, to take over financial control of the 1948 campaign. Johnson was able to collect large sums from wealthy Baltimore businessman James Bruce and American Oil Company founder Jacob Blaustein. Edwin Pauley, an independent oilman, also contributed heavily. He was subsequently blocked as Truman's Undersecretary of the Navy because of an allegation, which Pauley denied, that he offered to contribute several hundred thousand dollars more to the party if the Justice Department would drop its attempt to win control of the nation's tidelands for the federal government.

Large sums apparently also came from four major liquor distillers. A Department of Justice antitrust suit against the companies was dropped in 1949, and Republicans claimed it was the quid pro quo for the money.

Despite these contributions, funds were still so short during the campaign that checks were regularly kited over weekends. One fifteen-minute nationwide radio program was threatened with cancellation because the necessary $25,721 was not available. At the last moment a paper bag full of one, five, ten and fifty dollar bills arrived at Democratic headquarters in New York. It was rushed over to the radio station and the show went off as scheduled. According to several sources, the money had come from Greek-American restaurant owners in Manhattan.

During one cross-country campaign trip, cash to pay for the train ran out when Truman and his party reached Oklahoma. It was an embarrassing situation for an incumbent President to find himself in. A meeting was held between Governor Roy Turner and wealthy banker W. Elmer Harber of Shawnee. They threw a fundraising party in the President's private car and raised more than enough to pay for the rest of the trip.

In the last days of the campaign, Walter Winchell announced that the odds against Truman were 15 to 1. If true, it would hurt the campaign by drying up money sources and starting a bandwagon effect. Governor Turner once more came to the rescue by sending a $20,000 check (signed by Harber) to the campaign for the specific purpose of laying personal bets on Truman. This had the effect of lowering the odds—as far as 2 to 1 in New York and 4 to 1 elsewhere on the average—which in turn kept what little money was available flowing in and squelching the bandwagon effect.

In any election the time when money is contributed is often crucial. A thousand dollars in May, a politician will say, is worth $5,000 in October. Early money allows a campaign to be planned and executed properly. Late money often comes in when the odds begin to even out in the few weeks before election day. But in 1948 the Democrats had neither the advantage of early money nor the solace of late funds. However, the day after Truman's unexpected victory, a small blizzard of predated checks arrived at Democratic headquarters, many of which were followed up by telephone calls from eager donors explaining rather lamely why their check had been mislaid.

The years following Roosevelt's 1932 victory have witnessed a revolution in political communications, a revolution we are still engaged in today. Through radio, extraordinarily large audiences could be reached in a relatively short time and at a fraction of the effort and cost necessary to produce the same impact with the printed word. The cost of a 15- to 30-minute nationwide hookup in the late 1930's and early 1940's, according to Edward J. Flynn, was between $15,000 and $20,000. After World War II it rose to exceed $25,000. A full hour in 1944 cost around $195,000. Any one of these nationwide broadcasts might be heard by a minimum of 10 million voters. To reach as many people as effectively through the mails might cost as much as $1 million, if it could be done at all.

The 1952 Presidential election marks the beginning of the modern age of campaign financing. Television came into its own, as did the airplane, poll-taking, "Fat Cats," political consultants, computers and heavy costs.

This campaign was noted for its very heavy prenomination spending by Republican candidates. The chairman for Citizens for Eisenhower, for instance, reported that his group alone spent $1.2 million prior to the convention, mostly in Presidential preference primaries. This was then considered a large sum, 1920 notwithstanding, and was not revealed until after the election. Indeed, the law did not require that it be reported at all. Almost all of the money came from wealthy members of the Eastern Establishment.

Senator Taft appears to have spent even more money, in part because his campaign was launched much earlier. When his finance chief, Benjamin Tate, was queried about exactly how much was spent, he refused to divulge any figures on the grounds that he had neither files nor time. Some of Taft's funds came from General Motors executives who were subsequently so bitter over their hero's loss to Ike that for several years thereafter they refused to contribute to the GOP. This produced a severe financial problem in the party. Taft himself was sufficiently upset by his defeat to remark that "every Republican candidate for President since 1936 has been nominated by the Chase National Bank."

The big financial issue in the 1952 campaign was the existence of the Nixon Fund. Following Richard Nixon's election as senator from California in 1950, a few wealthy backers set up an $18,000 fund to help finance some of Nixon's political activities between elections on a year-round basis. The story of the "Checkers speech" has been told often enough that it need not be repeated here. Suffice it to say, in retrospect, the entire affair was blown out of proportion. There was nothing unique in the fund; many earlier politicians were beneficiaries of similar arrangements. Clearly the furor over Nixon's fund stemmed from hostility to the man rather than from any moral outrage.

What never received similar attention was the Stevenson Fund, revealed shortly after the "Checkers speech." While he was governor of Illinois, Stevenson had collected money, part of which was state campaign surplus, to supplement salaries of certain administrative state officials he believed were underpaid. When the existence of the fund was made known, Stevenson supplied the names of recipients and the amounts they received. It was not felt necessary for the candidate to go on television to explain his behavior.

Stevenson ran the vote-getting part of his campaign out of Springfield, Illinois, and the financial operation out of New York City. This decentralization created a certain chaos and confusion within the campaign, and inevitably took its toll on the amount of money raised. Nevertheless, Stevenson did receive heavy labor support and large sums from such Democratic regulars as Albert M. Greenfield, Joseph P. Kennedy, Herbert Lehman, Marshall Field, Sr., Averell Harriman and Joseph E. Davies. Beardsley Ruml's plan to finance the election with five-dollar contributions from the rank-and-file party faithful was a flop.

Eisenhower's campaign had few money troubles. All the traditional Republican money came through, even from the mossbacks who had pushed for MacArthur at the convention. During the campaign Ike advocated tidelands oil legislation favorable to the industry, and oil executives of the twenty-two largest firms swamped the campaign with funds.

Big-time money raisers came into their own in the 1952 election. The growing prosperity of the country, the increasing decentralization of the nation's financial power, and the rising costs of campaigns required specialist fund raisers: men who knew better than others a particular source of funds and how to milk it dry. The days when one man could cover Wall Street, and not concern himself seriously with other sources or areas, were over.

Some of those who raised money for the Democrats were Matthew McCloskey, with contacts all along the eastern seaboard; Wiley L. Moore, an Atlanta gas and oil man who scoured the South; Edwin Pauley, who tapped West Coast oilmen and all the Truman sources; George Killion, president of American President Lines, who covered California; House Speaker Sam Rayburn and Senate Majority Leader Lyndon Johnson who raised money in Texas and among oilmen; Milton Kronheim, a liquor importer with clout in Washington, D.C.; Abraham Feinberg, a wealthy New York garment manufacturer who solicited among Jews as an adjunct to his Zionist fund-raising activities; and Roger Stevens, who raised money among New York real estate developers and show business people.

Raising funds for the GOP were J. Clifford Folger who covered Washington, D.C.; philanthropist John Hay ("Jock") Whitney who covered New York contributions; investment banker Sidney

Weinberg who concentrated on Wall Street and the Jewish community; Boston industrialist Thomas Pappas who solicited money from New Englanders; and David B. Simpson, an Oregon realtor who covered the West Coast.

The financial aspects of the 1956 Presidential election were, in many respects, a repeat of the 1952 race. Most of the same fund raisers were active, and many of the same loyal contributors in both parties gave predictable amounts. Both sides even spent about the same amount—the GOP $7.7 million (up $1 million from 1952) and the Democrats $5.1 million (up only $100,000). However, there were a few distinct moments.

Television costs were beginning to hurt, and many campaign budgets were thrown into disarray to accommodate them. To replace *Hit Parade* in 1956, for instance, a candidate had to lay out about $45,000 to compensate the talent, another $50,000 or so for one-half hour of network time, and thousands of dollars more for his own production requirements. Yet, despite the ease with which Presidential candidates could now communicate with the public, they still felt compelled to continue spending money traveling frantically around the country in the manner of William Jennings Bryan, making as many as eight or ten speeches daily.

Several businesses were caught that year crowding the gray area of the law. The Guaranty Trust Company, for instance, ran an advertisement in September, 1956, decrying "public" ownership of electric power plants. The president of the company, under later examination by a Senate subcommittee, claimed the ad was nonpolitical because no candidate or political party was mentioned. At about the same time, the J. Walter Thompson Company circulated a memo among its executives suggesting that a Republican contribution was in order. "What would happen," the memo asked, "to the growth of our company if we faced an extended period of business uncertainty?"

The very thought of such a possibility was enough to make many Fat Cats reach for their checkbooks.

V

Big Money in Control

In the 1964 Presidential elections, Lyndon Johnson's victory enjoyed wide electoral support but was built on a narrow financial base. Goldwater, on the other hand, received relatively few votes but was financed by an extraordinarily large number of contributors. Costs continued to rise over previous elections; television expenditures cornered a larger share of the average campaign budget; selling candidates like headache remedies through the 10-, 20- and 60-second spot became commonplace; polls became more elaborate, more accurate and more expensive; and the phenomenon of the "campaign consultant" came to full flower.

For the Democrats, the only race was for the Vice-Presidential nomination. Money was spent by the President to create an ersatz competition between aspirants which he hoped would keep public interest from concentrating solely on the GOP race. Johnson's refusal to have Robert Kennedy on the ticket was based in part on the knowledge that no significant campaign funds would be withheld as a result. When Presidential adviser James Rowe was dispatched by Johnson to clear Hubert Humphrey's past in the event he became the nominee, one of the questions Rowe asked Humphrey was: "Do any contributors' liens exist on your future politics?" Humphrey replied no, there were none.

There were three primaries that were crucial to the Republicans in 1964: New Hampshire, Oregon and California. Of particular interest in New Hampshire was the Henry Cabot Lodge campaign, which spent less money than all the other GOP campaigns and yet won a clear victory. It was an example of how, with a modicum of zeal, good sense and a good candidate, an American political campaign can be run relatively inexpensively.

It began almost as a lark for Paul Grindle, David Goldberg, Sally Saltonstall and Caroline Williams, four Lodge enthusiasts who were unhappy that the GOP might nominate either Goldwater or Rockefeller. Their first effort on behalf of Lodge, then our ambassador in Saigon, was to spend $87 for a huge Lodge sign, one of the biggest expenses of the campaign.

The major problem was to persuade New Hampshire voters to write in Lodge's name, since the ambassador was neither an announced candidate nor on the ballot. To do this required two very complicated direct mailings to every Republican in the state, the first describing the ballot and how to write in a candidate's name on both paper and machine ballots; and the second to commit respondents to the first mailing to bring two other people to the polls and teach them how to write in Lodge's name. The response to the first mailing was extraordinary, nearly 40 percent of all letters sent out. But the campaign was so poor that it could not pay the postage due on the returns, so a compromise was struck: the postmaster allowed the Lodge workers to look at the mail immediately as it arrived at the post office and to take down addresses, and to collect it later as they had money to pay for it.

About $30,000 was spent by the Lodge forces in New Hampshire, $20,000 of which was a debt secured by Paul Grindle's personal note. (Rockefeller, in comparison, spent approximately $250,000 and Goldwater, slightly less.) Two $3,000 contributions came from Lodge friends; the Lodge family itself gave only several hundred dollars total. John Loeb, a senior partner in Carl M. Loeb, Rhoades & Company and a classmate of Lodge's at Harvard, put together a lunch on Wall Street that was a dismal failure. Over 500 Fat Cats attended but total contributions averaged only $6 per person. As one observer said, "They were scared to death that David [Rockefeller] was listening at the door."

Grindle, Goldberg, Saltonstall and Williams developed new techniques for saving money. They decided that they needed some television exposure for their candidate but realized that they did not have enough money. So Grindle went to New York City and tracked down some footage from 1960 when Lodge was Nixon's running mate. Eventually he found a suitable documentary which he and a friend then set about to update. Whenever Nixon's face appeared it was excised, leaving Lodge alone in the film. Sometimes it proved difficult to do: on occasion there were shots of Lodge with just Nixon's hands appearing on the screen. Likewise, the sound track had to be altered, blipping out "Nixon" whenever it appeared. An Eisenhower endorsement of the "Nixon-Lodge" ticket, for one, came out as an endorsement for "[blip]-Lodge." The show ran for fifteen minutes on the Manchester, New Hampshire, television station and cost $100. The final product was so spotty and unprofessional that the press, as Grindle described it, "fell out of their seats laughing." Goldwater, quite naturally, was furious that Ike had "endorsed" Lodge in a primary, and Rockefeller tried unsuccessfully to have the documentary stopped.

The Lodge team developed other ways to save money. One was to eat and drink off the competition. The Rockefeller campaign was lavishly run in New Hampshire, and the Lodge workers regularly invaded the buffets, cocktail parties and cook-outs to stoke up for the days ahead. Rockefeller's managers were too embarrassed to kick them out, fearing adverse press reaction.

Another ploy was to travel with the competition. Lodge workers regularly climbed into the second or third bus of the Rockefeller entourage and transacted their business wherever the bus stopped. They never knew from day to day where they would end up, but they figured that Rockefeller wanted to go essentially where they wanted to go, and whether one went there today, tomorrow or the next day made little difference. By the end of the primary Rockefeller buses were regularly distributing all of Lodge's press releases around the state.

Everything was anticlimactic for the Lodge forces after New Hampshire. Establishment Republicans took over the campaign in Oregon and robbed it of all its vitality and freshness. In the process they drove Grindle and company deeper into debt through their failure to raise any significant amount of money. The night before the Oregon primary, a sheriff told Grindle and Goldberg that he had an order to refuse to let them leave the state until an $8,000 printing bill was paid. Eventually, they were allowed to leave, but only because they signed more personal notes.

In California the Lodge campaign fell apart. It could not compete with the Goldwater or Rockefeller money after the Oregon defeat. One of its workers did receive, however, $20,000 in "hot" money, as it was described, which was eventually returned. This money supposedly came from a Rockefeller supporter in New York who wanted the Lodge camp to switch to the New York governor. One person told me that the money was meant to "strike a blow for Rocky" which, in turn, would put the contributor "in good with David at the bank" so that he, the contributor, would be appointed a director.

Nelson Rockefeller's campaign for the 1964 Presidency began early in 1963. He put together an elaborate team of experts—many of whom were also on the governor's staff in Albany—in the fields of television, radio, research, publicity, minorities, finance, and state, local and regional politics. By the spring of 1964 he was employing about 100 highly paid people in his New York and Washington headquarters. Spencer-Roberts, a consulting firm, was hired to handle the California primary. A family jet airplane was also put at the candidate's disposal.

Rockefeller spent about $3 million in all the primary races he entered, and virtually all the money came from his family. One of the reasons Rockefeller had to spend so much was the need to recruit paid staff down to the lowest organizational levels. Unpaid volunteers were not attracted to Rockefeller in any numbers.

The Goldwater campaign began even earlier than Rockefeller's —almost immediately after the 1960 election. A National Draft Goldwater Committee was established and in 14 months had raised $750,000. Once Goldwater announced his candidacy in January, 1964, the National Goldwater for President Committee took over the fund-raising chores, raising an additional $2.8 million by July. Several million more was raised separately for use in the California primary. Altogether, a total of $5.5 million was spent by Goldwater forces for the nomination. Much of the early money was used to sew up convention delegates from states in which no primaries were held, a tactic adopted by both Nixon and Humphrey four years later.

One new approach to raising funds was the "Gold for Goldwater" campaign which was active in a score of states prior to the candidate's nomination. The idea was to convince contributors to give funds by writing postdated checks which would be held in escrow by a bank and given to Goldwater when he was nominated.

It was hoped that this political dowry would give Goldwater leverage in the convention. A variation of this theme was "Millions of Americans for Goldwater," a plan to collect funds in advance of his nomination but to return the money if he lost.

The Goldwater campaign also raised money through the sale of a handsome book containing photographs taken by the candidate himself. Entitled *The Faces of Arizona,* a thousand copies were printed and sold for $1,500 each. Nearly all of these were snapped up by large contributors. Perhaps the most enterprising fund-raising effort undertaken by the Goldwater campaign was that conducted by Robert Gaston, then the autocratic boss of the Young Republicans of California. He heard that Rockefeller's organizers were paying their workers fifty cents per signature to qualify the New York governor for the primary election. Gaston mobilized his own conservative supporters and collected $3,500 worth of signatures for Rocky and turned the money over to the Goldwater campaign.

Most contributors to Senator Goldwater's prenomination, and indeed his general election, campaigns gave small sums. Approximately 650,000 individuals gave $100 or less each, an extraordinary number considering the fact that Goldwater's chances of becoming President were never considered very good. This outpouring is understandable, however, if one looks at Goldwater as a "minor-party" candidate, which indeed he was, despite the 27 million votes he received, since philosophically he stood somewhat outside the mainstream of the Republican and Democratic parties. All minor parties, from the Barnburners to George Wallace (in 1968), received or still receive the bulk of their campaign funds from contributors of $100 or less. What they lack in Fat Cats they make up in hordes of zealous small donors.

The Scranton campaign was a desperation drive by Establishment Republicans to stop Goldwater and was confined essentially to the last 30 days before the GOP convention. Over $825,000 was spent in that period, nearly 30 percent going for television and about 50 percent for delegate-hunting activities. The money was raised by three influential Pennsylvanians: Thomas S. Gates, Jr., chairman of the executive committee of the Morgan Guaranty Trust Company; Frank C. P. McGlinn, a senior vice-president of the Fidelity-Philadelphia Trust Company and a long-time GOP fund raiser; and Thomas McCabe, Sr., of Scott Paper. McCabe held luncheons for Scranton at which a fair sampling of Eastern Establishment Republicans would be present, such as William S. Paley of CBS, William Murphy of Campbell Soups, Walter Thayer of the New York *Herald Tribune* (and a financial adviser to John Hay Whitney), former Attorney General Herbert Brownell, Walter Annenberg of the *Philadelphia Inquirer,* and several Du Ponts, Mellons and Whitneys. All of them contributed generously.

Approximately $9.5 million was spent in the 1964 primaries, none of which had to be reported. Another $35 million was spent to elect a President, $17 million by the GOP, $16 million by the Democrats and labor, and $2 million by independent committees and minor parties. The Republicans, who lost, ended up with a surplus; the Democrats, who won, entertained a deficit. The total costs at all political levels were an estimated $200 million, up 12 percent from 1960.

About 70 percent of all contributions to the Johnson campaign came in sums of $500 or more, compared with only 28 percent to Goldwater's campaign. Less than 7,000 individuuals accounted for $9 million of the $35 million cost of the Presidential race. Nearly $900,000 in contributions to the GOP came from just 99 people, counting husbands and wives separately, while $1.2 million in Democratic contributions came from just 111 donors.

Of particular interest in the 1964 election was the crossover of traditional Republican money to the Democrats. Douglas Dillon, a bulwark of liberal Republicanism, and his wife contributed $42,000 to the Democratic party. In 1960 they had given over $26,000 to the GOP. Another switchover was Henry Ford II, who gave $40,000 to the Democrats; in 1956 the GOP had tapped him for nearly $19,000. Most of the crossovers gave through the National Independent Committee for Johnson and Humphrey, which was headed by banker Henry Fowler. On the committee were, among others, Robert B. Anderson, Secretary of the Treasury under Eisenhower; John T. Conner of Merck & Company (and later Secretary of Commerce); John Loeb, who had contributed to the Lodge nomination effort in the spring; Thomas S. Lamont of the Morgan Guaranty Trust Company; Wall Street financier Sidney J. Weinberg; General James Gavin; publisher

Cass Canfield; and several Cabots from Boston. Under normal circumstances most of these men would have contributed heavily to the Republican nominee.

Where traditional Republicans could not bring themselves to switch parties completely, they expressed their concern by splitting their contributions between the two parties. Gustave Levy, senior partner at Goldman, Sachs, and his wife, ordinarily the most loyal and conscientious of Republicans, gave $7,000 to the Democrats and $5,000 to the GOP. Mrs. Herbert A. May (Marjorie Merriweather Post), banker George S. Moore, Dallas oilman John D. Murchison, brewer R. J. Schaefer, and industrialists Norton Simon and J. Irwin Miller split their contributions in a similar manner.

Of further interest in 1964 was the emergence of new Fat Cats. Men who had made their fortunes following World War II, or old money which hitherto had not contributed, began to replace the old established sources of large contributions. The trend in 1964 was not pronounced, but was nevertheless clearly evident. If the Republicans were still being financed in part by an assortment of Pews, Mellons, Du Ponts, Olins and Whitneys, they were also being underwritten by a small group of newcomers such as oilmen D. D. Harrington and Henry Salvatori, Illinois banker R. W. Galvin and National Airlines president Lewis B. Maytag, Jr. The same was also true of the Democrats: they could still count on large sums from Thomas J. Watson, Jr., Frank Altschul and several Lehmans, but large contributions were also being made by the likes of Sol Linowitz of Xerox, railroadman Ben Heineman, actor Gene Autry, Lew Wasserman, Arthur B. Krim and several Spiegels of Spiegel, Inc., a large Chicago mail-order firm. In the years ahead this new money would come to dominate the old.

Simultaneously, a proliferation of national committees cropped up in the campaign. They were designed not only to squeeze every last dollar from donors but to evade the intent of the Corrupt Practices Act. Both parties made an effort to establish committees that covered every conceivable condition of life, occupation, relationship and ideological position so that there would not be any potential contributor who could not find a happy home somewhere for his money.

Besides the National Independent Committee for Johnson and Humphrey, which was designed to draw Republican Fat Cat money, the Democrats also set up committees appealing to artists and entertainers, builders, business and professional men, citizens in general, citizens who preferred "responsible leadership," educators, friends, lawyers, small businessmen, pharmacists, rural Americans, scientists and engineers, senior citizens, veterans and women. Altogether, these committees raised and spent $1.3 million.

The Goldwater campaign had a Brothers (but no Sisters) for Goldwater Committee, several citizens committees, one committee for Republican women and another for women in general, and one named Solid South Speaks for Goldwater Committee. All of them together raised less than $1 million.

Feeding the well-fed continued to be a prime means of separating cash from contributors. Not counting President's Club meetings (which were never made public), Johnson attended 26 fundraising events between March and election day in which $7.9 million was raised. Two $1,000-a-plate dinners, one $100 gala, one $100 dinner and a $5-to-$100 gala were held in New York and Washington over the course of two days in May and alone raised $3.1 million of the total. In contrast, Goldwater could only attract $4.2 million at all of his fund-raising events. A $1,000-per-person picnic at Ike's Gettysburg farm brought in thousands of dollars, and private citizen Richard Nixon raised considerable sums by speaking at Republican events.

Several bipartisan fund-raising efforts in 1964 failed to raise any significant contributions. The "Eisenhower-Stevenson Appeal" failed because fund-raising tends to be partisan, and because in this case the quality of the lists was poor. A community bipartisan political fund-raising effort in Saginaw, Michigan, was an experiment at the local level and raised a total of $411 at a cost of $2,800.

Labor continued to contribute heavily. Thirty-one national unions reported spending $3.7 million in 1964, most of which was transferred to local campaign committees to spend. This reflected a shift away from the 1960 trend in which labor spent most of its money directly in campaigns. Clearly, union officials were confident that their men were not needed to defeat Goldwater. Virtually all of labor's contributions went to Democrats. Even the small but traditionally Republican glass bottle blowers' and carpenters' unions put their money into Democratic war chests.

COPE was the biggest labor spender at $1 million. It was followed by the International Ladies' Garment Workers' Union ($426,000) and the United Auto Workers, Machinists, Steelworkers, and Teamsters (about a quarter of a million dollars each). The Seafarers' International Union, with only 80,000 members, mostly ordinary seamen, spent a surprising $121,000.

Offsetting labor's influence somewhat were several new organizations with a business bias. The American Medical Political Action Committee, or AMPAC, spent $400,000 on candidates opposed to or wavering on Medicare legislation. The Business-Industry Political Action Committee, or BIPAC, an organization designed to promote management views such as right-to-work laws, spent over $200,000.

Despite the ban on industry advertisements in convention programs, businesses still contrived to contribute directly by purchasing ads in a convention booklet dedicated to the memory of John F. Kennedy. A full-page ad cost $15,000 and at least 96 were sold, giving the Democrats about $1.5 million in campaign funds. Among those contributing were United Artists (courtesy of Arthur B. Krim, who was also president of the President's Club) and Avco Corporation, which took two full pages. The American Trucking Association, a highway lobby then run by Neil J. Curry, arranged for 16 pages of ads from 114 trucking companies at a cost of $240,000. Universal American and two of its subsidiaries all took full-page ads. Francis S. Levien, the president of the firm, and his wife contributed another $17,500 to the Democratic campaign.

Right-wing money was in evidence for the first time since 1952 when it backed General Douglas MacArthur for President. (Active right-wing money in 1960, the only other postwar election in which it played a role, was limited to anti-Catholics.) Americans for Constitutional Action, which was formed to offset the influence of the liberal Americans for Democratic Action, spent over $200,000 pushing candidates to the right of center. The Christian

Nationalist Crusade, run by aging anti-Semite Gerald L. K. Smith, reported spending $278,000 for far-right causes. The racist National States Rights Party spent $42,000 for the 7,000 votes its Presidential candidate received.

Left-wing or ideological liberal money was less in evidence, but was nevertheless still there. The ADA spent nearly $180,000 in support of liberal candidates. The National Committee for an Effective Congress, which dates back to 1948, spent over $300,000 on favored congressional candidates in marginal districts. The Socialist Labor party, the oldest Marxist party in the United States, spent approximately $65,000 for the 43,000 votes its candidate for President received; and the Socialist Workers party, Trotskyist and violence-prone, reported spending slightly less than $2,600 for the 22,000 votes its candidate received.

Costs continued to rise in 1964. Political broadcasting costs at all levels in the general election were up 75 percent over 1960 to $24.6 million. An additional $10 million, it is estimated, was spent in the primaries. The $34.6 million total represented 18 percent of all political spending in 1964. Democrats outspent Republicans on broadcasting throughout the election, $18 million to $16 million, although at the Presidential level Goldwater outspent Johnson $7.5 million to $5 million. Goldwater would have spent even more, but when he realized late in the campaign that he would lose decisively, he cancelled many last-minute programs to save money.

Radio continued to decline in importance as a political medium, although actual expenditures for AM and FM increased. In the election of 1952, for instance, $3.1 million was spent on radio, which represented 51 percent of all political broadcasting expenditures that year. In 1964, however, $7.1 million was spent on radio, but that represented only 29 percent of all broadcasting expenditures.

Broadcasting costs rose in 1964 for several unusual reasons. President Johnson laid out double the amount spent in 1960 because he wanted to win in a landslide and free his administration from the Kennedy aura and influence. Second, the 20-, 40- and 60-second spot took over as the favorite method of communicating on television. Spot announcements increased in number from 9,000 in

1960 to nearly 30,000 in 1964. A spot announcement is usually far more expensive per second used than a quarter hour of time or longer.

Although no systematic accounting of Democratic spending is available, it has been estimated that the Johnson-Humphrey ticket spent at least half a million dollars on advertising agency fees, a further million on payrolls, and $435,000 on campaign paraphernalia. Polls were popular with President Johnson, particularly those concerned with the "backlash" issue and his own standing among the voters. How much was spent on them, however, has never been revealed by the party. The fact that 1964 Democratic party campaign expenditure figures are still wrapped in a cloud of obscurity attests to the weakness of the campaign financing laws as they existed then.

In the same year, the Republicans spent a large $1.6 million on campaign salaries, underscoring the point that many individuals find economic security in our electoral process. Another $1 million was spent on mailings to soak up the small contributions. A further $165,000 went for surveys and polls, $750,000 to advertising agency fees, and $450,000 for telephone and telegraph service. The Goldwater campaign also found reliable mailing lists expensive. One of the most productive was the list of buyers for an automobile polishing cloth.

Republican liberals, following the 1964 defeat, set about to regain control of their party. Moderate Ray Bliss was brought in as chairman of the RNC, and he appointed General Lucius Clay to succeed Ralph Cordiner, the head of General Electric, as finance chairman. Together with C. Langhorne Washburn they slowly wooed back traditional party givers. They managed to raise over $7 million in 1966, not bad for an off year and a recently shattered party.

For the Democrats, however, it was mostly downhill after 1964. The party did manage to raise $700,000 with the publication of "Toward an Age of Greatness," a tribute to LBJ's Great Society. A full-page ad sold for $15,000 and some of the purchasers included defense contractors, regulated companies, all the nation's major airlines, and several subsidized shipping lines and railroads. However, the money was put in a special bank account after questions were raised concerning its legality, and was not released until 1972, when it was used for a bipartisan voter registration drive.

Slowly over 1965, 1966 and 1967 contributions from Democratic Fat Cats began to dry up. The primary reason for the defection, of course, was disillusionment over the war in Vietnam. The heavy electoral losses in 1966 were a manifestation of it, and many of those feeling particularly disaffected directed their contributions to new Republican or other anti-LBJ candidates.

Johnson's reelection bid in 1968 had hardly begun before it ended. He never declared himself and officially entered no primaries. However, at least half a million dollars was spent on his renomination effort, mostly in New Hampshire and Wisconsin.

Only $75,000 was reported spent in Wisconsin, but the true amount, admitted by several LBJ supporters, was closer to $200,000. Some of the money came from the Seafarers' Union, from Texas, Illinois, New York and California President's Club members, and from the Citizens for Johnson-Humphrey Committee (of 1964), which was still in existence.

Large amounts of unreported money also came out of the Democratic National Committee in the form of cash. This money was flown out periodically late at night to Wisconsin by a bagman for distribution. "I never knew his name," commented one campaign aide, "but I got to recognize his face." Toward the end of the Wisconsin primary, the bagman was approached by a young Democrat at a social gathering and asked for funds to cover a large advertising bill. Both withdrew into a bathroom where the bagman pulled out a huge packet of cash from his pocket. He then proceeded to count out—licking his thumb on each count—$100 bills on the toilet seat cover. "My God," thought the young Democrat at the scene before him, "and this is to renominate the President of the United States!"

Several days later Johnson took himself out of the running.

One measure of the President's deteriorating political position was the difficulty Wisconsin Democrats had in finding dummy names to account for the cash. Many stalwart Democrats refused to have their names used as having "contributed" money. Said one Johnson worker, "It was then that we realized how much trouble we were in."

Eugene McCarthy's campaign funds came mostly from both ends of the scale: there were many $100 and $1,000 (or more) checks, but very few in the middle range. Altogether about 600,000 people gave to McCarthy, nearly equaling Goldwater's 1964 total. About $11 million was spent at the national and state levels in behalf of McCarthy, roughly what Richard Nixon spent to win the Republican nomination.

Small contributions were solicited through the mails. The subscription lists of such publications as *Atlas, Commonweal,* the *New York Review of Books, Ramparts, Avant-Garde* and *Playboy* were purchased as were certain faculty and political lists. By mid-July they had yielded nearly $400,000, with costs running about one quarter of the take. Indoor and outdoor rallies were also used successfully to raise money, some of which were held in Madison Square Garden, the Boston Garden and Detroit's Cobo Hall. Several discotheques, a couple of which were named "Eugene's," turned their profits over to the campaign, which in one instance amounted to nearly $12,000 per week.

The bulk of McCarthy's campaign funds came from a wealthy few. Stewart R. Mott, a young General Motors heir, for one, contributed approximately $210,000 after having vainly spent $100,000 trying to persuade Nelson Rockefeller to run. Another large contributor was Jack J. Dreyfus, Jr., of Dreyfus & Company. He and his wife are listed as having given more than $100,000, although he may have given as much as $500,000, partly as "loans" which were forgiven. Dreyfus was a man of truly eclectic tastes in 1968, for he later gave at least $69,000 to Humphrey and other Democratic candidates and at least $76,000 to Nixon and various Republicans. Other $100,000 contributors included Martin Peretz, a Harvard assistant professor whose wife is a Singer heiress; Ellsworth Carrington, a wealthy broker; and Allan Miller, a Florida philanthropist.

Daniel J. Bernstein, then the president of the brokerage firm of D. J. Bernstein & Company, and his wife gave at least $75,000; Howard Stein, one of Jack Dreyfus's business partners, came up with more than $10,000; Yura Arkus-Duntov, president of the Equity Growth Fund, gave twice as much; and broker Richard T. Shields gave about $18,000. Blair Clark, McCarthy's campaign manager, Martin Fife of Fife Industries, and Samuel Rubin, a retired Fabergé executive, each donated $75,000. Mrs. June Degnan, a wealthy California philanthropist and money raiser for liberal causes, Robert Gimbel of Saks Fifth Avenue, and Chicago department-store heir Robert Pirie each contributed over $100,000. Several political appointees under LBJ contributed heavily using pseudonyms, including a former Secretary of the Navy and a few general and flag rank officers on active duty.

Influential McCarthy fund raisers included Stephen Quigley, the candidate's brother-in-law, Massachusetts industrialist Arnold Hiatt, and Degnan, Stein, Pirie and Clark. The intense antipathy of these four was well known within the campaign. Russell Hemenway of the National Committee for an Effective Congress, Larry Spicer of the American Civil Liberties Union, and Maurice Rosenblatt, a Democratic party insider, also raised funds. McCarthy himself was not a good fund raiser because, if he took a dislike to a person or was otherwise distracted, he made no effort to convince a potential contributor why he should part with his cash. Many contributions were lost for this reason.

The financial management of the McCarthy campaign was one of the most chaotic in American history. There was a fundamental split between those in the organization who believed that most of the money should be spent to promote the candidate on television and radio, and others who sought to keep the candidate "pure" by spending money at the grass-roots level to organize and convert.

As a result, a number of bootleg bank accounts cropped up, each of which drew contributions that were sympathetic to the account manager's particular point of view. For instance, Howard Stein raised money that never went through the campaign books, but directly into a private campaign fund which he wanted to use only for McCarthy television advertisements. Blair Clark, who fought continuously with Stephen Quigley over policy, set up a bootleg account, at the Freedom National Bank in Harlem, called "Clergymen for McCarthy." Arnold Hiatt's bootleg account was amassed by intercepting the mail before it reached campaign headquarters. By this move Hiatt hoped to bring Quigley around to his particular viewpoint. But at the last moment, Stein, by mistake, forwarded $50,000 to Quigley that kept the latter from capitulating. Some bootleg funds were still unreleased as late as mid-September, 1968, two months after McCarthy lost the Democratic nomination.

At one time there were twenty-six legitimate bank accounts holding McCarthy campaign funds, and the scramble within the organization was so acute to divert them to bootleg accounts that the signatures on all of them had to be changed at least eight times. Locks were also replaced periodically to keep rival factions from ransacking files and the petty cash drawer.

Factionalism within the McCarthy camp was so intense that it often provoked ludicrous incidents. On one occasion, June Degnan followed a man into the men's room in order to make sure that funds raised at a dinner for the national McCarthy organization did not go to the state organization. In another instance, a zealous worker printed up on his own initiative 30,000 flyers tying McCarthy to the Pope. The offending literature, however, was caught in time by more level-headed staffers and subsequently destroyed.

The ebb and flow of funds into the McCarthy campaign were unusually dependent upon events. Between the time McCarthy announced his candidacy on November 30, 1967, until the New Hampshire primary in March, 1968, funds trickled in at a most modest rate. Following the New Hampshire victory, however, funds began to pour in. When Robert Kennedy entered the race on March 16, contributions slacked off momentarily only to rebound vigorously. Some of this new money came from the Humphrey campaign, which sought to blunt the Kennedy drive. Some of it was simply anti-Kennedy money. The Wisconsin, Nebraska, Indiana and Oregon primary victories sent contributions climbing, the California loss and death of Robert Kennedy sent them spinning, and the surprising New York primary victory sent them climbing once more.

When money was tight the McCarthy managers began to kite checks at all the banks in which they had legitimate accounts that were not computerized. The usual procedure was to overdraw an account, rush in a deposit the next day from another bank, then rush in yet another deposit from a third bank to cover the second overdrawn account, and so on until the necessary campaign money came in. An efficient banking system in New York City and Washington, D.C., would have paralyzed the McCarthy financial operation, and thus the campaign itself.

By September, 1968, the campaign was $1.3 million in debt. Part of the debt was paid back through special fund-raising efforts, some was assumed by the DNC, and the remainder was negotiated for 36 cents on the dollar. Those companies that accepted a negotiated settlement were in effect making an indirect contribution to the campaign, which, according to the letter of the law, was and continues to be illegal.

Robert Kennedy's campaign lasted 80 days, and in that time approximately $9 million—or nearly a million dollars a week—was committed to be spent on his behalf. Half the money was spent in seven primaries, with California drawing the bulk of the funds. Heavy stress was also placed on a media campaign which cost around $2.4 million. At one point Kennedy's advertising agency, Papert, Koenig & Lois, had 51 employees assigned to the campaign.

The deficit of the Kennedy campaign totaled $3.5 million, $1 million of which was assumed by the DNC. The remaining debt was satisfied by paying off small creditors in full and settling the larger bills for 33 cents on the dollar.

Despite their great wealth, the Kennedys have always solicited others for supplementary campaign funds. However, the ease with which past funds were raised was nowhere in evidence in 1968. In fact, the Kennedy campaign opened in near pauperism. Female enthusiasts, for instance, were reduced to painting bobby pins red, white and blue as a badge of identification because there were no buttons available.

But the trouble ran deeper than that. By the time they were tapped, many traditional Democratic contributors had already been solicited by the likes of Los Angeles lawyer Eugene Wyman and Lew Wasserman in anticipation of Lyndon Johnson running again. Furthermore, the "ideological money," found in large quantities in Washington, Cambridge, Massachusetts, the upper east side of Manhattan, and the hills surrounding San Francisco and Los Angeles, had already been thoroughly milked by the McCarthy fund raisers. In addition, Humphrey had made a special effort to keep regular contributors in line. Union money was also unavailable because of RFK's racket-busting activities and his vendetta against Teamster boss James Hoffa.

Thus, it was a vicious circle for the Kennedy camp: because of the late start it was difficult to raise cash, and because there was a shortage of cash it was nearly impossible to make up for lost time. In the end, most of the funds came out of the Kennedy family treasury, which was being managed by Kennedy's brother-in-law Stephen Smith from the 230 Park Avenue headquarters.

The Humphrey prenomination campaign, from the best of estimates, cost $4 million. Very little is known of how the money was spent, although it is believed that a bare minimum of $1.5 million was spent on media. A quarter of a million was spent on the convention, and an unspecified but large amount on the private wooing of convention delegates, a practice Goldwater perfected in 1964.

Humphrey inherited some Johnson money, and after March 16 was inundated with anti-Kennedy money. The latter source dried up after Kennedy's death, and it is believed that many of these contributors switched their support to Nixon. But most of Humphrey's money came from Fat Cats, the same people who backed LBJ in 1964 and belonged to the President's Club. Humphrey's preconvention debt amounted to $1 million and was assumed late in the fall by the DNC.

One of Humphrey's major fund raisers in the prenomination period was Richard Maguire, a Boston lawyer and former White House staffer. While he was treasurer of the DNC, Maguire instituted a policy of financial secrecy which has lasted up to the present. It was also through his influence that the Democratic party became almost fully dependent on Fat Cats for its finances.

The Republican contenders collectively spent $20 million before they arrived in Miami: Nixon about half the total, Rockefeller about $8 million, Romney $1.5 million and Reagan $750,000.

Romney was the first announced GOP candidate and the first to fall. Originally his campaign was budgeted to spend $4.2 million between September, 1967, and the Miami convention the following summer. However, only a third of the money was ever committed. When it became clear early in the campaign to Republican power brokers, money raisers and contributors that Romney's chances of gaining the nomination were slim, his contributions dried up. Romney did not drop out thirteen days before his first primary test in New Hampshire because he lacked the funds, but for other reasons, chief among them being his unfortunate remark that he had been "brainwashed" by military and diplomatic personnel in South Vietnam.

Romney's funds came from half a dozen wealthy men, among them J. Willard Marriott of the food and motel chain, J. Clifford Folger, Michigan oilman Harold McClure, Jr., Detroit industrialist Max Fisher, and Nelson Rockefeller. Marriott, a Mormon like Romney, solicited additional funds among Mormons; Folger tapped Eastern Establishment sources; and Max Fisher, a former United Jewish Appeal chairman, raised funds in the Jewish community. An attempt to tap Howard Hughes and J. Paul Getty was apparently unsuccessful.

Early efforts to convince Rockefeller to run went aglimmering. Governor Spiro Agnew of Maryland spent campaign funds to open a National Draft Rockefeller '68 headquarters in Baltimore, but was discouraged from continuing the effort. By the time Rockefeller decided to run, when he needed all the help he could get, Agnew had switched his loyalty to Nixon.

Once Rockefeller did announce, the money flowed freely. Details of his campaign financing are few, in keeping with the family's tight-lipped attitude toward disclosure. But the best estimates, from reliable sources, put the money spent promoting the governor in 1968 at $8 million. Well over half of this sum went into television, radio and newspaper advertisements alone. Another $250,000 was spent on polls, and $750,000 was spent on the convention campaign.

The purpose of this financial blitz was not to fight any primary battles but "to get the polls moving in Rockefeller's favor" by showing that he could beat any Democratic candidate. Equally as important was to convince convention delegates to hold off voting for Richard Nixon, at least for the first ballot.

Most of Rockefeller's campaign funds came from either his own pocket or from members of his family. His stepmother, Mrs. Martha Baird Rockefeller, was, contrary to family practice, listed in a report filed in Albany as having contributed $1.5 million. (The gift tax on this amount would be about $840,000.) The four brothers—John D. III, Laurence, David and Winthrop—were reported to have given $750,000 each. An additional $2 million came from outside the family, from perhaps two dozen people. The remaining $1.5 million, it appears, came either from the candidate himself or was money channeled through family accounts and not assigned to anyone in particular.

Ronald Reagan did not announce his candidacy officially until the first day of the GOP convention. Prior to that time, approximately $750,000 had been spent by various groups promoting the California governor. Reagan kept himself in the limelight throughout 1966, 1967 and part of 1968 by speaking at various Republican functions around the country, a technique used by Goldwater in 1964 and Nixon in 1968.

Reagan's travels were financed from a trust fund set up by the Republican State Central Committee of California. The money was raised by charging the sponsors of the event at which Reagan appeared either a percentage of the gross or a fixed fee.

The California governor also received contributions from many very conservative and right-wing sources. Henry Salvatori, oilman A. C. Rubel and Ford dealer Holmes Tuttle, all big contributors to Goldwater in 1964, kicked in for Reagan. So did Walter Knott of Knott's Berry Farm, savings and loan tycoon Howard Ahmanson, and Taft Schreiber, a vice-president of the Music Corporation of America. Other donors included steel company founder Earle M. Jorgenson, J. Paul Getty, Leonard Firestone, Justin Dart of Rexall Drugs, movie producers Jack Warner, Walt Disney and Armand Deutsch, and screen actors Randolph Scott, Robert Taylor, Chuck Connors, Bob Hope, Art Linkletter, James Stewart and John Wayne. The Kern County Land Company, the Hollywood Turf Company and the Western Offshore Drilling & Exploration Company were also givers, since it is legal for corporations to contribute in California.

Several early backers of Reagan told Max Rafferty, then the conservative Superintendent of Public Instruction in California, not to oppose liberal incumbent Thomas Kuchel in the U.S. Senate primary because it would eat up conservative money for the Reagan effort. To political insiders, this news was a tipoff that Reagan backers were husbanding their resources for a major Presidential effort.

Richard Nixon had never really stopped running for President, but his effort to win the 1968 GOP nomination can be dated from the formation of Congress '66, an organization set up to help Nixon campaign for Republican candidates in that year's congressional elections. The impressive Republican showing in November revived Nixon's stock among rank-and-file Republicans, and from there on he was running hard for the Presidency.

About $10 million was spent to win the nomination for Nixon, $2.5 million of which went for advertising, another $1.5 million toward primary campaigns, and a large $3.5 million into overheads. Nixon's base of financial support was half Goldwater's in 1964 prior to the convention, but the sums raised and spent were twice as large. About 150,000 people gave $2.2 million. Another $4.5 million came from twelve hundred $1,000-or-more contributors to Richard Nixon Associates, the Republican answer to Johnson's President's Club.

The largest contributor to Nixon's prenomination campaign was W. Clement Stone, president of Combined American Insurance Company and a man of immense wealth. Stone and his wife are believed to have contributed at least $500,000 to Nixon prior to Miami, and another $200,000 divided between Nixon's general election campaign and several other Republican candidates. Stone's total financial contribution was the largest single husband-wife group contribution since the 1920's.

Other large prenomination donors to Nixon include Robert H. Abplanalp, the inventor of the aerosol valve; Elmer Bobst of Warner-Lambert; Mrs. Helen Clay Frick of Pittsburgh; entrepreneur John M. King of Denver; John M. Olin of the Olin Mathieson Chemical Corporation; Mrs. Charles Payson, owner of the New York Mets; Mr. and Mrs. Ogden Phipps of New York and Palm Beach; and California businessman Fred J. Russell, who was later appointed Undersecretary of the Interior.

The total cost of elective and party politics in 1968 at all levels of political activity was estimated at $300 million, up 50 percent over 1964. Of that total, the Presidential race, including the primaries, soaked up one third of the total, or $100 million. Of the $100 million, $20 million was spent by GOP candidates for their party's nomination, $25 million by Democrats seeking the nomination, $37 million by both major parties in the general election, another $7 million by Wallace (since 1967) and the remaining $11 million either was spent at the state and local levels or was not reported.

Costs rose over 1964 at all political levels because of inflation; antiwar activity, which expressed itself in the political process; the increased use of television; and the extra effort made to control state legislatures in order to control reapportionment in 1970. At the Presidential level, costs were driven up by the insurgent candidacies of McCarthy and Wallace and by the active campaigns of two very wealthy men: Robert Kennedy and Nelson Rockefeller.

The financial operation of Nixon's campaign was one of the best organized in American history. It was run out of a sixth floor office at 54th Street and Park Avenue in New York City under the direction of onetime Eisenhower budget chief and longtime Nixon friend Maurice Stans, who later became Secretary of Commerce. Stans organized his fund-raising events and money raisers so efficiently—right down to the local level—that there was never any serious financial problem. Money flowed in from the old stalwarts, the ditch-Johnsonites, people on the make, Fat Cats and others in such profusion that it became a campaign policy not to offer or promise anything in return—no jobs, ambassadorships, deals or privileges.

Yet, for reasons not very clear, this smooth-running machine became locked into a rigidity of purpose toward the end of the campaign that made it nearly impossible to switch financial priorities as the situation required. For instance, as Humphrey began to rise in the polls, no effort was made to shift financial imperatives to meet the threat. The result was simply to do more of what already had been done, which did nothing to halt the late Nixon slide. In the end, despite all the money spent to elect Nixon, it changed very few votes.

Humphrey's campaign finances, by contrast, were in chaos. Following Chicago, the DNC was so broke it could not pay for a band to greet the party's nominee; someone had to write a personal check for the music.

Money was desperately tight. Humphrey could not count on any "hate-Kennedy" or "hate-LBJ" or antiwar or Texas money. He could not even count on "smart" money, which usually bets on both sides if both have a chance, because his standing was so low in the polls. Nor was there any Fat Cat Jewish money out of California and New York, which a Democratic candidate counts on heavily. These givers had been tapped out in the primaries by McCarthy and Kennedy, and had turned ideological on him in the general election: an attitude considered not quite proper for such people to assume. There was only labor money and "love Hubert" money, and both were either in short supply or unenthusiastic.

The financial logjam broke somewhat on September 30, 1968, after Humphrey's Vietnam speech in Salt Lake City. Money began to flow in at an acceptable rate, but by then it was too late. Television time and general financial planning have to be laid out months in advance, and contributions coming in as late as this, less than 30 days before the election, are almost useless, except to be used for sudden media blitzes which ordinarily are a waste of money and sway few votes.

Altogether, the DNC and 55 committees spent over $10 million trying to elect Humphrey. Robert Short, the National Committee's treasurer, admitted that $3 million was raised that was never reported because it went directly to pay bills.

George Wallace's bid for the Presidency was the most costly minor-party effort in American history. Nearly $7 million was spent over an eighteen-month period. Even taking into account inflation and the high cost of new campaign techniques, the sum dwarfs the $700,000 spent by Theodore Roosevelt's Progressives in 1912, the $250,000 spent by LaFollette in 1924, the $1 million spent by Henry Wallace and $163,000 spent by Strom Thurmond in 1948.

Of all the candidates in 1968, only George Wallace could say that most of his money came from the "little people." In fact, the $500-and-under contributions amounted to 85 percent of everything his campaign took in. Small contributions to the GOP, in contrast, amounted to about 50 percent of all money collected, about 30 percent of Democratic funds.

Wallace's technique for collecting money from the average citizen was part southern revival, part racket. The partisan crowd would be warmed up with an impassioned speech by either the campaign finance chairman, Dick Smith, or some other talented Wallace follower. Then Wallace himself would appear: the Lord would be praised, anarchy damned, and "pointy-headed bureau-crats" and long-haired youths ridiculed. Then, as the cheers were still ringing through the hall, Wallace Girls with sudsbuckets passed through the crowd collecting the $10, $5, $1 bills and loose change. Wallace staffers could usually count on one in three mem-bers of the audience dropping money into the bucket, but the ratio rose to as high as one in two whenever there were particularly vocal and scruffy-looking critics in the galleries. The collection was then poured into a steamer trunk which was known as "the woman" because, as Smith was once reported as saying, "We never let our hands off her, not even at night."

Unlike the two major parties, Wallace sold most of his cam-paign gimmicks at handsome markups. Anyone who wanted to set up a Wallace storefront could buy a kit of campaign materials—buttons, stickers, hats, and so on—for $250 from the official cam-paign and sell them to the public for $350, the difference to cover the other costs of the storefront. But for the "little people" $250 was a large outlay. Thus arose the phenomenon of political middlemen, someone who would buy in bulk from the national campaign and sell in smaller quantities to the storefront operators at even higher markups. Straw hats, for instance, cost fifty cents wholesale in Montgomery, Alabama, and were going for one dollar in the small-town storefronts. Bumper stickers were ordinarily marked up five times the wholesale price, and buttons were marked up 250 per-cent. One Wallace zealot was supposed to have made more than $10,000 profit from this ploy.

If Wallace was genuinely dependent on the "little people," it was Fat Cats who supplied most of the money for the two major Presi-dential candidates in 1968. Nixon received nearly $8 million in campaign funds from 285 individuals, none of whom gave less than $10,000. Fifty-three of them also gave to the Democrats. Stone, Bobst and Abplanalp all came through with more money as did political eclectic Jack Dreyfus. Max Fisher and his wife gave at least $103,000 while Mr. and Mrs. Henry Salvatori put up $83,000. Howard Butcher III, of the Philadelphia investment banking house of Butcher & Sherrod, and his wife gave at least $40,000. Ford Motor Company executive John S. Bugas came through with $20,000; Robert O. Anderson, chairman of the board of Atlantic Richfield and supposedly the largest private landowner in the United States (mostly in New Mexico), gave $44,000; Gene Autry contributed $15,000; New York lawyer John P. Humes gave $43,000; architect Charles Luckman coughed up another $15,000; and Arthur K. Watson of IBM gave at least $55,000. Also contributing heavily were Seattle mortgage banker Walter Williams, DeWitt Wallace of *Reader's Digest,* banker Peter Flanigan of Dillon, Read, real estate speculator Walter J. Dilbeck, investment banker Richard C. Pistell, and Vincent DeRoulet, who married a Whitney heiress. Wealthy Greek-Americans with such names as Goulandris, Metaxo, Skouras and Pappas contributed heavily, undoubtedly out of admiration for Spiro Agnew.

The traditional Republican sources—the Du Ponts, Fords, Mellons, Olins, Pews, Vanderbilts and Whitneys—gave a total of nearly $860,000 to Republicans in 1968, mostly to the Nixon campaign. These same families also gave $71,000 to Democratic candidates.

As in the past, some large contributors were appointed to high office. Walter Annenberg, who contributed only $2,500 but who also gave heavy editorial support to Nixon in the Philadelphia area, was sent to the Court of St. James's. Tennessee insuranceman Guildford Dudley, Jr., who gave $51,000, became ambassador to Denmark. Anthony Marshall, who is Mrs. Vincent Astor's son by a former marriage, contributed $25,000 and became ambassador to the Malagasay Republic. Insuranceman J. William Middendorf gave $15,500 and became ambassador to The Netherlands. David Packard of the Hewlett-Packard Company, a firm that manufactures many defense-related items, contributed $11,000 and was appointed Deputy Secretary of Defense. Lawyer John Humes became ambassador to Austria, and businessman Arthur K. Watson became ambassador to France.

Humphrey, too, had his Fat Cats, but not as many, nor on the whole as generous as Nixon's. Half of Humphrey's general election contributions came from about 50 people in the form of either gifts or loans. John Factor and his wife contributed at least $100,000. Mrs. Albert Lasker, editor Norman Cousins, Lew Wasserman, New York motion picture theater owner Harry Brandt, and former ambassador to Ireland Raymond Guest all gave in the $30,000-to-$60,000 range. Other major contributors included Edgar Bronfman of Schenley Industries, Xerox inventor

Chester F. Carlson, international financier-gone-bust Bernard Cornfeld, *New York Times* State Department correspondent Benjamin Welles, Meshulam Riklis of the Rapid American Corporation conglomerate, producer Roger Stevens and Thomas J. Watson, Jr., of IBM.

Eclectic Jack Dreyfus was not alone in spreading around his contributions. Lester Avnet of Avnet Industries, John L. Loeb, H. L. Meckler of the Bermec Corporation, and Thomas S. Murphy of Capital Cities Broadcasting Corporation not only gave to the Humphrey campaign but to Nixon *and* the McCarthy prenomination effort. Those who simply gave to Humphrey and Nixon included Frank Altschul, Henry Ford II, Gustave Levy, Richard T. Shields, Henry Brown, R. J. Schaefer, Walker L. Cisler of Detroit Edison, Sidney Weinberg, and Maxwell A. Kriendler of New York's 21 Club.

Traditional Democratic families such as the Fields and Lehmans contributed a minimum of $34,000 to Democratic candidates and about $5,000 to GOP candidates. The Harriman family, traditionally Democratic, reported contributing no funds to Humphrey and $16,500 to Republican candidates.

Because voluntary contributions were scarce, Humphrey was forced to borrow money to finance his campaign. John Factor and Lew Wasserman each lent $240,000 in addition to their original contributions. Lenders in the $50,000-to-$100,000 class included investment banker Herbert A. Allen, oilman Jacob Blaustein, United Artists executives Robert Benjamin and Arnold Picker, New York real estate developers Arthur Cohen and Robert Dowling, investment banker John Loeb, Leon Hess of Hess Oil & Chemical, Arthur Houghton of Corning Glass, S. Harrison Dogole of Globe Security, Samuel Friedland of Food Fair Stores, and at least three members of the board of the Gulf of Western Corporation conglomerate.

Many of Humphrey's Minnesota friends also came through with loans: Jeno Paulucci of Chung King Chow Mein, trucker and ex-Washington Senators owner Robert E. Short, banker Deil Gustafson, and grain broker and longtime Humphrey money raiser Dwayne Andreas.

At one point early in the general election, Stewart Mott wrote to Humphrey on behalf of himself and purportedly a group of wealthy McCarthy backers, suggesting that money might be forth-coming if Humphrey's views were satisfactory to Mott and his friends. Mott suggested that a one-hour meeting be arranged at which Humphrey would be grilled on a variety of subjects. Humphrey turned Mott down cold.

Setting up committees to circumvent the intent of the Corrupt Practices Act reached a new peak of development in 1968. Beyond the continuing national, congressional and senatorial campaign committees, the Republican financial managers set up nearly two dozen Nixon-Agnew committees, including Independents, Democrats and Grassroots for Nixon-Agnew. There was also a Thurmond Speaks Committee and a Vote Getters for Nixon Committee.

But it was the Democrats under the clever leadership of Robert Short who turned the setting up of committees into a special art. Short created nearly fifty committees as conduits to receive money from big contributors and lenders. These committees in turn channeled the money to the permanent national committees. Names of the committees varied from Advertising Executives for Humphrey-Muskie to Women for Humphrey-Muskie. In between were specialized groups like Dentists, Jewelers, Librarians, Musicians, New Englanders, Pharmacists, Pilots, Sport Stars and Wholesalers for Humphrey-Muskie.

Each of these committees had a list of contributors and lenders, most of them a variation of the same people noted above. Many of the committees filed virtually identical reports, with identical contributions from the same people. In two particular cases—Entertainers for Humphrey-Muskie and Lawyers for Humphrey-Muskie—both filed reports showing contributions coming from a committee in Minnesota which had been typed in over the erased name of Dwayne Andreas.

Wallace, surprisingly, had his Fat Cats too. One of his biggest contributors was Leander Perez, Sr., then the boss of Plaquemines Parish, Louisiana, a swampy and oil-rich area south of New Orleans. Perez was one of the moving forces in the establishment of the segregationist Citizens Councils and a leader against school integration in his state. Other big contributors were Colonel Harland Sanders, the fried-chicken king; Paul Pewitt, who made a fortune in potatoes and oil; Edward Ball, who controls vast Du

Pont interests in Florida; and retired General Edwin A. Walker. Actor John Wayne, who gave the "inspirational" address at the GOP convention, also sent in some money. On the back of one of his checks he is supposed to have written: "Sock it to 'em, George!"

Labor committees reported spending $7 million in the 1968 election, although the true figure is probably closer to $10 million. In all, 37 labor committees contributed money, most of which went to Democrats. COPE continued to lead the list with a reported $1.2 million in contributions. The Garment Workers distributed slightly more than a million dollars, the Machinists spent $572,000, while the Marine Engineers and United Auto Workers each contributed in excess of $250,000.

Somewhat surprisingly, the union making the third largest political contribution in 1968 was the Seafarers' International Union. Despite its relatively small membership (80,000 compared to the 1.5 million Auto Workers), it still managed to contribute $947,000 to candidates in the election. Early in 1968 the SIU contributed $100,000—in twenty $5,000 checks—to LBJ's reelection campaign. Subsequently it was learned that shortly before the contribution was made the State Department had declined to issue an extradition warrant to surrender a Canadian SIU official wanted in Canada on bribery charges. The sequence of events may have been a coincidence, but there are many who wonder.

Antilabor business groups continued to be active. BIPAC spent $568,000 on a variety of candidates at the gubernatorial and congressional level. BIPAC supported, for instance, the incumbent and conservative Democratic senator from Ohio, Frank Lausche, in his unsuccessful primary battle against liberal John Gilligan, who was financed in large part by union funds. It then backed the Republican nominee, William Saxbe, who won.

AMPAC spent $682,000, the money going to 162 candidates in House races and 23 in Senate races in 1968. Money was generally channeled through state affiliates, rather than directly to candidates, so that the possibility of embarrassment would be minimized.

Nonpartisan liberal political groups, such as the National Committee for an Effective Congress and the Council for a Livable World, collectively spent over $600,000 on left-to-liberal candidates in 1968. But the nonpartisan conservative groups—the Americans for Constitutional Action, American Conservative Union, and the United Republicans of America (which is not affiliated with the GOP, despite its name)—far outspent the liberal groups with a total outlay of $1.7 million.

Minor political parties reported spending a total of $460,000. The Communist party spent $16,000 for its 23 recorded votes, and the Socialist Labor party spent $80,000 for its 52,000 votes. The Trotskyist Socialist Workers party spent $40,000 and received 38,000 votes. The racist and anti-Semitic Christian Nationalist Crusade and National States Rights party collectively spent over $300,000 pushing their views in 1968.

Where did all the money go? More and more of it went into media campaigns, particularly television. Nearly $60 million was spent in 1968 on television time, 70 percent more than in 1964. If production costs were added, the total would be close to $90 million. Fifty percent of Nixon's expenses and 61 percent of Humphrey's went for media advertising and agency fees. Both candidates also spent funds to advertise over cable television networks, and expenditures for AM and FM political advertising nearly doubled over 1964.

The Nixon forces further spent $384,000 on polling, $1.3 million for campaign materials (which was handled by the New York advertising firm of Feeley & Wheeler), and $83,861 for an "ethnic" campaign. Direct mail appeals cost $1.6 million, jet travel $1.3 million, and staff salaries and fees paid to consultants ran well over $1 million.

Few figures are available on the Humphrey campaign, although it is known that $260,000 was spent on polls. Campaign materials were generally in such short supply that many local Democratic candidates and bigwigs dug into their own pockets to pay for buttons and bumper strips. Fees for consultants such as Joseph Napolitan probably did not run more than $25,000.

The Wallace campaign spent $3 million of the $7 million raised on advertising, or 44 percent of the total. Every television show included a pitch at the end for money which, it was estimated, brought in $40,000 a day. Travel cost another million dollars. Wallace used a DC-7 rented from a Texas oil millionaire; later a

DC-3 and two propjets were added to the campaign fleet. Polling was not a significant expense, but the campaign did pay General Curtis Lemay, Wallace's running mate, a salary of $12,000 while the campaign lasted. Legal fees for qualifying for the ballot in all 50 states ran to $118,000, over half of which was spent in Ohio and California.

The 1972 election was marked by several notable developments. One was the passage of the Federal Election Campaign Act of 1971, which was signed by President Nixon on February 7, 1972, and went into effect on April 7. It was the first law passed since 1925 to grapple with the subject of campaign financing as a whole, replacing the Corrupt Practices Act in its entirety and applying to all candidates for national office: President, Vice-President, U.S. senators and representatives.

The new law contains the following improvements over the old legislation: It requires, first of all, that all campaign contributions and expenditures which exceed $100 during a calendar year be disclosed, including money raised and spent from the moment a candidate announces for office. This includes primary and runoff, as well as general, elections.

Second, each candidate and each political committee supporting a candidate or candidates must file detailed, periodic reports in both Washington, D.C., and the office of the Secretary of State in the home state. The regular filing dates are the tenth day of March, June and September, January 31, plus fifteen and five days before each primary, runoff and general election. Any sum of $5,000 or more received within the last five days must be reported within 48 hours. Section 305 of the act, furthermore, requires that every person who contributes over $100 during the year, other than by contributing to a candidate or political committee, file his own separate report.

The act does not require, however, a political committee taking in $1,000 or less during a calendar year to file a report, although it must still register as a political committee. In addition, convention financing must now be reported in detail.

Disclosure provisions require that every contributor giving over $100 be recorded by full name, address, occupation and principal place of business. A political committee that takes in more than

$1,000 in a calendar year must file statements listing its name, address, officers, scope and jurisdiction, the name of its accountants, the name of the bank in which the funds are kept, cash on hand, debts, transfers, loans outstanding, a list of all contributors by name, address, occupation, principal place of business, and date of contribution in excess of $100, even in aggregate. It must also list all expenditures over $100 in aggregate over the year, and the total sum of all contributions and expenditures during the year which were $100 or less.

Third, expenditures for media by anyone on behalf of a congressional candidate, authorized or not, are limited to $50,000, or ten cents for each person of voting age in the district, whichever is higher. Of that ten cents, however, only six can be used for television. Production costs are not included in this limit, but agents' commissions are. The ceiling is subject to a cost-of-living increase from the time the legislation became law.

Fourth, the act abolished the D.C. committee loophole, the nonreporting states loophole, the $3 million committee limit and the $5,000 personal contribution limit. A person can now give a candidate as much as he wants, although the law does put a limit on how much a candidate or his immediate family can spend of their own money: namely, $50,000 in a Presidential race, $35,000 in a Senate race and $25,000 in a House race.

The law also requires that most telephone and postage costs, previously exempted from coverage, be reported. Contributing money in the name of others is also prohibited.

Fifth, the new law reaffirms the prohibition against corporate and labor union contributions. Both, however, may still contribute through separate and voluntary political organizations such as COPE, AMPAC and the like. If they hold government contracts, then all such contributions are prohibited.

Sixth, all the financial information that must be submitted will be published periodically by the Government Printing Office and offered to the public at a nominal cost.

Seventh, and finally, violating the law brings a maximum fine of $1,000 or a one-year prison sentence, or both; but when a conviction does not bring a prison sentence, the conviction is deemed to be a misdemeanor only.

Another development influencing the 1972 election was the

passage of the Revenue Act of 1971. A provision of this act allows individuals filing a single tax return to deduct the first $50 of all political contributions made in a calendar year, or if filing a joint return, the first $100.

A further provision of the Revenue Act would allow taxpayers to deduct one dollar of their tax payment for the party of their choice, but because of the controversy that has surrounded this plan (see Chapter VIII), the money collected is not be be distributed until the 1976 Presidential nominees have been selected.

Yet another development bearing on the 1972 election was the Watergate Affair. This is a complicated story involving burglary, electronic eavesdropping, political sabotage and the laundering of campaign contributions. Only the financial aspects of the case concern us here.

The Affair first reached the public's consciousness on June 17, 1972, when five men, three of whom were closely associated with the White House, the Committee to Re-Elect the President and the Republican National Committee, were arrested early in the morning in the headquarters of the Democratic National Committee in the Watergate Office Building while apparently either repairing, installing or removing eavesdropping equipment. Among the items found on the men were 53 new $100 bills. They were traced to a Miami bank account in the name of Bernard L. Barker, one of the five arrested. Records later showed that at least $114,000 had been recently deposited in the same account. Of that sum, $89,000 had come from a wealthy Mexican lawyer, Manuel Ogarrio Daguerre. The deposits were in the form of four checks made out to Ogarrio by the Banco International in Mexico City. The remaining $25,000 came from Kenneth H. Dahlberg, the President's campaign finance chairman for the Midwest.

Subsequently, it was learned that both sums were "laundered" —that is, passed through several hands to hide the true source. Ogarrio's $89,000, it appears, was originally part of a $100,000 transfer from Texas. A House Banking and Currency Committee staff report revealed that on April 3, four days before the new campaign financing law was to go into effect, the $100,000 had been transferred by telephone from the account of Gulf Resources & Chemical Corporation in the First City National Bank of Houston to account number 99-600 in the Banco International.

Account 99-600 was assigned to Compania de Asurfe Veracruz, S.A., a subsidiary of Gulf Resources on which the parent company had taken a $12.7 million tax write-off in 1969. The FBI then reported that the subsidiary turned the money over to Ogarrio, who also happened to be Gulf Resources' Mexican attorney. The president of Gulf Resources, Robert H. Allen, was at the time chairman of the Texas Finance Committee to Re-Elect the President. (When Allen later heard how his money had been used, he demanded and received all of it back.)

The $89,000 was allegedly part of $750,000 or more in securities, cash and checks from Texas and southwestern Fat Cats. The money was stuffed into a suitcase and flown from Texas to the President's fund raisers in Washington just in time to beat the April 7 reporting requirements. All of it may have been laundered in Mexico. Some of it was kept in a safe in Maurice Stans' office, and some allegedly went to underwrite a campaign of spying and sabotage against the Democratic party and its Presidential nominee. The $89,000 reportedly passed through the hands of several Stans subordinates before ending up in Barker's Miami account.

It was later learned as well that the true source of Dahlberg's $25,000 had been wealthy Minneapolis banker Dwayne Andreas, already a heavy contributor to Hubert Humphrey in the spring primaries. Four days before the April 7 deadline, he reportedly offered a strictly anonymous contribution. Dahlberg allegedly telephoned Stans in Washington to have the sum recorded before the deadline, but the money was not actually delivered until several days later.

On August 22, the Comptroller of the Currency granted a national bank charter to a bank in Minnetonka, Minnesota, 86 days after the application had been filed by five persons, two of whom were Dahlberg and Andreas. Although neither man has been charged with wrongdoing, Congressman Wright Patman, chairman of the House Banking and Currency Committee, pointed out that the coveted charter was granted with unusual speed, two days before a hearing had been scheduled on a competing application.

Chairman Patman's committee also found evidence that there were other laundry operations besides the Mexican one. It obtained some pre-April 7 bank records of the Finance Committee to

Re-Elect the President, for instance, which showed that President Nixon's campaign received at least $30,000 through the Banque Internationale à Luxembourg just prior to the April 7 deadline. There may have been other foreign laundry operations as well.

Further efforts were made by the Committee to Re-Elect the President to muddy the waters. Patman's committee found in one instance that the CRP had credited an account in the sum of $2,453, whereas the credit should have been $242,547. In another case, $250,447 was deposited in an account of a nonexistent political committee.

Wherever possible, the laws were stretched or broken. The $25,000 Andreas contribution, for instance, technically made after April 7, did not show up on any subsequent disclosure forms. Some of the laundered funds kept in Stans's office safe were deposited on May 25 in the bank account of the Media Committee to Re-Elect the President and carried the notation "Cash on hand prior to April 4, 1972, from 1968 campaign," but a General Accounting Office report in August stated that Stans claimed the money was not left over from 1968 but represented 1972 collections. In addition, the contributions from the Mexican and Luxembourg launderers are apparent violations of Title 18, U.S. Code, Section 613, which prohibits contributions by foreign principals or their agents.

In addition to Maurice Stans's unaudited campaign account, whose funds were kept in his office safe, there existed at least two other similar accounts. One was under the control of H. R. Haldeman—until his resignation in April, 1973, President Nixon's White House chief of staff. This account allegedly contained $350,000 in cash and was kept in a White House safe. Its purpose was and still is unknown, although many observers believe that at least part of the funds was used as "hush money" to keep the Watergate conspirators quiet.

The other unaudited account was under the control of Herbert W. Kalmbach, for many years the President's attorney. It allegedly contained about $500,000, and at least some of the money, it is suspected, went to pay for acts of political sabotage and other undercover campaign activities during the 1972 election.

Between the first of the year and the April 7 deadline, the Nixon campaign financial managers, under the leadership of Maurice

Stans, began a drive to collect a $10 million reelection kitty, none of which had to be reported. He established a "conduit system" whereby corporations would solicit their senior employees for contributions (technically on a nonpartisan basis), the money to be contributed in the name of one or two top executives. Quotas were set for all large corporations. One firm, American Motors, which was assessed $100,000 in contributions, refused to play along, even when the Nixon fund raisers subsequently reduced the assessment to $50,000. Like Mark Hanna seventy-six years previously, Stans suggested that corporate Fat Cats contribute one half of one percent of their net worth, which was presumably their stake in the general prosperity.

A typical letter, sent out in 1972 by a California fund raiser, Thomas P. Pike, reads as if it could have been written by Hanna. Pike admitted in the letter that he was operating under the direction of Stans, and goes on to say:

The simplest and most painless way to [avoid gift and capital gains taxes] is by giving appreciated low cost securities to several committees (whose names I can supply) in amounts of $3,000 to each committee. In this way neither gift nor capital gains tax liability is incurred, and I can easily explain to you the mechanics of doing it.

The standard of giving is ½%, more or less, of net worth. This makes for a very substantial campaign contribution which will actually have a minimal effect on your life-style and personal estate, but will have a tremendous effect on your family's stake in the future of our economy and our country. . . .

We have a deadline of April 7th to meet for this important major gift-phase of the drive, because this is the effective date of the new Federal Campaign Financing Law [*sic*] which will require reporting and public disclosure of all subsequent campaign contributions in excess of $100, which we all naturally want to avoid.

Later in the campaign Common Cause, the citizens' lobby, filed suit against the CRP to require that the names of contributors and sums raised prior to April 7 be revealed. To reduce the pressure, the CRP agreed to publish a list of contributors and their donations who gave between January 1, 1971, and March 10, 1972 the latter being the last reporting date required under the old Corrupt

Practices Act. Significantly, the critical twenty-seven days prior to April 7, when the laundered Watergate money, among other funds, was in transit, was not included. Some observers believe that as much as $20 million was raised in this four-week period, although a more accurate total might be closer to $10 million.

Nevertheless, the pre-March 10 list did reveal that a mere 283 Fat Cats had given close to $5 million to the Nixon campaign within the fifteen-month period. The two largest contributors were W. Clement Stone, who gave $2 million, and Richard Mellon Scaife, who was reported as giving $990,000 (although there are those who say he actually gave a million but that $10,000 was lost in the shuffle). Scaife avoided the gift tax by making out a series of $3,000 checks to the required number of committees, all of which were located in Washington.

Other $100,000-and-over GOP Fat Cats included Leonard Firestone, Raymond Guest, John P. Humes, New York industrialist John A. Mulcahy, Music Corporation of America founder Jules Stein, Arthur K. Watson, and DeWitt and Lila Wallace of the *Reader's Digest.* In the $25,000-to-$100,000 class were J. Paul Getty, Gustave Levy, Vincent DeRoulet, Thomas A. Pappas, Taft Schreiber, and Undersecretary of State John N. Irwin II. In the $2,000-to-$25,000 class were such Fat Cats as Elmer Bobst, Stephen D. Bechtel of the Bechtel engineering and construction firm, Ambassador to El Salvador Henry E. Catto, Jr. (son-in-law of Mrs. Oveta Culp Hobby), Benson Ford, Helen Clay Frick, E. Roland Harriman, James S. McDonnell of the McDonnell-Douglas Corporation, Jeremiah Milbank, Sr. and Jr., John M. Schiff, entrepreneur Nicholas Varvinaganis of Athens, Greece, and no less than 16 partners in the brokerage firm of Salomon Brothers who gave between $3,000 and $15,000 each. The milk lobbies of TAPE, SPACE and ADEPT were also reported contributing over $200,000 in this period, although the true figure is closer to $322,000 (see Chapter VI).

From April 7 to mid-October, the Nixon moneymen raised an additional $16 million, about half of it in the six weeks following Labor Day. Among those contributing not noted previously were Walter T. Duncan, a Texas entrepreneur reported to have many financial problems who still managed to contribute $257,000 to

Humphrey's primary campaign before giving an additional $305,000 to Nixon's general election campaign (because of his financial woes he later asked for and got his money back); John J. Louis, Jr., chairman of the Combined Communications Corporation of Phoenix (over $286,000); Ray A. Kroc, founder of the McDonald's hamburger empire ($255,000); Kent Smith, honorary chairman of the Cleveland-based Lubrizol Corporation ($244,000); Jack J. Dreyfus ($198,000); Foster G. McGaw, founder of American Hospital Supply (over $196,000); Charles and Sam Wyly of Universal Computing (over $149,000); Joseph Segel, president of the Franklin Mint (over $99,000); two members of the Johnson's Wax family ($84,000); and various members of the Pew family ($54,000).

Also contributing during this period was Robert L. Vesco, an international financial operator then under investigation by the SEC for allegedly looting over $220 million from Investors Overseas Services, Ltd. and its family of mutual funds. Vesco contributed $200,000 in cash to the Nixon campaign three days after the April 7 deadline, but the money was not reported by the Committee to Re-Elect the President. Another $50,000, given by checks, was contributed by Vesco and properly reported by the Committee. When this information became public knowledge nine months later, in January, 1973, the entire sum was quietly returned to the donor.

On May 10, 1973, Vesco, Stans, former Attorney General John N. Mitchell, and one other individual were indicted by a federal grand jury and charged with, among other things, conspiracy to obstruct justice by interfering with the SEC investigation. At this writing, the case had not yet come to trial.

Dr. Ruth L. Farkas, along with her husband, the founder of Alexander's Department Store in New York, together gave approximately $300,000 to the Nixon campaign in 1972. Their contribution was considered by many observers to be unusual because about $200,000 of the gift was actually delivered after election day and just prior to the White House announcement of Dr. Farkas' nomination as Ambassador to Luxembourg. Dr. Farkas explained to the Senate Foreign Relations Committee that no quid pro quo was involved, that the actual commitment for the

$300,000 had been made a year previously but that she had held off delivery until she could sell the necessary securities at the most advantageous price.

Democratic finances during the 1972 election were another story. Once the nomination campaigns began in earnest, the party's 1968 debt, the object of much breastbeating the previous four years, was forgotten. American Telephone & Telegraph threatened to cut off the party's telephone service unless it posted a $2 million bond to guarantee payment of the 1972 bills. American Airlines continued the harassment by bringing suit against Eugene McCarthy and the estate of the late Robert F. Kennedy for unpaid 1968 bills. Both actions were brushed aside by the party because they were considered the result of GOP pressure to keep the Democratic party on the defensive. Ordinarily no corporation, particularly those so heavily regulated by government, would choose to threaten its regulators unless some extraordinary pressures had been applied.

Aside from Senator Fred Harris, who dropped out early claiming lack of sufficient money, the horde of Democratic candidates appeared to have no serious campaign financing problems. Senator Henry Jackson complained that a photograph taken during the Florida primary showed him making a speech to only two people (when in fact the crowd numbered several score), and that the publicity had scared off his financial supporters. "One picture," he said, "is worth 10,000 words," and added, "It might be worth $10,000 in campaign funds." Despite this momentary setback, Jackson's campaign, while unsuccessful, ended in the black.

John Lindsay planned to spend $1 million on two primaries alone, Florida and Wisconsin. Much of his money came from Indiana industrialist J. Irwin Miller and the John Lindsay Associates, the latter a New York–based organization designed to raise "seed money" from his patronage appointees. By March, Lindsay had raised half the sum from only 1,000 people, most of them New Yorkers.

Senator Birch Bayh's campaign was also well-heeled, and was one of the few that flaunted its wealth, as if to give the campaign a sense of inevitability. On one occasion, for instance, Bayh took Al Barkin of COPE to a fund-raising dinner in a chauffeur-driven Rolls Royce.

As was the case in 1968, Wallace received most of his campaign funds from contributors of $100 or less and from contractors doing business with the state of Alabama. An exception was a $15,000 contribution from the Leander Perez family of Louisiana.

Humphrey received mostly traditional Democratic money. Between October, 1971, and mid-March, 1972, he received over $838,000 from 2,400 Fat Cats, among the most generous being Dwayne Andreas, S. Harrison ("Sonny") Dogole of Globe Security Systems, Jeno Paulucci, John ("Jake the Barber") Factor, Meshulam Riklis, San Francisco real estate developer Walter Shorenstein, Eugene Wyman, C. Douglas Dillon, TV star Lorne Green, Eugene V. Klein, and Samuel Rothberg of Peoria, a director of the Witco Chemical Corporation and the American Distillery Company.

House Ways and Means Committee chairman Wilbur Mills's campaign was also lavishly financed. Most of his funds came from lobbyists eager to tell their corporate and union superiors that they had actually spoken several words with the shy but immensely powerful legislator.

Muskie's nomination campaign was also financed by traditional Democratic Fat Cats. Approximately $4 million was raised and spent in the 18 months of the campaign's life. Among the big contributors were Arthur Krim, Robert S. Benjamin and several other United Artists executives who gave a total of $77,000. Muskie's chief fund raiser, Arnold Picker, also of United Artists, gave an additional $53,000. Other Fat Cat contributors were Lawrence and Preston Tisch of the Loew's motion picture and hotel empire, David Flexner of In-Flite Motion Pictures, Michael Redstone of the Northeast Theatre Corporation, Xerox chairman Joseph C. Wilson, Edwin L. Weisl of Paramount Pictures, lawyer Clark Clifford, Thomas J. Watson, Jr., Barry Bingham, Sr., of the Louisville *Courier-Journal,* Mrs. Marshall Field, and former government employees Paul C. Warnke, Milton Semer, Townsend W. Hoopes, Newton Minow and Najeeb Halaby.

Most of Muskie's Fat Cat money was hidden from public view through the use of nonreporting D.C. committees, still legal until the last few weeks of his campaign. Arnold Picker alone contributed his or other people's money to no less than 82 committees. There were 147 other committees available as well for Fat Cat money. Some of them carried creative names such as Jewish Grandmothers for Muskie, Lobstermen for Muskie, and the rather enigmatic Mondays for Muskie. Most of these committees were run out of the desk drawers of Washington lawyers. The Muskie Fair Play Committee, for instance, was run by Barry Chase, a lawyer with Wilmer, Cutler & Pickering. Ohio Muskie was chaired by Jay Gallagher of Sellers, Connor & Cuneo in downtown Washington. When sending money to the latter, contributors were instructed to "use [a] plain envelope."

The moment Muskie began to falter in both votes and the public opinion polls, his money began to dry up. Following his poor showing in Wisconsin, he invited 450 of his Fat Cats around the country to a meeting in Chicago to reinvigorate the campaign financially. When only 64 showed up, he and his advisers knew that the handwriting was on the wall. His opponents, particularly Humphrey, also saw their opportunity and wasted little time wooing his Fat Cats away. Three weeks after the meeting Muskie withdrew, claiming that he did "not have the money to continue."

With Muskie's withdrawal, many Democratic contributors either swung their support to Humphrey or stayed home. Once McGovern won the nomination, a few defected to the GOP, among them Eugene V. Klein, John Factor, Thomas J. Watson, Jr. and Jeno Paulucci.

McGovern's Fat Cats, for the most part, were loyalists from the start, and unlike other campaigns they provided only one third or so of the total McGovern kitty, the remainder coming from unsolicited contributors of $100 or less, fund-raising events and mass mail appeals. Altogether McGovern spent about $9 million winning the nomination and about $25 million in the race against Nixon. Unlike 1968, he ended up with virtually no debt at all, although about half the debt from the 1968 campaign remained unpaid.

McGovern's financial backers tended to be young, idealistic, generous and former supporters of Eugene McCarthy. Among his largest contributors were Stewart R. Mott; Alan Davis and Julian Price, whose families made their fortunes in the insurance business; book publisher Morris Dees; cosmetics heir Max Factor III; and Harvard assistant professor Martin Peretz. Two heirs to the Eli Lilly pharmaceutical fortune, David and Nicholas Noyes, lent the campaign a total of $500,000. All of the above Fat Cats were under forty years old at the time, Davis and the Noyeses in their early twenties.

Other sizable funds came from Henry Kimelman, a Virgin Islands industrialist and McGovern's finance chairman and chief fund raiser; Los Angeles businessman Miles Rubin; publisher Hugh Hefner; Dr. Alejandro Zaffaroni, who developed a birth control pill; Howard Metzenbaum; Washington, D.C., author and philanthropist Philip Stern; Arnold Hiatt; New York realtor John L. Tishman; Howard Samuels, head of New York State's Off-Track Betting Corporation; and George Weissman, a Phillip Morris executive.

As has become customary among Presidential contenders, Mc-Govern set up a club for his Fat Cats called the Woonsocket Club after the town in South Dakota where he and his wife met and fell in love. It cost a minimum of $25,000 in contributions to join, and at its peak late in the 1972 campaign, there were about 35 members. For lesser folk there was a Washington-based club called VICS, for Very Important Contributors, which cost only $5,000 to join.

Labor tended to sit on its hands for the Democratic nominee in 1972. McGovern did receive money from the United Auto Workers, Retail Clerks, Communication Workers and Machinists Non-Partisan Political League, but mostly in the form of loans, not the usual outright contributions. COPE raised and spent nearly $2 million, more money than it had ever spent in an election before. It went almost entirely to Senate and House candidates.

Business-oriented political action committees were also active in 1972. AMPAC reported spending $855,000 between April 7 and August 31. Most of its contributions went to supporters of free enterprise medicine such as Congressmen William E. Minshall, Samuel L. Devine and Paul G. Rogers. Minshall serves on the House Appropriations Committee overseeing health legislation, Devine is the senior Republican on the House Interstate and Foreign Commerce Committee and Rogers is chairman of its health subcommittee. On the Senate side, Wyoming's Clifford Hansen, a sponsor of the AMA's "Medicredit" plan; Illinois' Charles Percy; and Mississippi's James O. Eastland, chairman of the Judiciary Committee, all received contributions.

BIPAC was just as active, contributing to 29 GOP and Democratic House and Senate incumbents and 20 Democratic challengers prior to Labor Day. The milk producers lobby, in addition to what it gave President Nixon, spread its money among legislators in charge of dairy legislation (House Agriculture Committee chairman W. R. Poage, House Agriculture dairy subcommittee chairman Frank Stubblefield, etc.). The Restaurateurs Political Action Committee, representing establishments seeking exemptions from the minimum wage laws, spread nearly $100,000 among members of the House Labor, Rules, and Ways and Means Committees. The Securities Industry Campaign Committee, the political arm of Merrill Lynch, Pierce, Fenner & Smith, rifled contributions totaling $200,000 to appropriate legislators. Large donations were also made by the likes of the American Dental Association PAC, Savings and Loan PAC, the Real Estate Political Education Committee, the Builders Political Campaign Committee, and perhaps a score of other political action committees. All of them tended to concentrate their funds on House and Senate incumbents with seniority.

Many of these organizations tried to hide the source of their funds by earmarking their contributions through various Senate and House campaign committees. For instance, the Builders Political Campaign Committee, an affiliate of the National Association of Home Builders, acknowledged on registering with the Clerk of the House that it expected to receive and transmit earmarked funds. In its May 28 and June 2 reports it said that it had received contributions totaling $3,600 for transfer to Senators Sparkman of Alabama and Hatfield of Oregon, and Congressmen Baring of Nevada, Anderson of Tennessee and Annunzio of Illinois. The original donors were not named. Each of the candidates subsequently reported contributions from BPCC, or its predecessor, but none disclosed the original contributor or the earmarking. BankPAC, the Real Estate Political Education Committee, and General Telephone's Employees' Good Government Club, among others, also used this device to good effect in 1972.

Altogether, the 1972 election at all levels of endeavor cost an estimated $400 million, up 33 percent from 1968. The Presidential race consumed 15 percent of that total. As in the past, most of the money went to pay for television and radio time, travel expenses, polls and computer and telephone services. The GOP, for instance, set aside an unusually large $3 million just for a last-minute crash telephone contact effort.

The biggest growth area in costs, however, was in mailing lists which, unlike the media, are not subject to expenditure limitations under the new law. The McGovern mass mail fund-raising effort seems to have been more effective than the GOP mail solicitation drive. About half of all McGovern's money was raised through the mails, an extraordinary feat under any circumstance.

McGovern's mail-order experts shunned the computerized, one-page begging letter, complete with the recipient's name sprinkled throughout it several times, in favor of a reasoned and frank approach. In one case this took the form of a seven-page letter that described in detail why the money was needed and how it was to be spent. The success of McGovern's mail-order fund raising appears to have been in its concern for details. Stationery and envelope colors, for instance, were carefully coordinated, the size of both were reduced to give the "package" a more personal touch, stamps were chosen for eye appeal, names and addresses were not printed on mailing labels, and computerized blank checks were enclosed for the convenience of the donor. Between 50 and 80 commercial mailing lists were tested prior to Labor Day. Approximately 250,000 individuals had responded by mid-September. Obviously, many were taking advantage of the tax-deduction provision in the Revenue Act of 1971. The average donation ran to $40 for a total of $10 million. By the end of the campaign, mail-order donations had pushed the total up close to $15 million.

All in all, if one had to sum up the 1972 election, it could be described, like the 1904 and 1920 elections, as one in which campaign financing was an issue but had no appreciable influence on the outcome of the Presidential or other races. It was, furthermore, a preliminary testing ground for the 1971 reforms which will undoubtedly lead to a prolonged struggle in the years ahead between opponents and proponents of the new law.

Finally, it was an election in which none of the major candidates for President had serious money problems. Even Senator Vance Hartke, who ran in a fit of vanity, had no trouble raising a respectable campaign kitty (even though he later claimed that it was lack of money that lost him the nomination); and George McGovern, who by any measure fared rather poorly at the polls, still managed to spend record amounts and end up with virtually no deficit at all.

PART TWO

THE
PRESENT

VI

Fat Cats and Serious Money

W. Clement Stone gave to Richard Nixon in 1968 and 1972 because he believes he is changing the course of history. He claims he speaks with the President over the phone about once a month, and has expressed a desire in public to be appointed to some important job, preferably Secretary of the Department of Health, Education and Welfare or ambassador to Great Britain. He likes being invited to the White House and mixing with other powerful and influential people, and he believes in the idea of large campaign contributions because, he says, they offset the power of entrenched machines.

The recipients of Martin Peretz's large contributions have changed over the years, in line with his developing philosophical and ideological position at any one moment. He supported the Student Nonviolent Coordinating Committee, then moved on to *Ramparts* magazine until it chose the wrong side in the 1967 Six Day War. He then turned his generosity toward helping peace groups and new political organizations. Generally, he seeks a third way between "confrontationists" and "vacillating, vapid liberals," which is what led him to back McCarthy so heavily in 1968 and McGovern in 1972. Today, he would tend to support any candidate advocating radical economic and social reform.

There are Fat Cats who give for the same reasons as J. Clifford Folger, long a top GOP fund raiser and contributor: he is more amused by politics than government, more interested in picking a winner than ideology. Most "smart money"—either early money or long-shot money—is given for this reason. Instead of buying works of art before they are recognized as such, some monied contributors, particularly the radical chic Fat Cats who orbit the society pages of New York, Los Angeles and San Francisco, consider it amusing to back a potential political winner before he breaks out of obscurity.

J. Irwin Miller, who regularly gives to between 75 and 100 promising candidates at all levels of political activity, most of whom are Republicans, actually wants good men in office. His contributions also enhance his business and social image. Originally, he tended to give money based on the enthusiasm of the pitch made to him, but then he hired half a dozen men to work out a rational approach to his contributions. Only about one in four candidates under consideration eventually gets a contribution, and the amount is usually no more than $3,000 to $5,000.

Miller's systematic approach, coupled with his idealism and the esteem with which he is held in Republican circles, has encouraged other liberal GOP Fat Cats to organize their contributions in a similar manner, among them John Hay Whitney in New York, Norton Simon in California, and Sam Wyly of Universal Computing and Stanley Marcus of Neiman-Marcus in Texas.

Nobody knows exactly why H. L. Hunt gives contributions except Hunt himself. Contrary to common belief he does not give only to right-wingers. While he put up $150,000 in 1952 in support of General Douglas MacArthur's campaign for President, he is also believed to have given $100,000 to the Kennedy-Johnson ticket in 1960 because of his long-standing friendship with the Vice-Presidential candidate. Generally, though, Hunt has a reputation for eccentricity (he believes, for instance, that the rich should have more votes than the poor), and it laps over into his political contributions for which no clear pattern has ever been discerned.

Stewart R. Mott gave in 1968 because he wanted an antiwar candidate elected President. He appears to have given heavily to McGovern in 1972 because he wanted to both influence and change the course of events. More than anything, however, he likes the personal publicity that comes with giving large sums. In the 1969 New York City mayoralty race, for instance, he offered to buy full-page newspaper advertisements on behalf of Lindsay. He was eventually turned down, but throughout the negotiations, while the terms of a possible agreement over copy matter were being thrashed out, one point remained nonnegotiable: Stewart R. Mott's name in large type at the bottom of the advertisements was not to be changed. This is in keeping with his belief that "people who give money ought not to do so quietly if they want to get leverage."

Max Palevsky gives in part because he has been a success in business and seeks other worlds to conquer. He is also concerned for the future of the country. "If this society gets torn apart," he once said, "it won't help me or my kids to be rich." Cornelius Vanderbilt Whitney contributes because, among other things, he wants to be ambassador to Spain. Eugene Wyman, until his death recently, both gave and raised money because it was good for his law practice. "People figure," he said, "if a man's a good fund raiser, he's a good lawyer."

Howard R. Hughes apparently gives because it is good for his business. While he was living in Nevada, he regularly gave to city councilmen, county supervisors, tax assessors, sheriffs, state senators and assemblymen, governors, congressmen, senators, Vice-Presidents and Presidents. He is supposed to have contributed to Hubert Humphrey in 1968 with the understanding that President Johnson would be pressured into halting atomic testing in Nevada because Hughes believed it was hurting his business. Humphrey had opposed the tests prior to Hughes's contribution but made no subsequent overture to Johnson to stop them.

Martin Stone, the chairman of the Monogram Industries conglomerate, gives at least in part because he wants the ear of the President. In 1972 he was an early backer of Muskie before the latter's campaign collapsed, and was quoted as saying: "I've never asked for a favor from anyone I've backed. Of course, I would hope to have an influence on Muskie in terms of an immediate Vietnam withdrawal, European troop cutbacks, a new welfare approach and public tax structures."

There are some Fat Cats who give serious money hoping it will give them leverage against tax investigations, antitrust suits and unfriendly legislation. A few give seeking favors or social position. Others are looking for contracts, licenses and purchasing orders.

Giving to both sides, known as "double riding" in the trade, is a preferred tactic of a few Fat Cats because they believe that such largesse will cover all bets. George Eccles, president of the First

Security Corporation of Utah, contributes to both parties because, he said, "I believe in the two-party system."

Sometimes a Fat Cat simply likes to feel he "owns" a candidate by becoming the principal supplier of campaign funds. This motivation has been dying out at the federal level, primarily because it costs too much, but in many states it continues to thrive. Jess Unruh, for many years a power in the California legislature, was one who resisted the temptation to be owned, much to the irritation of many Sacramento lobbyists. "Those bastards hate me," he once said, "because they never could own me. When I ran the Assembly, I let them buy chunks of me—in fact, you might say I sold 125 percent—but I never let anyone buy a controlling share."

One of the principal, and often overlooked, reasons why Fat Cats give is that they simply like the candidate and want to help him win. Humphrey's old Minnesota friends gave primarily for this reason, as did McGovern's liberal constituency, Muskie's New England friends and Nixon's various acquaintances. The same could be said for most big contributors to House, Senate, statewide and local candidates.

In liking a candidate, a contributor presumes that he and the candidate share a common view of life, compatible interests and similar political attitudes. If the giver did not believe this, in all probability he would not contribute money. Thus it can be said that a candidate is an extension of the political views of those from whom he receives money. Therefore, it would be wrong to assume that, because a politician votes down the line in a way that pleases his financial backers, he has, ipso facto, sold his soul. In all likelihood he would have voted that way in any event.

This is not to imply, however, that WASPs finance only like-minded WASPs, or Jews only other Jews, or Irish other Irish. What is important to a Fat Cat is a candidate's outlook, not his background or religion, however much they all may be entwined. Thus Jewish money will support a Catholic like John F. Kennedy or Protestants like Harry S. Truman, Dwight D. Eisenhower and Lyndon B. Johnson because of their sympathetic attitude toward Israel and approach to solving domestic problems, while a candidate like Barry M. Goldwater, whose grandfather was Jewish, will not get much Jewish money because of his independent domestic and foreign policy views.

Often, when mutual compatibility is assumed from the start, a contribution is given to cultivate a climate in which it becomes difficult, if not impossible, for a candidate to distinguish between his own convictions and his friendship for the donor. The crunch comes not on fundamental issues and questions, on which they both agree, but on the hundreds of peripheral issues and questions on which many men of good will might disagree. Here, the Fat Cat hopes that his contribution, combined with the weight of friendship and shared attitudes, will provide the necessary difference when it matters. All big contributors know that, unless a candidate is corrupt, no amount of money will change his basic views. They also know that on lesser issues and questions money can be used to keep a man in line. This is the true power of money in American politics, and most Fat Cats understand this.

If one accepts the belief that large political contributions are made for some purpose, no matter how selfish, egotistical or altruistic, then there is a right and a wrong way of giving serious money at all levels of American politics.

There are seven ironclad rules of behavior to which a Fat Cat must subscribe if he wishes to get the most mileage from his contribution. Surprisingly, no more than one in five Fat Cats understands how the game is played.

The first rule might be called *Don't Just Write Out a Check*. The usual procedure in giving large sums to a candidate is for a Fat Cat to sit down at his desk, write out a check for $3,000 or so, hand it to his secretary for mailing, and then turn his mind back to his business or personal affairs. Unless the Fat Cat is a close personal friend of the candidate, this routine offers the contributor no benefits at all. No one in the campaign knows his face, his name will simply be added to the campaign's "sucker list," he will not even be able to tell his family a good story connected with his contribution that does not sound like bragging, and he will not even have a chance to put in a good word for his projects. All he can show is a standard thank-you letter that in all probability was signed by a machine.

This manner of giving is best illustrated by the story told by a powerful New York Republican fund raiser who was working for John Lindsay in the latter's 1969 reelection campaign. In an effort to cover every possible source of money, the fund raiser one day walked unannounced into a firm's head office, asked for the president (whom he did not know), and proceeded to give the standard fund-raising pitch. Hardly had he begun before the president turned around in his chair and shouted to an employee in the back, "Hey, write out a check for my friend here for five thousand bucks." Then, turning back to the fund raiser with his pen poised to fill in the recipient's name, he asked, "Now, who do I make it out to? . . ."

The second and third rules might be called *Find Yourself a Key Man with Access* and *Do a Little Dance*. Both are usually applied back-to-back because they cannot easily be separated. Key men with access are a special breed of political moneymen. They not only contribute their own funds and raise money from others, but they have clout among their peers and exert great influence over the candidate and his campaign. They are discussed at length in the following chapter.

A smart Fat Cat will attach himself to one of these key men and insist that, before he gives his money, he be introduced to the candidate. The two men, the candidate and the contributor, then meet for ten minutes or so, perhaps at a small cocktail party before a fund-raising dinner, exchange small talk and then part. The Fat Cat then writes out his check for a large sum and directs it to the proper committee. This political minuet, while appearing trite, means everything to the Fat Cat who wants to milk all possible benefits from his contribution: his face is now known, he can say he "knows" the candidate, he has increased his "recognition factor" as politicians like to say, the meeting itself might produce a story worth repeating to family, friends and those he wishes to impress, and it was all done relatively properly and in good taste.

Furthermore, as one Washington key man told me, "Anyone who gives money through me will get double value. I'll make sure he meets the candidate and, in addition, he knows I'll go to bat for him at the appropriate time."

The fourth rule is: *If You Give Cash, Make Sure Your Name Is on It*. There is nothing illegal about making a political contribution in cash, unless it is not reported like any other gift. However, a contributor who favors cash over checks usually has something, either real or imagined, to hide, and he invariably prefers that the cash pass through an intermediary's hands before it reaches the candidate. But because he is preoccupied with so many other matters, a candidate may associate the cash with the go-between and not the original donor. Thus, the Fat Cat may be denied future access to the political power brokers and the contracts, licenses and concessions they dispense because no one recalls that it was *he* who originally gave the cash.

Ken Birkhead, a veteran politician and a member of Senator Thomas J. McIntyre's staff, claims he recently saw a candidate for the Senate (not his boss) shake hands with a contributor and come away with a $1,000 bill stuck to his palm. For all the risks of misunderstanding such a transaction incurs, it is still the best way to give cash because there is no doubt who gave it.

Some cash contributors go to extra pains to make sure the recipient knows from whom the money came. Noah Dietrich, a longtime aide of Howard Hughes, for instance, recalls that during the 1948 election his boss contributed $12,500 in cash to the Truman campaign. The money was in an envelope and delivered by Neil McCarthy, one of Hughes's lawyers. However, it soon occurred to Hughes, who was in the adjoining room, that the President might not fully appreciate from whom the money had come since it was being delivered in cash by an intermediary, so the billionaire stalked into the President's suite and said, "Mr. Truman, I want you to know that that is *my* money Mr. McCarthy is giving you."

The fifth rule is: *Use a Rifle Rather than a Shotgun.* That is to say, a clever Fat Cat will rifle his contributions to candidates who, if elected, can be of specific help to him. At the federal level, this means giving to a Presidential candidate himself, or to a specific House or Senate committee chairman who has the power to make decisions beneficial to the contributor. At the state and local level it means giving to a candidate for governor, or a powerful state senator, or an influential mayor. A Fat Cat would not waste his money giving to the Democratic or Republican National Committees, the various congressional campaign committees or the many state and local political organizations unless there was a particular individual in one of those groups who had clout in the political arena. Power and tenure in these organizations tend to be fleeting; thus a Fat Cat contribution made yesterday may be forgotten tomorrow.

Fat Cat lobbyists have long understood the value of rifling. This is why so many contributions from military contractors flow to members of the House Armed Services and Appropriations Committees, why the highway lobby pumps so much money into gubernatorial races, and why suppliers of goods and services contribute so heavily to the local mayoralty race. These candidates, once elected, have the power to grant or withhold business contracts. Such power is not vested in general political fund-raising committees.

Shotgunning contributions is the weakness of ideologues. It is not unusual for a conservative Fat Cat like Patrick J. Frawley of Eversharp-Schick or a liberal Fat Cat like Harvard assistant professor Martin Peretz to scatter their contributions among a large number of ideologically compatible candidates. The Pews of Sun Oil and GM heir Stewart Mott behave in the same manner. All of them seek to tilt the general political climate in their ideological favor, but when it comes to influencing the course of events within government, their money is wasted.

The sixth rule is: *Lend Rather than Give.* Many Fat Cats have learned that it pays to contribute money borrowed from banks rather than their own personal funds. Many Humphrey backers in 1968 and McGovern followers in 1972 used this technique to good effect. Such a ploy has the advantage of making a big contributor seem generous, yet it costs him nothing but the interest, which is deductible. If the loan is not repaid then no gift tax need be paid. Loans for this purpose cannot be made by national banks; thus state charted banks and savings and loan associations receive all this business.

It is also doubtful whether big lenders who are not repaid, such as may be the case with some of Humphrey's 1968 backers, will ever suffer much of a financial loss. A precedent was set, back in 1948, when the IRS ruled that 90 percent of the money former DNC Treasurer Richard J. Reynolds contributed to various Democratic committees in the immediate postwar years, which was listed on his books as business loans, could be regarded as a non-business bad business debt which could be offset against capital gains. Similar consideration was given to a $50,000 "loan" by Marshall Field.

The final rule is: *Whenever Possible, Hide the Source.* There are several standard ways in which this can be done illegally—not reporting the contribution, offering services in kind and deducting them as business expenses, dipping into general union or business funds for the money, and so on—but they are not of concern to us for the moment.

Currently the favorite legal method of hiding the source of funds is through the practice of "earmarking." It works in the following manner: A Fat Cat, wishing to contribute to a candidate but also mindful of the troublesome publicity that may accompany his gift, gives his money to a campaign committee with specific instructions that the funds be passed through to the candidate. In this way any link between the donor and the contributor is effectively hidden. How? When the candidate files his disclosure report, he simply lists the total contribution from the campaign committee, only part of which represents the donor's gift; the campaign committee, when it files its report, lists various contributions from Fat Cats, but there is nothing in the report to indicate any ties between a particular donor and a candidate.

Party officials encourage earmarking because it makes points for the contributor with the committee, then with the candidate, and in the case of labor funds, with the state organization from which the funds came. Some people contribute to opposing candidates and use earmarking as a way to keep one side from knowing about the other contribution. Earmarking also keeps contributors' names off sucker lists, and avoids any connection between a contributor's personal interests and the compatible powers of the legislator receiving the contribution.

There is no guarantee that if a Fat Cat rigidly followed these seven basic rules of behavior, his contribution will automatically bear fruit. But it is almost certain that if he does not follow them, the road to whatever he seeks to achieve will be strewn with many unnecessary stumbling blocks.

When one speaks of Fat Cats today, one is referring to approximately 130,000 individuals in the United States who are willing to contribute $500 or more in a federal, state or local election. About

30,000 of these people concentrate their gifts at the federal level, and slightly less than 1,000 of them qualify as Extra Fat Cats by virtue of their willingness to give $10,000 or more.

Any contribution of $500 or over today is considered by politicians to be serious money. Why $500 was chosen as the sum worthy of more consideration than a lesser offering is unknown. Part of the answer, no doubt, lies in the fact that, on a person-to-person basis, $500 is worth making an effort to get, and worth making a fuss to give, while a lesser sum is not. From a fund raiser's point of view, it is better to consign a potential $100 contributor to the computer than to waste a person's time telephoning, writing letters and arranging personal meetings. Furthermore, a $500 donor probably knows other $500 donors, which makes soliciting him worthwhile; a $100 contributor, on the other hand, probably only knows men of similar means, and it is often not worth a fund raiser's time to seek them all out.

There are roughly 90,000 people in the United States who are millionaires, counted by personal assets. If it is assumed that all 30,000 of the $500-and-over contributors in federal elections are millionaires, although many are not, it would still mean that only one in three millionaires in the country bothers to contribute any sizable sum to House, Senate and Presidential races. The remaining resident millionaires, some 60,000 of them, it can be assumed, either give only token amounts, refuse to give, are not asked to give, are below or beyond the age of cognizance or, like 30 to 45 percent of the eligible voters who never exercise their franchise, are disinterested and unwilling to take part in the game.

Who are the Fat Cats? Any generalization about 130,000 individuals is risky, but nevertheless certain traits appear to predominate over others. Most serious money in federal elections does not come from members of established monied families as is so commonly believed. Large contributions from families like the Fields, Harrimans, Lehmans, Vanderbilts and Whitneys, for example, no longer have the relative size or importance they did in the 1920's and previously. Even Du Pont, Mellon, Olin and Pew contributions, still large today, do not carry the impact they did prior to World War II. Only Rockefeller and Kennedy money has had an impact over the past two decades equal to or greater than Fat Cat contributions in, say, the 1896, 1904 and 1920 elections.

The more typical big contributor is usually self-made and absolute or near-absolute ruler of his own business empire. He made his money quickly over the past quarter century, and the bulk of his personal wealth is not tied up in trusts, which allows him to give freely and spontaneously. Big contributors today are more likely to be investment bankers rather than commercial bankers, wildcatters rather than oil company executives, sports equipment manufacturers rather than professional athletes, fast-food-chain tycoons rather than restaurateurs, real estate speculators rather than landed gentry.

Large contributors tend to be found more in relatively new businesses such as electronics, aerospace, pharmaceuticals, beauty products, business machines and conglomerates rather than older ones such as retailing, utilities, steel and shipbuilding. They are concentrated in five major areas of the United States: New York City, Washington, D.C. (usually in the form of a lobbyist or corporation lawyer), southern California, the Dallas–Ft. Worth area and the eastern Florida coast. Secondary concentrations can be found in big cities such as Boston, Philadelphia, Chicago, Atlanta, Phoenix, Denver and Seattle. The Democrats tend to find more money in midtown Manhattan and Beverly Hills, while the Republicans tend to find more in Wall Street and downtown Los Angeles. Wealthy Jews tend to give to Democratic candidates, while rich WASPs and Catholics tend to give to GOP candidates.

Typical of the new breed would be Jack Dreyfus, Elmer Bobst, Gustave Levy, Lew Wasserman, Henry Salvatori, Bob Hope, W. Clement Stone, Max Fisher and Charles Revson. The late Sydney Weinberg, Jacob Blaustein, Lester Avnet, Howard Ahmanson and Chester Carlson would also qualify. Put another way, it means that the A. T. Stewarts, John Wanamakers, Henry Clay Fricks, James J. Hills and Mark Hannas, who were running the relatively new businesses of yesterday, have been replaced by the David Packards, Thomas J. Watson, Jrs., Leon Hesses and J. Willard Marriotts, who are running the relatively new businesses of today.

In state and local elections, serious money comes from those who sell goods to the government, such as police cars, ambulances, helicopters, snowplows, uniforms, hospital and office equipment, and food. Those who perform services such as collecting garbage, providing heat and light, brokering municipal and state bonds, providing insurance coverage, and holding bank deposits all contribute heavily. So do concessionaires (newsstands, pushcarts, fairgrounds, sightseeing buses, highway services, and so on), construction firms, architects, bail bondsmen, real estate developers, theater and restaurant owners, saloonkeepers, taxi fleet owners and labor unions. Illegal businesses such as bootlegging, gambling, narcotics, prostitution and shylocking also kick in heavily.

There is nothing to indicate that today's Fat Cats crowd a particular band of the political spectrum. There is a clear bias toward conservatism and the status quo, but it does not follow that most givers of serious money are members of the John Birch Society, racists or fascists. Nor does it follow that the GOP is the party of old money and the Democratic party the party of the nouveau riche. For every conservative like Henry Salvatori, John Factor, J. Howard Pew and John Wayne there are an equal number of liberal Fat Cats like Norman Cousins, June Degnan, J. Irwin Miller and Martin Peretz. The truth of the matter is that the views of the vast majority of the $500-and-over givers at all political levels, like the views of the public at large, fall comfortably somewhere between these two poles. Most big contributors are not ideologues but practical people who, as noted previously, choose to give heavily for a variety of other reasons.

The link between what is desired and what is actually obtained is sometimes long and tenuous, and the question that really must be answered is: what does a Fat Cat actually get for his serious money?

More than anything, regardless of whether or not a contributor has anything specific in mind, serious money buys access. It may not be used, but it is there to be used until the next election period when subscriptions to the access are up for renewal.

Having access to men in power in Washington, in the statehouse, or down at city hall means that doors are opened, the way is greased, red tape is cut and one is put toward the front of the line. The kind of access big political money buys is no different than what it buys when a man gives money to a university because he has a fifteen-year-old son who might want to go there. It does not guarantee anything, but it certainly helps.

At the federal level, having access means that one can wangle a White House invitation, get one's passport issued overnight, extend the visa of one's alien-resident maid, or have a nephew appointed to the Air Force Academy. At the state and local level having access means that you can get to see the governor, that your name goes to the head of the list of favored suppliers, that you can get a state pollution abatement order softened, that you can argue for lower rates before the insurance commissioner himself and not one of his aides, or that you can find a job for an out-of-work brother, or have a speeding ticket fixed.

There is no standard way in which a large contributor exercises his access options. The routes are as varied as there are grievances needing redress. To take one's friend off the hook for tax evasion requires one particular route, to win a big printing order from the Pentagon requires another, and to have one's tobacco allotment increased requires a third.

However, the White House usually is the primary focal point for contributors who seek access to the federal government. In every recent administration, be it Republican or Democratic, there have been men on the White House staff whose job, in part, has been to satisfy the particular problems of big contributors. These men are the pivot point at which access is either gained or not gained. Sherman Adams and General Wilton B. Persons were the two to see in the Eisenhower administration. During the Kennedy years it was Lawrence O'Brien; with Lyndon Johnson it was Joseph Califano or Marvin Watson. With the Nixon administration it has been Harry Dent for southern, textile and special Fat Cats, Charles Colson for moneybags in general, and Peter Flanigan for Wall Street and Social Register Fat Cats. These men know their way around government and, because of their closeness to the President, can reach virtually anyone they want on short notice.

The very fact that a man gave $1,000, $10,000 or $100,000 in the last election means, unless he is terribly naïve, that he knows someone important in the party hierarchy. If this particular big contributor has a problem that he believes can only be solved by the federal government, he might call up his friend in the party who, in turn, would contact the White House; the key man, if he believed the problem was one the government could legitimately solve, would then make a few telephone calls around town. A meeting would then be arranged between the contributor and the proper bureaucratic power, the problem would be discussed, and something would be done or not done according to the merits of the case and the amount of pressure being applied by the White House. By no means are all Fat Cat problems resolved in the contributor's favor, but the advantage the Fat Cat gains over the small or noncontributor is the opportunity for a speedy and sympathetic hearing with those in government with the power to change things.

If a contributor's problem can be solved through a change in federal regulations, then the person is steered to the proper bureaucrat for a hearing. A private session with an undersecretary of the Interior, for instance, may lead to an innocuous-sounding change in departmental regulations governing, say, national forests which will mean the difference in profit or loss to a strip mining company, an all-terrain vehicle manufacturer, or a lumber company using clear-cutting techniques. Thus a $10,000 contribution might be the necessary wedge to a million-dollar profit.

For instance, until early 1970, Peter Flanigan, one of Nixon's chief fund raisers and contributors, was president of the Barracuda Tanker Corporation, owner of the Liberian flag tanker *Sansinena*. Under United States law the ship was ineligible for U.S. coastal shipping unless a waiver could be granted by the Treasury Department. Without the waiver the *Sansinena* was worth only an estimated $4.5 million, with it approximately $11 million. In late February, 1970, Flanigan, then a White House aide, sold his 200 shares in Barracuda to others in the firm. Less than a week later the Treasury Department granted an unusually broad waiver for the tanker, on the grounds that national security required it. Overnight the ship jumped in value by $6.5 million. The waiver was subsequently cancelled, but only after potentially embarrassing questions were raised in the Senate.

The International Telephone & Telegraph case of 1972 is another good example of this. Although it is difficult to know exactly where the truth lies, the volumes of testimony seem to indicate that the billion-dollar conglomerate was pleased to underwrite part of the cost of the 1972 GOP convention, then planned to be held in San Diego, with the apparent expectation that in return the Justice Department's Antitrust Division would not pursue its case to prevent the company from keeping the huge Hartford Insurance Company. While the story is Byzantine in its complexity, it can be boiled down to the fact that, over the many months that the antitrust action was being put together, IT&T's problem was of no extraordinary concern to the White House; but the moment IT&T became a Fat Cat all sorts of doors opened, and the White House went out of its way to help the company find relief. Had the company refused to contribute, had its contribution been perfunctory, or simply had the company been relatively small and insignificant, it is questionable whether it would have been treated with as much consideration, regardless of what problem it may have had.

Another access route is through the Senate. In spite of the Hatch Acts, many senators still control certain patronage appointments in their home states and in select federal bureaucracies. A prospective federal judge, for instance, is first cleared with the senator or senators in whose state or states he will sit. Therefore, if a Fat Cat seeks to influence whether or not a particular person is appointed to the federal bench, his route of access in all probability will take him to a senator.

Senators also try to place as many of their men as possible in positions of power in the federal bureaucracy. One of the favorite agencies to control is the General Services Administration which lets millions of dollars of construction, supply and service contracts each year on a variety of government projects. Anyone wanting some of this business might go to the senator with the most clout in the agency. For years, Senator Dirksen controlled GSA through the appointment of men loyal to him to the top jobs, but following his death this power passed to Senator Hugh Scott, who replaced Dirksen's men with his own. As a result, access to GSA and its contracts can currently be found through the office of Senator Scott.

Often, access will first be gained in the White House, and the Fat Cat then directed to the appropriate senator; but more and more contributors with a problem are contributing directly to a senator's reelection campaign (even when it is four or five years away) without giving to the President first. This is true not only of senators with allies in the bureaucracy, but of senators who have the power to report out bills that might benefit or harm a particular individual, business or industry.

One of the best ways to tell from whom an incumbent senator receives campaign contributions is to look at his committee assignments. A senator like John Tower, for instance, sits on the Armed Services and Banking and Currency Committees. In his 1972 reelection campaign, a sizable portion of his funds came from bankers and individuals who had or sought military contracts.

To give another example, Daniel B. Brewster, while he was a senator from 1963 to 1969, served on the Senate Post Office and Civil Service Committee which, among other things, sets postal rates. In 1972, he was found guilty of accepting an "unlawful gratuity" (which means he accepted the money without corrupt intent) from a Washington lobbyist to influence his Senate vote on postal rate legislation. Brewster claims the money was actually a campaign contribution. The lobbyist, Cyrus T. Anderson, was a Washington representative of Spiegel, Inc., a Chicago-based mail-order house. He was found guilty in the same district court of bribery. As of this writing, both men are appealing their convictions.

Since many problems of wealthy givers are often financial, a well-trodden access route is to the tax-writing House Ways and Means Committee. For years the chairman of this committee has been Wilbur Mills, who is personally incorruptible and gives the appearance of being slightly naïve about the behavior of his fellow committee members. Nevertheless, he is extraordinarily astute and knows how to get things done.

Several members of the committee specialize in handling tax problems for various industries. The automobile industry is usually handled by either Martha W. Griffiths or Charles E. Chamberlain, respectively Democratic and Republican representatives from Michigan. James C. Corman of California covers aircraft industry problems; and until his death, John C. Watts of Kentucky oversaw the tax problems of the liquor, sugar, wine and tobacco industries.

At various intervals during a legislative session, in closed-door meetings from which the public is barred, private member's bills are discussed, perhaps two dozen or so of which are eventually reported out each session for a vote. Many of these bills spring from the special tax needs of ordinary citizens, but many more spring from the specific problems of Fat Cats. Usually all of them are opposed by the Treasury Department and the crusty chairman of the House Banking and Currency Committee, Wright Patman of Texas.

On the surface these bills appear to benefit every taxpayer, but on closer inspection restrictive provisions make it clear that the benefits are limited to a particular industry, business or individual. All of the bills are introduced either in the last days of a congressional session when everyone is eager to go home, or when things are busy, so that they receive minimum scrutiny and debate. Once these bills reach the floor of the House or Senate they are rarely ever challenged. When Patman took exception to several of them in 1972, for instance, it was considered big news.

Typical of the way these bills are processed occurred in late December, 1970, and early January, 1971, during the last hours of the lame-duck 91st Congress. Twenty of these special bills were rushed through the legislative process with almost no debate. They benefited such industries as medical equipment manufacturers by reducing the duty on imported stethoscope parts; liquor distillers by reducing tariffs on certain imported spirits and by reclassifying other tariffs on certain imported sugars, syrups and molasses; aircraft engine overhaul firms by providing drawback privileges; cement-mixer body manufacturing firms by providing certain refunds; the beer industry by allowing certain tax breaks; rubber companies by providing credits or refunds for the tax paid on tread rubber used in recapping and retreading; and bicycle manufacturers by suspending the duty on certain imported parts.

Another of the bills allowed the heirs of one individual to donate $1 million from the estate and an additional $4 million of their own money to a university and to deduct the lot as a charitable contribution.

Perhaps the most famous of this type of bill was what has come to be known as the Louis B. Mayer Bill. It allowed the movie mogul to receive all future profits from his company to which he was entitled after retirement in one lump sum, and to pay taxes on this money at the 25 percent rate rather than at his higher personal income tax rate. The legislation was written in such a way that virtually no one but Louis B. Mayer could benefit from it.

Another special bill once made fat profits for the Milwaukee-based Mortgage Guaranty Insurance Corporation, one of whose stockholders was Robert G. ("Bobby") Baker. The company lost money its first year, 1957, and struggled on with indifferent success for several years more. According to Wisconsin law, MAGIC, as the firm was called, was required to put half its premiums into a contingency reserve for fifteen years, thus tying up funds that could be used to expand the business. MAGIC officials argued that it should not have to pay income taxes on this money until the fifteen years were up and it had full use of the funds. Twice the IRS refused to change the rules, so company officials went to Ways and Means Committee member John W. Byrnes of Wisconsin, who introduced a bill that, if enacted, would have given MAGIC the tax break it desired. As a result the company's stock soared.

In September, 1960, Byrnes himself purchased a large block of MAGIC stock at its depressed price. By the time the news of the transaction had leaked out, the price of the stock had risen over 1,000 percent. Byrnes defended his action on the floor of the House, saying that he would donate the stock to a nonprofit foundation (which he subsequently did). His fellow legislators stood and gave him a rousing ovation.

Another instance of favorable treatment occurred in 1971 when Congress eased the minimum tax law. This tax, part of the Tax Reform Act of 1969, was designed to make sure that individuals with large incomes paid at least some federal taxes each year. Late in the lame-duck session of the 91st Congress, Republican Senator Jack Miller of Iowa introduced an amendment, in typically opaque wording, to an unrelated bill, which in effect created a giant loophole for Fat Cats, allowing some to escape most if not all of the minimum tax. Debate on this amendment, which subsequently reduced tax revenues by about $100 million annually, filled only two columns of one page of the *Congressional Record.*

Lest there be any doubt as to the power of a large contributor who has access, consider the words of two professionals, Ken Birkhead and Secretary of Agriculture Earl Butz. In describing the behavior of an average senator, Birkhead said, "If there were two people in a senator's waiting room, and one was a contributor and one wasn't, it would only be natural for the senator to see the contributor first." Butz is even more blunt. He believes that Fat

Cats should be used directly to pressure legislators. "That's the way I worked to beat a bill raising price supports 25 percent," he said. "It would have been disastrous for our farmers. I called up one chap," Butz continued, "and started to explain the bill. He said, 'Hell, don't bother. I'll just tell the congressman I don't want it.' He did. That was it."

Sometimes, however, pressure from a Fat Cat can backfire or fall on deaf ears. For example, a very wealthy and powerful Pennsylvania businessman is supposed to have called up Senator Richard Schweiker in late 1969 and said, "Damn it, I gave you $10,000 for your campaign [in 1968], and I'd appreciate it if you'd vote for Clement Haynesworth." Schweiker is supposed to have replied, "Look, I just bought $10,000 worth of your stock, but I don't tell you how to run your business."

In 1970, the son of a trading-stamp-company lobbyist offered his political support to Sargent Shriver in the latter's bid for the Maryland Democratic gubernatorial nomination. But the nomination was locked up by the incumbent governor, Marvin Mandel, and Shriver's chances went aglimmering. Mandel, however, apparently did not forget whose side the lobbyist's son had been on, because shortly after the primary the Maryland legislature passed a bill allowing trading-stamp holders to redeem their stamps in cash rather than in consumer goods (which is where a trading-stamp company makes its money).

Contributing serious money at the federal level brings with it certain privileges. One is being asked to the White House. At most White House functions, whether it be a dinner, an entertainment or a reception, the number of wealthy contributors usually falls somewhere below government officials (many of whom are themselves large contributors), show business and sports figures, and influential businessmen, but above artists, writers, philosophers, academics and clerics. As a Presidential campaign nears, however, the number of Fat Cats in attendance rises noticeably.

For instance, a cursory glance at four representative White House functions in 1971—honoring, respectively, Prince Juan Carlos of Spain, singer Beverly Sills, Prime Minister William McMahon of Australia and President Emilio Medici of Brazil—shows that of the more than 500 total guests in attendance, less than 5 percent were visible Fat Cats. But at a White House white-tie dinner in January, 1972, honoring Mr. and Mrs. DeWitt Wallace of the *Reader's Digest* with Medals of Freedom, Fat Cats numbered nearly half of all the guests. Among those present were Nixon's three major fund raisers—John Mitchell, Maurice Stans and California lawyer Herbert W. Kalmbach—and no less than eight individuals who contributed $10,000 or more in 1968.

The Nixon-Cox wedding in June, 1971, contrary to popular belief, was not simply a family affair but in part one more opportunity to reward contributors of serious money. Invited were such names as Robert Abplanalp, Elmer Bobst, Bob Hope, J. Willard Marriott, Henry Salvatori, Richard Mellon Scaife, DeWitt Wallace and Thomas J. Watson, Jr., and their respective wives. None gave less than $10,000 in 1968.

Also invited were such influential Republican Fat Cats as Walter Annenberg and his wife; Norman Chandler, of the *Los Angeles Times,* and his wife; Mr. and Mrs. Leonard K. Firestone; Mr. and Mrs. Peter Flanigan; Patrick J. Frawley of Eversharp-Schick, a backer of many right-wing causes, and his wife; Bernard ("Bunny") Lasker, a powerful New York Republican fund raiser; Mrs. Mary G. Roebling, of Roebling Steel and a power in New Jersey Republican politics; and wealthy John W. Rollins, of the Rollins broadcasting chain in Delaware.

Being a Fat Cat means you can join an "exclusive" club such as Kennedy's and Johnson's President's Club or Richard Nixon's RN Associates or Lincoln Club. All it costs is $1,000 or so a year, although George McGovern's Woonsocket Club cost a minimum of $25,000 to join. These types of club were outgrowths of earlier groups such as the Eisenhower Fund, the Democrat's 750 Club, and the GOP's 1,000 Club, which were organized almost exclusively to pay off campaign debts. The idea soon expanded, however, to include giving the contributors something more concrete for their money, such as invitations to special functions, secret briefings on government policy and a forum through which members could advise the President.

It would appear that membership in such clubs would guarantee a solid-gold pipeline to government power brokers. But, in fact, it has not worked out that way. A pervading sense of cheapness and shoddiness, and an occasional cloud of scandal, have hung over all these clubs, and to many members the pipeline had turned out to be gold-plated.

In the first place, membership in these clubs has been and continues to be secret, which does not promote public confidence. Second, despite the high-blown rhetoric that usually accompanies their formation, these clubs are little more than a gathering of rich men on the make who are willing to part with large sums of money in the hopes of some tangible personal return. During his tenure in office, President Nixon has invited many Fat Cats to the White House, most of whom presumably belong to RN Associates or the Lincoln Club. He has fed them dinner, listened to their complaints and words of advice, given a short speech praising their work, and then withdrawn to allow his hard-nosed fund raisers to tighten the screws. What makes this practice unusual is that previous to the Nixon administration the White House was considered off-limits for such behavior.

Third, anyone who can produce $1,000 or so (McGovern's club excepted) can join, which lowers the quality of what constitutes "exclusive." "Hell," said Paul Grindle, "you can't get into a golf club for that." Grindle also tells the story of a southern California rancher who told him he once contributed $1,500 to the Eisenhower Fund, and as a result was invited to the White House twice every year Eisenhower was President. He boasted to Grindle: "It was the best $1,500 I ever spent!"

These clubs are so nonexclusive, in fact, that Lyndon Johnson once found to his embarrassment that a well-known Bircher had joined his club.

Finally, hints of scandal have touched these organizations. In the spring of 1966, for example, top executives of the Anheuser-Busch brewery in St. Louis and their wives contributed $10,000 to the President's Club, and shortly thereafter a long-pending anti-trust suit against the company was dropped by the Justice Department without any explanation.

In the same year, as reported by Senator Charles Goodell in the *Congressional Record,* large contributions were made to the President's Club and the DNC by a senior vice-president of Consolidated American Services, Inc. Shortly thereafter a million-dollar Office of Economic Opportunity poverty contract was awarded the company, despite the fact that Consolidated did not meet the agency's own specifications, and that OEO passed over four other fully qualified bidders.

Also in 1966, George R. Brown, chairman of the board of the huge Texas-based construction firm Brown & Root, and members of his immediate family contributed $25,000 to the President's Club, $23,000 of which was given between the time a House Appropriations subcommittee cut funds from the 1967 budget for the multimillion-dollar deep-sea study, Project Mohole, and the time President Johnson sent a special message to Congress pleading that the money be retained. It so happened that Brown & Root was the prime contractor for the job.

In 1972, *Life* magazine charged that the Nixon administration had "tampered with justice" by blocking legal action against C. Arnholt Smith, a self-made millionaire from San Diego and a prominent Lincoln Club member. *Life* claimed, among other things, that the administration had squelched an investigation by a federally organized crime strike force that was looking into purported violations by Smith and others of federal tax law and the Corrupt Practices Act during the 1968 election. As of this writing, the charges that the Nixon administration had tampered with justice remain unanswered.

Serious money buys other things besides access and privileges. One thing it buys is consideration for appointment to high office. Not all Fat Cats who lust after appointive offices win them, but a surprising number do, and the tradition which dates back to Andrew Jackson's time shows no sign of dying out. Ordinarily between 10 and 15 percent of a President's top appointments go to contributors of serious money. The reason the percentage is not higher, according to one knowledgeable Massachusetts politician, "is that once a politician takes office he tends to prefer higher types."

Although it cannot be denied that our system has prospered by the infusion of outside talent into the government, clearly many appointments would not have been considered seriously had the individuals not given large contributions. Eisenhower, for instance, appointed Maxwell H. Gluck, the owner of a dress-shop chain and a $26,500 GOP contributor in 1956, as ambassador to Ceylon. At the time Gluck was so unversed in the requirements of the job that he was unable to name the country's prime minister during the Senate hearings on his nomination.

President Kennedy appointed Matthew McCloskey, a big Democratic fund raiser and contributor, as ambassador to Ireland. McCloskey, who spent most of his working life in the construction business, was not known for any particularly subtleties of thought, word or action that might be appropriate to the job. Lyndon Johnson appointed Edward Clark, a wealthy Texas lawyer and political crony with no known diplomatic skills, as ambassador to Australia.

Nixon appears to have outdone his predecessors. He appointed newspaperman Walter Annenberg, a man with few apparent diplomatic skills, as ambassador to Great Britain. He appointed John G. Hurd, a member of a Texas oil and cattle company and his 1968 campaign manager in Texas, as ambassador to South Africa. He appointed Vincent DeRoulet, whose only qualification for a diplomatic post seems to be the fact that his wife is a Whitney heiress, as our ambassador to Jamaica.

Henry E. Catto, Jr., son-in-law of Oveta Culp Hobby (a former Secretary of HEW, and president of the *Houston Post*), according to a former *Newsweek* editor, asked several White House reporters during the 1968 campaign how much he had to contribute to be considered for an ambassadorship to a Latin American country. He subsequently contributed $10,750 to the Nixon campaign and later was appointed ambassador to El Salvador.

Historically, many Canadians have viewed our ambassadors as of such mediocre quality that it prompted one Canadian diplomat to confide in me his government's policy of demanding privately that every third or fourth nomination for the job be a "serious" person—in other words, a diplomat, whether amateur or professional, rather than a run-of-the-mill party moneybags. The same is true to a slightly lesser degree of our ambassadorial appointments to Luxembourg, New Zealand, Mexico and several Latin American and Caribbean countries.

At the state level, it is much the same thing. When Estes Kefauver died in 1963, Governor Frank Clement of Tennessee appointed 71-year-old Herbert S. ("Hub") Walters to the vacant Senate seat. Walters, an east Tennessee building and highway contractor, banker and oil and gas distributor, had no particular qualifications for the job except that he had played a big role as Fat Cat contributor in every gubernatorial election in Tennessee, save one, since the 1930's.

Of the hundreds and often thousands of appointive offices under the control of governors and mayors, relatively few go to contributors of serious money. Those Fat Cats who contribute at this level are usually more interested in the access they might gain to business contracts than in a steady job. Furthermore, most jobs available at the state house and city hall do not have enough prestige to interest a big contributor.

The one exception is judgeships. The pay is usually fairly good and the job is secure, which appeals to many Fat Cat lawyers who want to escape from private practice. It has long been known that most judgeships in New York are up for sale, and the going price is around $50,000 for a state supreme court or appeals court appointment, payable into a candidate's campaign chest. In a state such as Maryland the price in the mid-1960's for a run-of-the-mill judicial appointment was about $5,000.

The Lindsay administration made an effort to halt this practice, although the word never reached some aspirants for judicial office. During the 1969 campaign, for instance, one individual worked his way through the Lindsay campaign hierarchy asking how much it would cost to have his lawyer-wife appointed judge. In each instance he was thrown out. As one astonished aide told me, "He was shopping as if he were buying groceries."

Big money will also buy some insurance against government retribution, both real and imagined, although such efforts are often fruitless. Near monopolies such as IBM contribute to lessen the possibility of antitrust suits. Executives of gasoline-station gimmick-game companies, pharmaceutical houses and conglomerates kick in heavily to dampen the government's enthusiasm to prosecute. Major polluters such as steel, paper, chemical and utility companies contribute all down the line to take off the political heat.

For example, the 1968 Nixon campaign was financed to the tune of roughly $500,000 by oil and gas company executives, of which $44,000 alone came from Robert O. Anderson of Atlantic Richfield. President Nixon subsequently appointed Anderson and several other gas company executives to the National Gas Survey

Executive Advisory Committee, which advises the President on natural gas policy. In 1971, of the 41-member committee, 32 men were executives of gas companies. Thus, for a relatively small sum, the gas industry insured itself control over a committee which has the power to influence decisions worth hundreds of millions of dollars in profits to it.

The Armco Steel case is another example. It was one of the heavier polluters of the Houston ship channel, dumping an average of half a ton of cyanide into it every day. Its executives were also reported to have contributed $14,000 to the 1968 Nixon campaign.

In December, 1970, after extensive negotiations with the firm had failed, the Environmental Protection Agency filed an action to force the company from discharging any more of the toxic substance into the channel. Nine months later a federal district judge issued an order requiring that the cyanide discharge cease forthwith. Shortly thereafter, the president of Armco wrote to President Nixon, asking him to look into the court's decision. The problem was turned over to Peter Flanigan, who called the EPA and the Justice Department. A few days later government lawyers added a stipulation to a modification of the court's decision, deferring the court's order for another six months.

Occasionally, serious money will buy, or attempt to buy, a quid pro quo, which is often a polite way of describing a bribe. Such was the case in 1958, when Frank Moss of Utah heard that a $5,000 contribution was available for his campaign for the U.S. Senate if he publicly declared himself in favor of the 27.5 percent oil depletion allowance. Moss turned the offer down and never received the money. However, he did manage to win the election.

In May, 1969, White House aide Harry Dent sent a memo to Secretary Robert H. Finch of the Health, Education and Welfare Department informing him that several Fat Cats had offered substantial contributions to the Georgia Republican party if federal funds were restored to a school district there. Federal funds for the Washington County school system had been cut off previously for failure to desegregate, but were restored three months after the memo was sent—not by HEW order, however, but as a result of a federal court order requiring the school system to desegregate.

Two years later, Deputy Attorney General Richard Kleindienst testified before a federal judge that he had received an offer of a $100,000 campaign contribution to Nixon's 1972 reelection campaign if he would help quash pending conspiracy, bribery and perjury indictments against a former administrative assistant of Senator Hiram Fong. Somewhat surprisingly, Kleindienst said that he did not at the time consider the offer a bribe.

Early in the 1972 campaign, a potentially big donor approached Edmund Muskie and offered to contribute $200,000, with more to come later. "You understand," said the Fat Cat, "there will be a quid pro quo. I want to be an American ambassador. Not a big country, you understand, not France or England, I couldn't afford those anyway. But can you give me a little one, Switzerland or Belgium?" Muskie turned the man down flat, claiming that while he had heard that such things happened, never had such a crass proposal been made to him before during his many years as a public servant.

There are various levels of quid pro quos. At the lowest it requires cash in the bag and immediate results, like the man shopping for a judgeship for his wife. At this level, quid pro quos are not very sophisticated, and it is these that are most easily exposed.

At the highest level, quid pro quos are very subtle and sophisticated. They are arranged by men of substantial means who have sufficient financial reserves that it may be several years before they call any one of them in. Often these men have many quid pro quos out at the same moment, the same way a Senate Whip may have hundreds out among his colleagues. Often the quid pro quos are implied rather than baldly stated, the same way a debt is implied when a friend does a slight favor for you. Most political quid pro quos operate at this upper level, and as a result, few examples ever surface. It is no wonder for, indeed, they are at the core of all political effort.

Serious money will also buy government business, although it is not so widespread as most people believe. No doubt contributions by builders Matthew McCloskey and William J. Levitt and architect Charles Luckman, and the like, have helped them to win government contracts, but by no means is the business guaranteed. Most of them realize that if it is government contracts they want, contributing to a candidate is not the best way to secure them. Power in the federal government is sufficiently diffused that for a

President or legislator to wangle a contract out of the multilayered bureaucracy for a Fat Cat contributor can be time-consuming, frustrating and fraught with political danger. As a result, most of these contracts are won by Fat Cats who seek out and win over the right government employee rather than by contributing to a candidate.

Nevertheless, the acquisitive instinct is far from dead at the federal level. To cite but one example, in 1971 the newly organized Postal Service decided to issue $250 million worth of bonds. It was decided that the bonds should be sold on Wall Street rather than through the Treasury, that federal guarantees would not be in effect (which would raise the price of the bonds), and that the underwriting would be accomplished by negotiation rather than through competitive bidding. Not unsurprisingly, the firm of Dillon, Read & Company, of which Peter Flanigan had once been a vice-president, was selected to sell the bonds. In testimony before the House Committee on Post Office and Civil Service in 1971, Congressman Morris Udall noted that a "strong appearance of impropriety has arisen" in the case and that "there is ample evidence to indicate that [Flanigan] has been involved in discussions and meetings involving this issuance of the bonds by the Postal Service."

At the state and local levels the link is more obvious. The power to dispense such favors in the states, counties and towns is still for the most part in the hands of the top elected officials themselves, and the business can be handled with dispatch and a minimum of publicity. Take the case of Alameda County, California. In 1955, funeral directors contributed to the campaign of a candidate for coroner. Once elected, the man appointed his funeral-director contributors as deputy coroners, which entitled them to be paid nine dollars for every body removed from the scene of death. This kind of thing still goes on today, not only in California, but in all states where these types of job are elective.

The H. J. Heinz Company, to cite another example, sells more than $100,000 a year of catsup to the city of New York. Coincidentally, one member of the Heinz family makes sure he turns up each year on the mayor's list of contributors.

In 1966, Vince Albano, the Manhattan Republican party chairman and a political patron of John Lindsay, told James Marcus, then the city's commissioner of Water Supply, Gas and Electricity, that the $800,000 contract to clean Jerome Park Reservoir should go to the S. T. Grand Company because its president, Henry Fried, was a big contributor to the GOP. (Fried, in fact, regularly gave heavily to both parties.)

A further example would be the manner in which Democrat Arthur Levitt, since 1955 New York State's controller, distributes the $4 billion in state funds under his command. Some of the money is deposited in selected banks, particularly those whose executives and major stockholders have contributed generously to his campaigns. Other funds are invested in companies whose executives and major stockholders make a similar effort. It is not surprising therefore to find that some of the money has been invested in United Artists, for one, whose president is Arthur Krim, a major Democratic fund raiser and contributor.

Sometimes profits can be made by contributing to those with the power to assess or tax. In 1971, for example, investigative reporters discovered that P. J. ("Parky") Cullerton, Illinois' Cook County tax assessor, had granted millions of dollars in tax breaks to real estate developers who were contributors to Cullerton's reelection campaign. Sometimes it is even more blatant than that. In the early 1960's, it was discovered that firms could buy changes in city zoning ordinances and contracts on the Frankford Elevated system in Philadelphia in return for "campaign contributions" to the Democratic County Executive Committee. One contractor claimed he "contributed" $3,000 to win an extra $650,000 of repair work on the line.

In 1970, a series of investigative reports in *Newsday* revealed that the Nassau County Democrats, under the leadership of Eugene Nickerson, were financed by businesses who received building contracts in return for their contributions. Between 1963 and 1969, it was found, $36 million in personal service contracts, which require no competitive bids because of the supposedly unique talents and services of the contractors, were awarded. They produced $833,000 in campaign funds for the Democrats. Some of the money was used by Nickerson in his race for the U.S. Senate in 1968 and governor in 1970.

Most of the firms were told they would have to contribute a minimum of $500 to have their names put on the list under consideration, and that they would have to contribute an additional 5 percent of the total amount of any contract they received. The Nassau County Democratic fund raisers, said one contractor, "didn't have to get nasty with us. We're pretty big boys and we go after big stakes. You can't make a $150 contribution or you'll wind up with some two-bit job. You've got to be important to them. . . ." Besides, he added, "contributions are chargeable to the job."

The general party rule was, "no contributions, no work," and the articles showed a clear pattern of contributions being followed by the awarding of contracts. One of those who contributed and subsequently received a contract was famed architect Edward Durell Stone.

Around the country, however, the link between contributions and government contracts at the state and local level is just as firm but usually less spectacular than in the examples just cited. It is part of the routine, generally accepted by those who are aware of what is going on, and is usually anything but glamorous or even profitable.

Snowplow contracts are a case in point. A young Boston politician close to former Democratic Governor Endicott ("Chub") Peabody, and one who is quite knowledgeable about plowing snow, described the reality to me: A snowplow contract, he said, "is what the cocktail party circuit in Washington likes to talk about as if it's an important thing in the political world. But it's not. When you get a snowplow contract, and they call you up at two o'clock in the morning, you've got to get your plow out. Okay? Well, that's something the boys in Washington drinking cocktails don't know about.

"What you find," he continued, "is that it's not all that sensational. When you get it all down, you'll find it's all what I call 'shaving'—what honorable men do to make a deal but on a sleazier basis. It's very popular for people who are supposed to be honest gentlemen to say, 'Oh, yes, the disgusting snowplow contracts,' but what you'll really find is that those with contracts are nothing more than basically honest men who want to use their trucks in the winter. And they're willing to give $1,000 to the governor or city council to be in a good position to get a couple of hundred thousand dollars worth of work."

The truth of the matter, he concluded, is that guardrail contracts are much more lucrative than snowplow contracts. "Jesus," he said, "you know, if you can get twenty-five miles of guardrails, *you're all set!* You gotta plow snow for *ten years* before you can do as well as you can with guardrails."

Wealthy candidates are a special breed of Fat Cats whose existence seems to generate considerable emotion among both observers of and participants in the American political arena.

It is rare that a man who has made his own money has not thought seriously at one time of running for office. He has done what he set out to do, and has captured a particular center of power, usually in business; he sees that he has a long life ahead of him, and he believes it only natural that he should push on to the next power center, which is in politics. It seldom occurs to him that he should solicit others for campaign funds; the money he has made, he believes, should be used to promote his political activities, just as it was used to promote his business ventures.

Party regulars invariably welcome wealthy candidates because assessments and money-raising efforts are lightened all the way down the line. Since so much money in a campaign goes for basic equipment and organizational efforts such as automobile and office rental, telephones, mimeographs, registration drives, mass mailings, public meetings and election-day expenses, everyone else on the wealthy candidate's ticket gets at least a partially free ride.

Wealthy candidates are not particularly welcome if they show too much independence. Party workers, like other individuals, want to feel that they are needed. A man like Franklin D. Roosevelt was welcomed by politicians because he was just rich enough to pay his own way and to attract new Fat Cat contributors to the party. A person such as Nelson Rockefeller, on the other hand, generally has not been welcomed by party regulars because he is so rich they believe he pays everybody's way and does not need anyone else to help him. As a result, the rank and file feel both useless and helpless.

Such candidates are also not welcomed by rivals with less financial resources available to them. They claim with considerable justification that rich candidates can up the ante to such a level that good but less wealthy candidates lose interest in running for office. In addition, they say that a wealthy neophyte forces the public to pay attention to him, whether or not he deserves it, which in turn may reduce the amount of time the electorate should be spending judging more qualified candidates, however rich or poor they may be.

It is a mistake to think that money is all that is needed to win an election. As Fergus Reid, a Wall Street investment banker and an influential GOP fund raiser, once put it: "The graveyard of American politics is strewn with the bones of rich guys who didn't make it." Cleveland parking-lot millionaire Howard Metzenbaum, for instance, spent over $800,000 of his own money in 1970 trying to win the U.S. Senate seat from Ohio. Edward Wittenberg, a wealthy Texan, spent $200,000 seeking the Democratic nomination for governor of Texas. Norton Simon, a wealthy Los Angeles food executive and art collector, spent $1.9 million trying to win the Republican nomination for U.S. senator from California. Other names come to mind: wealthy insuranceman E. Clayton Gengras of Connecticut, wealthy actress Shirley Temple Black of California, wealthy businessman Sam Grossman of Arizona, wealthy drugstore chain owner Jack Eckerd of Florida, fried-chicken entrepreneur John J. Hooker, Jr., of Tennessee, and Baggies tycoon Howard J. Samuels of New York, to name but a few of them. All of them have one thing in common: at this point in time each one is a political loser.

What none of these wealthy and unsuccessful candidates had or have is what professional politicians call a "track record." What constitutes a track record that will attract votes depends on the time, the situation and the individual. Being the first American to orbit the earth was still not a good enough track record to most Ohio voters to warrant electing John Glenn to the U.S. Senate. Yet being a song-and-dance man was good enough for most Californians to elect George Murphy to the Senate. The conditions are never constant.

There is no such thing as a foolproof formula for high office, particularly one based on money. Some individuals like Senator Charles Percy find that business success is sufficient to carry them far. Others find that success in sports (Congressmen Bob Mathias and Jack Kemp, for example) or farming (former Senator John J. Williams of Delaware) is sufficient. Most successful politicians establish their track records by diligently working their way up the political ladder. Yet a particular individual who is rich, has been successful in business, has a pleasing personality, is active in community affairs and is willing to work hard to be elected may, because of the alchemy involved at the moment, be a monumental political loser. Most wealthy political losers fail to realize that money in itself is not a track record, but simply a tool that can either build or destroy an existing track record.

It would be a mistake to think that all rich men in high office are flukes. On the contrary, it is difficult to find a single wealthy man who has reached high office who at the same time is not a good politician.

A candidate's track record will only take him so far, and no amount of money will materially advance his political career further. Nelson Rockefeller's millions could win him the governorship of New York, but not the Presidency. Richard Ottinger's money could help him win a seat in Congress but not in the Senate.

It is not as true, of course, in the least competitive states, of which there are perhaps a dozen, where a rich man with no other qualifications can both win and maintain his seat through the sheer power of his money. In competitive states like New York, California, Illinois and Massachusetts, a rich man must have something more to offer than just his money.

At the lower and middle levels of American politics, it is still possible for rich men with no track records to buy their jobs. Andrew Stein, son of wealthy Democratic fund-raiser Jerry Finkelstein, admitted spending nearly $300,000 to win his seat in the New York State Assembly. Wealthy jetsetter Carter Burden likewise spent tens of thousands of dollars to win his seat on the New York City Council. Yet, surprisingly, the buying of seats at these levels of American politics is relatively rare because people with that kind of money usually think in terms of running for high office.

With few exceptions, most successful wealthy politicians seldom if ever spend any of their own money to win office. The Lodge and Saltonstall families, for instance, have never spent more than token amounts of their own money in their campaigns. Nor have Senators Goldwater, Long, Percy, Proxmire, and Harrison Williams, Mayor John Lindsay or Governor Ronald Reagan, all of whom are quite rich. Millionaire State Senator Roy Goodman of New York could easily finance his campaigns out of his own pocket, but he prefers to seek support among a variety of financial sources. Usually, a successful politician who must rely solely on his own checkbook for funds does not last long on the American political scene.

For the past several decades, no two Fat Cat families have been more active, or spent more money in politics, than the Kennedys and the Rockefellers. How each of these families has handled its campaign funds tells us not only how other Fat Cats behave but helps to illustrate the role of money in American politics.

To understand Kennedy money one must first understand the late Joseph P. Kennedy, who made the family's fortune. His political contributions were always family-oriented and always given after a cold-blooded analysis of the political benefits that would or might accrue to him.

Several examples will suffice. During the 1932 campaign, whenever contributions were given anonymously, Joe Kennedy would forward the money to Roosevelt's managers by means of his own personal check. This enhanced his position, magnified his contributions and undercut his opposition. He also made points by lending the Democratic party between $50,000 and $65,000 and then later letting the note default.

In 1942, John F. ("Honey Fitz") Fitzgerald, then nearly 80, decided to oppose a New Deal congressman in the Democratic primary for the U.S. Senate. The winner would face incumbent Republican Henry Cabot Lodge, Jr. Clearly, Fitzgerald was an underdog and, in fact, lost the primary election by a substantial margin. Records show that Joe Kennedy contributed only $1,000 to his father-in-law's losing effort.

In 1952, Joe Kennedy found reasons to contribute money to both conservative Republican Robert Taft's prenomination campaign for President and liberal Democrat Adlai Stevenson's general election campaign.

In 1962 the elder Kennedy was supposed to have said to his sons John, then President, and Robert, then Attorney General, when the latter two raised objections to brother Edward running for John's old Senate seat: "Look, I spent a lot of money for that seat. It belongs in the family." Although the story is probably apocryphal, it still accurately reflects the father's attitude.

Kennedys have always spent what it takes to win: about $100,000 to keep John Kennedy in the House of Representatives, another $350,000 to $500,000 to put him in the Senate in 1952, almost $1.5 million to win reelection in 1958, approximately $3 million of their own money to win the Democratic nomination and the Presidency in 1960, another $1.2 million to put Edward in the Senate in 1962, and similar amounts to reelect him in 1964 and 1970, about $1 million to put Robert in the Senate in 1965 and another $3 million or so on his race for the Presidency in 1968. Altogether, the family has spent a minimum of $14 million on themselves in politics since 1946. This represents about 5 percent of the family's estimated fortune of between $200 and $300 million. Put another way, it means that the Kennedys probably never had to dip into capital to finance their many campaigns.

None of the children ever had to ask their father for the money. It was simply provided, like allowances, tuition and travel money. Most of the brothers never knew exactly how much their father gave and in all probability did not care because they knew it would be enough.

Like many Fat Cats, the Kennedys are extremely tight-lipped about their political finances. Nothing is given out that does not have to be given out, and even then many figures are often understated and hidden in the balance sheet.

A typical example is Edward Kennedy's race for the Senate in 1962. Veteran political analysts estimated then that a campaign for major office like U.S. senator in a state the size and complexity of Massachusetts would cost a minimum of $700,000 and could easily exceed $1.25 million. Those who witnessed the 1962 race agreed that money was spent freely in Edward McCormack's primary challenge to Kennedy and in George Lodge's Republican campaign, but that Kennedy's campaign was one of the most carefully planned, expertly staffed and lavishly financed in recent memory. Only Independent candidate H. Stuart Hughes seems to have run a shoe-string operation.

Kennedy reported spending only $421,000, and that included the fight for convention endorsement, the primary nomination and the general election. Hughes, on the other hand, who most people believe reported his expenditures accurately, waged a low-budget campaign which observers considered a curiosity. Yet he still reported spending nearly $166,000, or 40 percent of Kennedy's reported total.

The Kennedy campaign also reported spending only $14,139.93 on television and radio, a very low figure for a big-state Senate race. By contrast, Hughes, whom most Bay Staters never remember having seen on the tube during the campaign, reported spending $21,500.

Stationery costs also appear to have been grossly understated. It is conservatively estimated that the Kennedy campaign sent out an absolute minimum of 1.5 million letters during the entire campaign. A 1.5 million mailing involves 1.5 million envelopes and 1.5 million letterheads. Kennedy's letterhead was in three colors and contained a photograph of the candidate. Three large stationery houses reported that these items, if purchased in bulk, would cost around $18,000. Yet the Kennedy campaign reported spending only $2,119.37 on stationery.

Most of this information was first revealed by Murray B. Levin, associate professor of government at Boston University in his book *Kennedy Campaigning*. When the Kennedys heard that this and other embarrassing information was about to be published, they dispatched no less than a learned Harvard professor to Beacon Press to try to persuade it to withdraw the book. To its credit, Beacon refused, and no one has yet challenged Levin's facts in public. While the Kennedys lost this battle of censorship, it illustrates the lengths they will go to to keep their political finances from becoming public knowledge.

Unlike the Rockefellers, the Kennedys solicit others for funds. Such was the case in the 1960 campaign, when it was understood that Joe Kennedy would tap his Wall Street friends for contributions. But the fund raising is carried on right down to the level of extracting fifty cents out of ghetto blacks. This is not done, however, as some believe, to lighten the Kennedy load, but to buy a future commitment. A person who gives fifty cents and cannot afford to do so is the same person who will lick stamps, register voters, round up volunteers and do odd jobs for a Kennedy victory. The Kennedys have never underestimated the commitment that comes with giving, and they have exploited it well. Robert

Kennedy, for instance, was never just content with getting a huge contribution from some rich man; he wanted to know what the Fat Cat was planning to do tomorrow for the campaign down at headquarters.

Kennedy candidates never solicit money personally from wealthy contributors but are reserved to clinch a deal made by their staff. Stephen Smith, the family's current financial overseer, for instance, would make an overture; a private meeting, or a party, or some other type of gathering would be arranged, and then the Kennedy candidate would be presented—in the words of one close Kennedy friend, "like a birthday cake"—to the contributor. A large part of any Kennedy campaign is spent in this manner. The Kennedys are also very careful about whom they ask for contributions, because they tend to take a refusal to contribute as a personal affront.

Contrary to widespread belief, the Kennedys seldom contribute heavily to friendly or so-called "pro-Kennedy" candidates. When they contribute at all, it is usually a token amount. John Glenn's several tries for public office were not underwritten by the Kennedys. Nor have Pierre Salinger, Theodore Sorenson, Kenneth O'Donnell, Arthur Goldberg, Sargent Shriver, John Tunney, Jess Unruh, Adam Walinsky and George McGovern, to name but a few of the Kennedyites who have run for office, received anything but nominal contributions from the Kennedy family. In fact, the Kennedys will seldom if ever help even the national or state Democratic parties. The Massachusetts and New York Democratic parties, for two, have yet to be enriched by a Kennedy candidacy.

Eugene McCarthy, an early Kennedy type, received only $1,500 from John F. Kennedy in his successful 1958 run for the U.S. Senate from Minnesota. Apparently he expected much more, and some people date the McCarthy-Kennedy antipathy to this time. Most Kennedy contributions of this size are given to incur an obligation that can be cashed in at some future date. McCarthy, clearly, did not see it that way.

There is a certain arrogance about Kennedy money. Kennedy money means that you rent *two* Teleprompters in case one breaks down. It means that in Indiana in 1968 you put out two different versions of the same literature in the same state: one in the north advocating civil rights, and the other in the south advocating law and order. It means that when your opponent rents the best head-quarters in town, the Kennedys will offer double the price to the landlord (as also happened in Indiana). It means that in the 1968 California primary, you buy up all a radio station's air time the last three weeks of the campaign.

Like most large contributors, the Kennedys do not believe that their money is safe. There is not only a feeling throughout the entire campaign that the money might run out but a tendency to poor mouth in public. One story is particularly illustrative. In the 1960 Presidential election, one group of Kennedy supporters wanted to free enough money to buy millions of "Coffee with Kennedy" cups. Stephen Smith, on the other hand, was more interested in pushing 100,000 45-rpm records of a tune entitled "High Hopes," the Kennedy theme song for that year. Eventually Smith released the money for the cups, but by then the campaign was nearly over and most were not used. Nevertheless, they were certainly not thrown away. They were stored in cartons and later turned up in Robert Kennedy's 1968 primary campaigns. Much the same fate awaited "High Hopes," which was a flop in 1960. Most of the records are now piled in a warehouse awaiting the day they once again can be used to promote a Kennedy.

Rockefeller money is quite different from Kennedy money. It is secure money, patrimonious and "in good taste." It is quietly powerful, rather than "pushy," money and is never seen. To talk about it in a Rockefeller race would be considered gauche, because it is assumed by everyone that it will never run out. There is a feeling in any Rockefeller campaign that the money is there not only in greath depth, through at least three generations of active Rockefellers, but also in breadth, from the many financial resources of their empire.

The Rockefellers try but are never successful when they solicit at a general level. Too many people think of the name as "the bank," and for them to give even five dollars to participate in a Rockefeller event makes them feel silly. Nelson Rockefeller has always had difficulty lining up serious money for this reason. His failure to win electoral support during the 1960, 1964 and 1968 Presidential primaries was due in part to his financial independence.

He has, as have other members of the family, received contributions from a few equals. Douglas Dillon, John Hay Whitney and William Paley, for instance, all contribute during a campaign. It is a very sophisticated level of giving. Each knows what is expected of him, no favors are asked or given, and a certain reciprocity is understood. It is a personal touch among equals who take care of their own. In a sense, it is a true Establishment because everything has been understood since their nannies first exchanged gossip in Central Park.

Whenever a Rockefeller runs for office, whether it be Nelson in New York or nationally, Winthrop in Arkansas, or John D. IV in West Virginia, the family chips in. Exactly how this is arranged is not clear, but it is known that the senior brothers—John D. III, Nelson, Laurence, David and Winthrop (until his death in 1973) —and on occasion their sister, Mrs. Jean Mauze, apportion the costs among themselves. No doubt J. Richardson Dilworth, the financial mastermind of the entire Rockefeller empire, would be consulted. He would tell how much cash is available, how much money might have to be diverted from the investment income account, and so on. Ordinarily, it would not be a difficult task arranging the financing.

Unlike the Kennedys, the Rockefellers do contribute to others, and sometimes quite generously. They contributed $39,000 to Louis J. Lefkowitz's campaign for mayor of New York in 1961, and another $100,000 to John Lindsay's campaign in 1965. They underwrote most of George Romney's primary expenses in 1968, and they have singlehandedly propped up the Republican State Committee in New York. They also put their considerable financial resources behind an unsuccessful effort to defeat Congressman Ogden Reid in 1972, who defected to the Democrats.

Similar to the Kennedys, however, is the family's tight-lipped attitude toward revealing campaign expenditures. Generally, they will report only what has to be reported, lest the omission be discovered by the press. An example illustrating the family's attitude occurred in 1970 following Nelson's fourth successful race for the New York governorship. Herbert Alexander, head of the Citizens' Research Foundation and an unbiased authority on campaign financing, wrote to George L. Hinman, Rockefeller's closest political confidant (and perhaps the only man in American history who, with such massive financial resources, has engineered three losing efforts for the Presidency), asking if it would be possible to stop by at a convenient time to discuss the finances of the campaign. Hinman returned the letter to Alexander with the words "Don't bother" scrawled at the bottom.

How much money have the Rockefellers spent on their own campaigns since Nelson first became politically active in 1958? Estimates run between $36 and $64 million, with most knowledgeable observers settling on $58 million as the most reasonable figure. This would include Nelson's five campaigns for governor (including the 1974 race, which is underway), the last four of which have cost the family between $4 and $8 million each, and his three tries for the Presidency, the first two of which cost between $3 and $5 million and the last of which cost $8 million. It would also include Winthrop's various campaigns for governor of Arkansas and John D. IV's three campaigns in West Virginia.

To the $58 million must be added perhaps another $10 million contributed to other candidates and political committees over the years. Measured against any other family's contributions, $68 million is a large figure, representing an average yearly outlay of over $4.5 million. Yet, measured against the Rockefeller family's estimated $2 to $3 billion collective fortune, it represents roughly 3 percent of assets. In other words, $68 million represents less than what the family earns as income on its investments *in one year*.

Despite the mannered way in which the money is handled, most Rockefeller campaigns, particularly Nelson's, still come across in the end as arrogant. It means that if you are a Rockefeller running for governor for the fourth time, you can pay 370 campaign workers full-time, versus 35 for your opponent, and that does not include hundreds of paid volunteers. It means you can draw the best talent from the family foundation, the family fund, "family" banks like the Chase Manhattan, "family" law firms such as Milbank, Tweed, Hadley & McCloy and Debevoise, Plimpton, Lyons & Gates (some of whose partners sit as directors of Rockefeller interests), "family" advertising agencies like Jack Tinker Associates, and "family" employees holding sinecure jobs. It means that you can also hire potential troublemakers and pay them large salaries to do nothing in a campaign.

It means you have your own private airline: a helicopter, a

Gulfstream jet and a four-engined Fairchild. It means that as a matter of course you print over 30 million pieces of campaign literature, which is nearly two pieces for every person living in New York. It means that when you campaign in a bowling alley you have a man spend part of the week before making absolutely sure that the proper size bowling shoes are available. Finally, it means that when you are asked how much you are prepared to spend to win, you can answer, "Enough."

After nearly two decades this arrogance has begun to irritate people. For instance, in 1968 many powerful Wall Street money-men delighted in thumbing their noses at the Rockefellers by raising money for Richard Nixon, whom Nelson detested. In fact, Nelson's arrogance in particular even provoked a minor revolt among the brothers themselves in 1970. Apparently they had become tired of the obligatory four-year payout that was expected of them. They contributed the amounts they promised, but much later in the campaign than usual. To sophisticates in the Rockefeller campaign, this was a serious slight.

VII

Key Men with Access

The man who raises the money is the prince of American political campaigns. While he may initially bring notice to himself as a large contributor, he stands apart from the run-of-the-mill Fat Cat because of his ability to tap sizable sums from others. More often than not his legal, business and financial acumen, plus his social contacts, make him invaluable as a general political strategist as well. During a Presidential election year, there would be approximately 3,000 major fund raisers actively engaged in raising money for candidates at the federal level, and an additional 15,000 to 20,000 working in state, county and municipal elections around the country.

Of the estimated 500,000 elective political offices in the United States, 96 percent would require a candidate to raise and spend less than $10,000. In fact, $1,000 would be closer to the median expense, the heaviest cost being the filing fee. For certain elective party jobs such as delegate or committeeman, seldom are personal campaign expenses ever incurred. Whenever it is necessary to spend money on campaigns for, say, county clerk, township supervisor, borough humane officer (once known as dogcatcher) or recorder of deeds, the candidate acts as his own fund raiser, and receives his contributions either from a few friends and business acquaintances or from his own pocket. Success at this level of American politics depends less on having funds to promote one's candidacy than on one's party (or lack of party) label. Clearly, there is no need for fund raisers here.

But the other 4 percent of elective offices in the United States require the near-full-time services of skilled political fund raisers. These 20,000 or so offices are where power lies at the federal, state and local levels. As a result, most of them are subject to stiff competition, which usually runs up the costs beyond the point where they can be managed without the help of fund raisers.

The cost of running for any one of these particular offices is never constant. In North Dakota, for instance, the average cost of running for the U.S. Senate is about $50,000, but in the special election of 1960 the successful Democratic candidate spent $100,000 and the Republican candidate about $250,000. In Vermont, the cost might run to $100,000 on average, but in 1968 Senator George Aiken spent $17.09 to be reelected, down $2.12 from what he spent in 1962. In Wisconsin, Democrat John A. Race spent $6,000 in 1964 to win a seat in Congress; two years later he spent about $85,000 and lost.

To run for the California Senate in a competitive district cost about $10,000 in 1962, and double that in 1970. A Democrat in Portland, Oregon, however, can still win a state senate seat for as little as $5,000. To run for county executive in populous Montgomery County, Maryland, or Suffolk County, Long Island, costs a minimum of $100,000. To win reelection as mayor in a city the size of Gary, Indiana (1970 population: 175,000), would cost around $175,000, as it did Richard Hatcher in 1971. To become mayor of a city the size of Boston (1970 population: 641,000), assuming there is no knock-down primary, would cost a minimum of $500,000. It takes several million dollars to run a respectable campaign for mayor of New York City.

To run for governor in a predominantly rural state like Idaho costs a minimum of $35,000, in large industrialized states a minimum of $1 million. Even so, Milton Shapp spent $3.8 million of his own money running unsuccessfully for governor of Pennsylvania in 1966, Ronald Reagan spent between $5 and $6 million to be elected governor of California the same year, and Nelson Rockefeller spent about $8 million to be reelected governor of New York in 1970. On the other end of the scale, J. J. Exon won the governorship of Nebraska in 1970 with an outlay of only $20,000.

Running for Congress as an incumbent in a safe rural district might cost a token $5,000; to run as a challenger in a competitive urban district might cost as much as $200,000 (which is what Richard Ottinger spent in 1964 to win his New York seat in Congress). Most congressional races, however, cost in the $25,000 to $50,000 range, which is expensive considering that the sum has to be raised every two years. To run for the U.S. Senate from a sparsely populated state like New Mexico might cost $300,000, which is roughly what Peter Domenici spent in 1972 to win. In a big state like California or New York, the general election costs alone would run over $1 million. Richard Ottinger set some sort of record in 1970 by spending $1.8 million of his own family's money just to win the New York Democratic party's *nomination* for U.S. senator, which was six times more than his three primary opponents spent together. Robert F. Kennedy spent about the same amount to beat incumbent Kenneth Keating in the 1964 general election, but not all of it was his own money. In most states, however, anyone thinking of running for the Senate should make plans to raise and spend at least $300,000.

Obviously, campaign funds in these high ranges are beyond the capacity of most candidates to raise and spend personally. In most instances these matters are handled by a fund raiser—the key man in a campaign who has access to the necessary money sources.

Key men with access in American politics are part of a loose-knit national association of equals. This association has many of the earmarks of tribal behavior. Most key men in a particular city or area, for instance, know, or know of, each other; if they do not, it is easy enough to set up an introduction through mutual friends, as is done every day in the business world. Socially, they treat each other more or less as equals, they help each other out on occasion, and they are strengthened and fortified against adversity by the knowledge that they have the same general objectives.

These individuals, by being economic and social powers in their respective communities, can produce campaign cash in large amounts, some of which is their own, some of which is other people's money. They can, by virtue of their position, also make independent political decisions which may vitally affect a candidate's campaign. They can also open doors, influence the behavior of others and even produce votes, all of which are essential in winning an election.

It is not good enough simply to be a bright and eager banker, lawyer or businessman. A key man with access must have clout. He must have many IOU's out in the community, the city, the state or across the nation that he is willing to call in for his candidate; he must be the kind of power that when he telephones others, they drop whatever they are doing to answer the call; he must have some organizational ability, a fairly thick skin and, as a protégé of the late Senator Robert Kerr once put it, "the balls to ask for the money." If he is rebuffed the first time around, he must have the nerve to go back a second, third and even fourth time for the money.

He must know who has the money, who is currently "heavy" and who is "light," how and when to tap a potential contributor, and how much to ask for. He must know when he can return a check as not enough, and how many times he can go back to a money source for additional funds before the latter is "tapped out." He must also know enough not to solicit a "hard case" alone since it is too easy to say no. He must be very good at timing because he knows that the competition for a Fat Cat's cash is fierce—from local, state and national political groups, his church and college, the Red Cross, and so on. He must realize that he can call on the richest man in America at the wrong moment and come away with only $100.

He must be able to use the candidate beneficially to extract maximum contributions from Fat Cats. Typical of the manner in which this is done is reflected in a memorandum from Dick Kline, the key finance man on Muskie's 1972 campaign staff, to George Mitchell, one of the three campaign managers. The memo was written just after Muskie had "abandoned" the New Hampshire primary and was turning his attention to the Florida primary. It carried the notation "Personal and Confidential," and read:

We would like to have the Senator make the following Florida finance calls:

JAKE ARVEY [longtime Cook County, Illinois, Democratic power]. Arvey has offered to help, but has not actively raised any money yet. The Senator should ask him if he is going to help raise money now, and particularly if he will motivate Henry Crown [of General Dynamics] to help us. According to Paul Ziffren [a Los Angeles lawyer and big Democratic fund raiser], Arvey is extremely close to Crown.

ALBERTO VADIA [of Coral Gables, Florida]. Vadia was the host to the meeting the Senator attended in Coral Gables early this month [February], but so far only $7,400 of Vadia's pledge of $50,000 has been sent in to us. The Senator should express disappointment at Vadia's sending in only so little money and ask him if he can come up with at least $25,000 more, in terms of a self-liquidating loan if not a personal contribution.

RICHARD F. HOYT [of Surfside, Florida, a Miami suburb]. He was one of the key people who was invited to Arnold Picker's [Muskie's chief fund raiser's] party two weeks ago which was cancelled. The Senator should apologize for his inability to go to the party and ask for Hoyt's direct financial help.

RICHARD REYNOLDS [of the Reynolds Metal Company]. He was also invited to the Picker party. The Senator should handle him the same way that he handles Hoyt.

A key man must have a story to tell. Flagwaving and pleas of poverty will not ordinarily shake loose large campaign contributions. He must "find the common ground," as they say in fund-raising circles: that is to say, if he is raising money for a party or candidate out of power, he must argue the sad state of the economy to a wealthy broker whose portfolio has performed poorly; if he is raising money for a party or candidate in power, he must cite the administration's most recent political achievements. If Democratic, he might remind Jewish contributors, for instance, that it was Harry S. Truman who first recognized Israel; and if Republican, he might convince prosperous businessmen that the country's economic health will be maintained.

Key men know enough not to make promises they cannot keep in return for a contribution; they realize that they must be candid about a candidate's financial needs; they must anticipate put-offs ("I can't afford to contribute . . ."; "I already gave . . ."; "I'm registered with the other party . . . ," etc.) and try to answer them; they must have a particular sum in mind for a Fat Cat to contribute ("We believe you should contribute $25,000 . . ."), and they must keep an eye peeled for corporate or union checks which are illegal. Most important, they must develop a facility for names and faces, since there is no worse blunder in American fund-

raising circles than not recognizing a Fat Cat three months after he
gave his $25,000.

A good key man will also leverage his own commitment by
parceling out his chores to donors by asking each of them to ask
five or six of their friends to give. Thus, the original fund raiser
ends up giving less but raising more.

A key man with access is often asked to do double duty, by also
serving as a candidate's finance committee chairman. If he accepts,
he must bring to bear all the legal, business and political skills he
possesses.

The first job of a finance committee chairman is to raise what is
known as "seed money" or "venture capital," money that is
needed to set up the campaign organization itself and its fund-
raising arm. This money comes from only twenty or thirty wealthy
individuals, depending on the size and needs of a particular
campaign. Each pledges a large sum, say $20,000, which is
secured by a personal note from a bank. Ordinarily the campaign
committee would not guarantee it. The individual then goes out
and raises as much of the $20,000 as he can among his friends to
pay back the note. What he is unable to raise is, in effect, his own
contribution.

A great deal of seed money comes from the Jewish community,
primarily because Jewish financiers tend to be more risk-oriented
and because they have had many years' experience raising money
for long-shot causes (such as Israel). Virtually all the early
moneymen in the 1972 Presidential election, for instance, were
men who had great clout among fellow Jews: Milton P. Semer,
Arnold Krim and Arnold Picker in Muskie's camp; Henry L.
Kimelman in McGovern's campaign; Joe Rosenfield in Senator
Harold Hughes's brief campaign; Milton Gilbert in Senator Birch
Bayh's camp; and Marvin D. Rosenberg, who raised some of
Humphrey's early money.

A good finance committee chairman must maintain a clear distinction between his duties and responsibilities and those of the
campaign manager, who spends the money, or those of the campaign treasurer, who pays the bills and tries to control spending. If
there is confusion or competition among the three, and there often
is, chaos can result.

A typical example is the manner in which oilman Henry Salvatori almost lost the California primary in 1964 for Senator Barry Goldwater. Salvatori mistakenly believed that being a key man with access made him a campaign expert. He set up a procedure, for instance, which his staff derisively called the "requisition inquisition," wherein *all* matters concerning the campaign had to have his signature. He ran his staff as he would a business, cutting it to the bone and thus angering loyal party workers; when he wanted to expand it later, he found that there was no readily accessible labor pool available to him. If he thought a bill too high, he would hold up all deliveries and schedules until it was settled. He even thought of himself as a television expert and interfered with producers and technicians in the course of their work. As a result, the vital mechanics of the campaign—releases, mailings, meetings, programming, and so on—broke down time and time again, and it is a reflection of the resilience of the Goldwater followers that they prevailed at all.

A good finance committee chairman must not give the impression that his candidate is loaded with money (if he is); he must argue for spending the money late in the campaign even if he raised it early; and he must warn the others in the campaign not to spend any money until it is actually in hand.

He must also organize his money raising at several levels. Usually he works personally with a small team of three or four other key men—again, depending on the needs of the campaign—who divide up the task of tapping bankers, brokers, doctors, lawyers, manufacturers, contractors, service companies, unions and other sectors of wealth in the area. Federal employees are also tapped where they are found in plentiful supply, although it has been against the law since 1939 to do so. Those most often solicited are individuals who owe their jobs to a particular political patron. (In 1972 a three-man federal court voted 2–1 to end the Hatch Acts' ban on political activities, although the ruling was later reversed by the Supreme Court.)

Of increasing importance in all major political campaigns are mass mailing appeals for contributions. An average well-run campaign can raise as much as 40 percent of budgeted money through the mails. Thus it is important that a good mass mailing operation be established (or purchased), preferably with an expert in charge.

Finally, a good finance committee chairman must pick a team to run his fund-raising events, a major source of all campaign contributions. These men must be well versed in three talents: the basic needs, the tricks of the trade, and the trends of the day.

Basics involve knowing when to throw a fund-raising event (mostly in late winter or early spring so that the money is acquired early), how to avoid conflicting with a competing event (nothing can destroy a fund raiser faster than scheduling it, say, the same day the Philadelphia Orchestra comes to town), how much to charge for an event (too little and not much money is raised, too much and not many people buy tickets), and what the profit margin might be (a $100-a-plate fund raiser for 300, for instance, costs around 12 to 15 percent of the gross; a $50-a-plate function costs about 25 to 30 percent of the gross).

Basics also involves acquiring good solicitation lists, known generally as "milk" or "tickle" lists. It requires lining up good speakers, clamping down on the giving away of free tickets, and keeping a sharp eye out for freeloaders.

Each fund raiser must make an effort to give his or her gala a different theme, a new twist, so that it will attract maximum attendance. Some hold bean feeds, corn roasts, picnics or bake-ins. Others buy discount tickets to sporting events and then ask the Fat Cats to buy them at a premium. Still others invite contributors to meet the famous (Lady Bird Johnson, Mamie Eisenhower, and so on) or to visit interesting houses (Mrs. Robert F. Kennedy's "Hickory Hill" in McLean, Virginia, is a favorite for liberal Democrats in the greater Washington, D.C., area). In 1958, some Republican women wanted to hold a striptease to raise money; in the mid-1960's, a GOP enthusiast from Baltimore proposed $25- to $100-a-plate "fun nights" featuring "plenty of pretty girls and booze" to loosen money from contributors, plus gambling with "play money." Such is the pressure to raise campaign funds and to be different.

More than anything, basics require that the fund raiser make it clear how the proceeds will be divided. An example of the chaos that can ensue occurred in 1964. John Volpe, who was running for governor of Massachusetts that year, held a meeting of all Republicans on the state ticket and convinced them that it would be more efficient if all fund raising were centralized in one big event. Every candidate was to submit a budget, and the proceeds of the event, an estimated $350,000, were to be apportioned on a pro rata basis. Most of the candidates were confident of getting their money and, accordingly, went out and made financial commitments for time, services and material. But the entire sum went to Volpe's campaign because his managers claimed they needed it all. (It may have been done without Volpe's knowledge.) The rest of the ticket was left holding the bag. Some of the candidates went deeply into debt as a result.

Knowing the tricks of the trade means that you hold a fund raiser in an enclosed area so that the audience cannot escape giving. One young Iowa Democrat recalls going to a fund raiser that was held on the patio of a farmer's house; when the pitch for money was made, he said, about half the crowd scattered through the corn field.

It means that, when considering seating arrangements, certain people who do not get along are seated at separate tables. It means that all contributors are coded with a pin when they hand in their check (a cowboy hat, say, for $500-and-up contributors, a sheriff's badge for the $100-to-$500 givers, and a lariat motif for the under-$100's) so that the candidate knows how much of a fuss he has to make over a particular individual. It means, finally, keeping a photographer handy, avoiding chicken, rice and peas, keeping mum when a Fat Cat's front man shows up with the tickets, and having a neutral collect the money so that the party workers do not appear greedy.

A good fund raiser at this level also tries to keep up with the times. He would know, for instance, that there is a trend away from head tables and windy speeches, and a move toward spreading the powerful and influential among the tables and scheduling nothing but the briefest of political speeches. The trend is also toward "entertainments," most consisting of either political humorists or a Hollywood-type review of stars.

The pressure for money is so great that some states are experimenting with credit card arrangements to encourage the affluent to part with their cash, although their use is attacked as inflationary. Other state parties have worked out a system of postdated checks from contributors which has two advantages: it spreads out the bite, and it is difficult for the giver, once involved, to back out. Still other state parties are considering a pledge system which is tied into one's bank account, so much being deducted automatically every month and transferred to the party's account.

There are certain chores in a political campaign that finance committee chairmen must be prepared to do, regardless of their own personal sense of propriety. One is setting up a network of bagmen to make cash deliveries. In spite of all the past campaign financing laws, including the Federal Election Campaign Act of 1971, which have sought to eliminate campaign financing abuses, a significant part of most campaigns for the top federal and state offices has been and continues to be paid for with unreported cash. The Watergate caper of 1972, described in Chapter V, is a recent example. The pressure to "wash," "bleach" or "launder" money by hiding the source through the use of cash usually comes from political professionals, and is strong and persistent enough to force most finance committee chairmen, at a minimum, to bend their scruples.

There are varying levels of bagmen. At the most basic, a bag-man is a full-time political worker in the employ of a local boss. He ordinarily makes his money by skimming 10 percent off the top of any delivery. At a more sophisticated level, bagmen are usually called agents or couriers, and might be recognizable public figures. In 1957, a cab driver found a paper bag containing $11,200 in his back seat shortly after having Carmine DeSapio, then Tammany boss, as his passenger. DeSapio's claim that he did not know to whom the money belonged brought loud laughs from cynical New Yorkers. In 1961, W. Alton Jones, chief executive officer of Cities Service Oil, and a major Republican fund raiser, was killed in a plane crash; in his briefcase was found $61,000 in cash and traveler's checks. In both instances no explanation was ever offered why such large cash amounts were in transit, but many political observers believe that, at best, both men were acting as couriers for their respective political parties.

Robert G. ("Bobby") Baker, while he was secretary to the Senate Democratic Majority, was bagman for a number of politicians on Capitol Hill, in particular Senator Robert Kerr and Senate Majority Leader Lyndon Johnson. In 1962, he collected nearly $100,000 in $100 bills from the officers, directors and lawyers of three powerful California savings and loan associations, one of which was Howard F. Ahmanson's Home Savings & Loan. The money was to be spent by Kerr on the campaigns of eight incumbents. However, some of the money allegedly ended up going to Baker himself. Shortly after Senator Kerr died in January, 1963, a safe deposit box in his name was discovered containing $41,300 in cash.

This was not the only instance in which Baker handled large sums of cash. While he was in prison serving out his sentence for income tax evasion, conspiracy to defraud the government, and theft—charges that grew out of the above incident—he admitted that he had handled cash contributions because he was told to do so and because that was the way the system worked. "I was the guy," he said, "whom they could trust not to say anything about the money. I've handled millions in cash." He even claimed he saw one senator in the Senate chamber pass $10,000 in cash to a colleague known for his righteousness; the recipient, claimed Baker, overcame his scruples in time to pocket the money.

Prior to the passage of the 1971 law, hiding cash was easily accomplished. If a finance committee chairman did not choose to go the unreported cash route, he could assign cash to state employees or campaign staffers, like LBJ's men tried to do in the 1968 Wisconsin primary.

In 1964, as an example of how contributions may be falsely attributed, a patrolman from the Bourne, Massachusetts, police department claimed he gave $100 to Governor Endicott Peabody's reelection campaign, and he produced the check to prove it. Subsequently the patrolman was appointed an examiner of elevator operators. The campaign's financial report, however, showed the former patrolman as having given $1,000, and in cash.

In the 1970 Pennsylvania gubernatorial race, the Republican State Committee telephoned the campaign headquarters of Ralph Scalera, the party's nominee for lieutenant governor, and asked for the names of his staff. The committee, it appears, was the recipient of a large cash contribution that it wanted to hide by assigning it to party workers as ordinary contributions. Thus, many Scalera staffers were listed as having given as much as $1,000, when in fact they gave little or nothing.

Fictitious names were often used in lieu of assigning cash to anyone in particular. So, too, were nonreporting committees in the District of Columbia, Alaska, Delaware, Georgia, Illinois, Louisiana, Nevada and Rhode Island. Cash could be pumped into them and none of it had to be reported publicly.

Nonreporting committees were also the favored device for hiding the names of donors prior to the passage of the 1971 act. Conservative James L. Buckley, for instance, confessed after his election to the Senate in 1970 that over $400,000 in campaign cash flowed through more than 50 D.C. committees. They carried such names as "Scientists for a Sensible Solution to Pollution" and "Committee to Keep a Cop on the Beat." Buckley's campaign manager admitted that the only reason the committees were set up was to hide the names of donors, many of whom were conservative Republican Fat Cats.

More commonly, finance committee chairmen were interested in minimizing the impact of a donor's contribution, rather than hiding it, since they realized that some disclosure takes the pressure off press curiosity. The preferred method was to obscure the size of the total donation by giving part of the whole at different times, from different locations and under variations of one's own name.

For instance, nine-month receipts for the GOP's Booster Club in 1966 revealed, among other things, that Thomas B. McCabe, Sr., of Scott Paper gave three contributions totaling $4,000 from Philadelphia and another $1,000 from his summer home in Northeast Harbor, Maine. Mrs. McCabe gave an additional $1,000 from the Northeast Harbor address. In the same report, Washington, D.C.–based businessman and government appointee Arthur Gardner contributed $1,000, the Honorable and Mrs. Arthur Gardner contributed $2,000, and Mrs. Arthur Gardner contributed $1,000 on her own and another $1,000 as Suzanne A. Gardner. In addition, there was a $1,000 contribution from an A. Gardner, also from Washington.

On the surface, the passage of the Federal Election Campaign Act brought many of these practices to an end. But the pressure to hide cash and donors' names is still so strong in American political life that many finance committee chairmen are turning their minds toward developing new ways to conceal the facts (see Chapter X). In fact, when it became known among my political acquaintances that I was studying American campaign financing practices, I was queried on numerous occasions by interested political figures on how one could legally evade the new law's disclosure requirements.

Who are these key men with access? Generally, they fall into two groups: those whose influence tends to be national or at least regional, and those whose influence tends to be limited to a particular metropolitan area or one or two states.

In New York, nationally and regionally oriented key men tend to be investment bankers. There is a reason for this. In the first place, investment bankers, because they are a major source of business capital, carry great clout in the business world. They sit on boards of, and act as financial advisers to, hundreds—even thousands—of large and small businesses in every state of the union. As a result, their contacts and influence are national in scope.

Furthermore, investment banking is one of the last industries in which most of the firms are still privately held. Thus, when a senior partner says "I support so-and-so for President [or mayor, or senator, or whatever]," it carries great weight because he speaks as near or absolute owner of his business and does not have to go before a board of directors for approval of his actions. As a result, such an individual has far more clout then, say, Gabriel Hauge, chairman of the board of the Manufacturers Hanover Trust Company, or Donald Regan, chairman of the board of Merrill Lynch, Pierce, Fenner & Smith (whose separate corporate assets dwarf those of even the largest investment banking houses), because they tend to be inhibited by the need to report to their respective directors and stockholders.

The most successful Republican investment bankers in recent years have been Gustave Levy of Goldman, Sachs; Al Gordon of Kidder, Peabody; Bernard Lasker of Lasker, Stone & Stern; John Schiff of Kuhn, Loeb; Peter Flanigan of Dillon, Read; Joseph Gimma of Hornblower & Weeks–Hemphill Noyes; and Fergus Reid of Roosevelt & Son and Clark, Dodge. Howard Stein of the Dreyfus Fund and John Loeb of Loeb, Rhoades & Company are well-known Democratic fund raisers. Loeb has an advantage over other key men in that his wife, "Peter," has built a reputation as an efficient political fund raiser in her own right.

New York City is not a place where lawyers carry much clout as fund raisers. Although Arthur Krim and Walter Thayer are both New York lawyers and well-known fund raisers, Krim is better known as president of United Artists and Thayer as an investment adviser to John Hay Whitney. John N. Mitchell (prior to Watergate) and Richard Nixon, when they were practicing law in New York, would be the exceptions to the rule.

A major concentration of key lawyers is found in Washington, D.C. Among the heavyweights are Thomas G. ("Tommy the Cork") Corcoran and James Rowe of Corcoran, Foley, Youngman & Rowe, who have been powers in Democratic fund-raising circles for over thirty years. Also very influential are former Defense Secretary Clark M. Clifford; Oscar Chapman, a Secretary of the Interior under Truman; Thomas Hale Boggs, Jr., son of the Democratic Whip who disappeared in Alaska during the 1972 campaign; Donald S. Dawson of Dawson, Quinn, Riddell, Taylor & Davis; Paul Porter of Arnold & Porter (formerly Arnold, Fortas & Porter); and Gerald D. Morgan, a lawyer serving as AMTRAK's vice-president of government affairs.

Most of Washington's blue-ribbon law firms—Covington & Burling; Wilmer, Cutler & Pickering; and Sellers, Connors & Cuneo, to name but a few—spurn political fund raising as an activity beneath their dignity. In spite of the fact that nearly all of them began as fund-raising, string-pulling, power-peddling firms, they progressively withdrew from the sweat-stained arena over the years as their clientele grew in both number and quality. Occasionally, one of the partners will serve as secretary or treasurer to a political fund-raising committee, wherein he becomes the initial collection point for campaign funds, but seldom do they go beyond that.

Another concentration of lawyers exists on the West Coast. Herbert W. Kalmbach of Newport Beach, California, for one, is influential among Fat Cat Republicans. He is the major force behind the success of the Lincoln Club, and prior to the Watergate Affair was so close to Richard Nixon that he was known as "the President's lawyer."

Eugene Wyman of Los Angeles, who died in early 1973, was another well-known West Coast lawyer–fund raiser. Wyman's influence derived from the fact that no other fund raiser apparently had as many Fat Cats in the $10,000-and-up bracket who were willing to follow his judgment. Many Democrats claim that Wyman was so talented at raising money that he was in a class by himself, although his reputation took a beating in the last years of his life by his backing a string of losers, the last being Hubert Humphrey in 1972.

A third West Coast source of fund-raising talent is the Los Angeles law firm of O'Melveny & Myers, some of whose partners raise funds for Republicans and others for Democrats. Sometimes they find themselves opposing each other in the same election.

Commercial bankers who raise campaign money are not concentrated in any particular areas of the country as investment bankers and lawyers tend to be. Thus you will find Maurice Stans (prior to his government service) in California, Sinclair Weeks (in the 1950's and 1960's) in Massachusetts, True Davis in Washington, D.C., David Rockefeller in New York City, various Mellons and Scaifes in Pittsburgh, David Kennedy in Chicago, Frank C. P. McGlinn in Philadelphia and Dwayne Andreas in Minneapolis.

The same is true with key men in the business world. A few of the better known ones whose influence is national or regional include Arnold Picker and Jerry Finkelstein of New York City, Henry Kimelman from the Virgin Islands, Tom and John Pappas of Boston, Max Fisher of Detroit, Robert S. Strauss (who is also a lawyer) of Texas, S. Harrison Dogole of Philadelphia, Robert Short of Minneapolis (and owner of the Texas Rangers baseball team), Joe Rosenfield (also a lawyer) of Des Moines, J. Irwin Miller of Indiana, and Max Palevsky, Lew Wasserman, Eugene V. Klein and Taft Schreiber, all of California.

These many diverse fund raisers do not solely solicit within their own professions. Businessmen Wasserman and Schreiber and lawyer Arthur Krim, for instance, are adept at milking the entertainment world. Businessmen Fisher, Palevsky and Picker and investment banker Gustave Levy are similarly adept at shaking the Jewish money tree. Before his death in early 1973, Eugene Wyman was unexcelled in both worlds.

Some fund raisers fit into no precise category. Anna Chennault, widow of Flying Tiger founder General Claire Chennault, is one example. She raises money from the pro-Taiwan lobby for the GOP. Another example is philanthropist June Degnan who raises funds from liberal Democrats on the East and West Coast.

The influence of most key men with access, however, is usually limited to a particular city or state. Nevertheless, they must be courted with the same ardor one must reserve for nationally and regionally oriented key men when running for President. They are crucial to any campaign for senator and governor, and sometimes congressman, mayor and state legislator. Inevitably, of course, there is considerable overlap between nationally and regionally oriented and locally oriented key men, since an individual with contacts around the nation will usually still take a special interest in his home town or state affairs.

In Massachusetts, for instance, if one is a moderate-to-liberal Republican, it would be wise to have Bruce Crane of Dalton on your side. Crane is president of Crane & Company, the quality-writing-paper manufacturing firm, and his name is considered solid gold on fund-raising literature. John Volpe always put Crane's name on his fund-raising letterhead, and as a result never had any serious money-raising problems.

Frederic C. ("Buck") Dumaine, Jr., of Weston is another key man to see. He is president of Amoskeag Mills in New Hampshire and a former Republican State Committee chairman. On at least one occasion he has bailed out the state GOP with a generous loan.

Tom Pappas of Belmont, who has extensive business interests in both New England and Greece, is another key man in moderate GOP circles in Massachusetts. He has been raising money for the Republicans at least since 1952 and, like Joseph P. Kennedy before him, has perfected the technique of raising money from friends and taking full credit for the contributions.

Other Republican key men in Massachusetts include Boston investment bankers Henry Vance and Forrester Andrew Clark. Both were backers of George Lodge in 1962. Harcourt Wood, Senator Edward Brooke's principal fund raiser, Robert Chapman Sprague of the Sprague Electric Company, and William Dwight, publisher of the Holyoke *Transcript-Telegram,* would also be worth courting.

If one's ideology is to the right of center, it would be beneficial to see Jack Molesworth of Boston and Lloyd Waring of Rockport, the latter a partner in Kidder, Peabody. Although both were Goldwater supporters in 1964, it would be unwise to mention the name of one in the presence of the other, since they have been feuding for years over what exactly constitutes the proper right-wing philosophy.

A moderate-to-liberal Democrat, on the other hand, might begin his courtship of key men by seeing Robert P. Fitzgerald, president of the Harbor National Bank of Boston, a Kennedy relation and one of Edward M. Kennedy's principal moneymen. He should also see Eli Goldston, a Boston utility executive; Joseph T. Benedict, president of the First Federal Savings and Loan Association in Worcester, who could tap all the financial sources not covered by Fitzgerald in Boston; John ("Judge") Pappas, Tom's brother, who covers the Democratic bets in the family; racetrack owners George Reynolds, Joe Linsey and George Carney; Lester S. Hyman, a Washington lawyer and former Massachusetts Democratic party power with many contacts in the state; Arnold S. Hiatt of the Stride Rite Corporation, who raised money for McCarthy in 1968 and McGovern in 1972; and Robert Pirie, a Boston lawyer whose family made a fortune in the Chicago department store of Carson, Pirie & Scott.

In New York, key men to see for state and local elections, particularly for mayor of New York City, include Harry Van Arsdale, Jr., president of the Central Labor Council; Anthony Scotto, Brooklyn waterfront leader with apparent ties to the Mafia; Peter Brennan of the Building and Construction Trades Council (and Secretary of Labor in Nixon's second administration); and stockbroker John A. Coleman of Adler, Coleman & Company, who, as a fund raiser for Roman Catholic causes, has great clout among his fellow Catholics.

Of particular interest in New York City is the real estate industry which, like investment banking, is still tightly held by a relatively few individuals and families. The key real estate developers whose voices and money carry weight in political circles are Jack, Lewis and Samuel Rudin of the Rudin Management Company;

Harry B. Helmsley of Helmsley-Spear, Inc.; Richard Ravitch of HRH Construction; Laurence and Robert Tisch who own a string of theaters (Loew's) and hotels; and various family members of the Tishman, Uris and Minskoff construction and realty companies. Generally, they support liberal candidates of both parties.

In Wisconsin, key men with access in moderate GOP circles include the senior members of the Uihlein family, who control both the Joseph Schlitz Brewing Company and the First Wisconsin National Bank; the Brumder family, who are in real estate and are related to the Uihleins; Walter J. Kohler, Jr., the moderate Republican governor from 1951 to 1956, and son of the man who for years refused to allow union representation in the family's plumbing supply firm; John and Frederick Stratton of Green Elevator, who also own stock in the Briggs & Stratton Corporation; and William S. Carpenter of Rexnord, formerly Rex Chainbelt, Inc.

Also influential are members of the Vollrath family, who are related to the Kohlers and carry just as much weight in the Milwaukee, Kohler and Sheboygan areas; Ody Fish, a successful businessman and a former chairman of the Republican party in Wisconsin; William Dickerman Vogel, whose family was once big in tanning but has now moved into warehousing; lawyer John McIvor, who ran Nixon's 1968 campaign in the state; seed merchants Walter and Wilbur Renk of Sun Prairie, and benefactors of the University of Wisconsin; Bernard C. Ziegler, an investment banker with ties to West Bend Aluminum Company; Victor Ivan Minahan of Green Bay, who has extensive financial interests in lumber companies, newspapers, and radio and television stations; and Melvin Laird's family, who made their money in lumber and are a power in the Marshfield-Wausau area.

Wealthy businessmen Harold and Louis Falk are key men with access to very conservative and right-wing sources of money in Wisconsin. Both are directors of many businesses and civic organizations in the Milwaukee area. Harold is also a director of the Marshall & Ilsley Bank, many of whose other directors and stockholders are key men in the state Democratic party. The Falks are adept at extracting large sums from such well-known industrialists as Walter Harnischfeger, William J. Grede and Fred F. Loock. Harnischfeger has been associated with such right-wing groups as the Manion Forum and the Citizens Foreign Aid Committee; Grede with the John Birch Society. Loock was tied to the Great Electrical Industry Conspiracy of 1961 in which the Allen-Bradley Company, of which he was president, was convicted of collusive bidding and illegal price-rigging. Their money is always welcome, even by moderate-to-liberal GOP fund raisers, but their names seldom appear on fund-raising literature, and they are rarely asked to raise money for others, because it would be a kiss of death to a Republican candidate in the state.

In the Democratic camp, key men with access would include Richard Cudahy, a West Point and Yale graduate, lawyer and chairman of the Democratic party in Wisconsin, whose family made a fortune in the meat-packing and processing business. He managed Senator William Proxmire's reelection campaign in 1970 and is considered to be the state's most effective fund raiser within the liberal Democratic establishment, particularly among bankers, Catholics, Jews and home-construction executives. Another with extensive influence is James C. Windham, president of the Pabst Brewing Company. He is to the Democrats what the Uihleins are to the Republicans, although all the big Wisconsin breweries have a reputation of giving to both sides in the important campaigns.

Additional key Democrats include W. D. Pavalon who owns the Milwaukee Bucks basketball team, a string of nursing homes and Career Academy, a national correspondence school; Gerald S. Colburn of Fox Point and plumbing contractor Burton J. Zien, both of whom have clout in the Jewish community; Martin Hansen of Mellen, Wisconsin, whose family made a fortune in furniture; Howard Meister, president of the Continental Bank and Trust; Elmer Winter who owns Manpower, Inc.; John Schmidt of the state AFL-CIO; Sherman Stock in Senator Gaylord Nelson's Milwaukee office; and Martin Lobel, a former aide to Senator Proxmire.

In a state like Wisconsin, it also makes sense to seek out key men with access in various unions and lobbies, since they are a prime source of campaign funds. Wisconsin COPE is a major source of Democratic funds, as are the Steelworkers, Railway Clerks, Machinists, Meatcutters and Teamster unions, as well as farm lobbies such as ACT (Agricultural Cooperative Trust) and

ACRE (Action Committee for Rural Electrification). Many of these organizations are located in Washington, D.C., and are discussed in more detail in the following chapter.

In Pennsylvania, GOP key men with access include Thomas B. McCabe, Sr., of Scott Paper; Thomas S. Gates, Jr., former Secretary of Defense and retired head of the Morgan Guaranty Trust Company (who commuted between his home outside Philadelphia and his New York office); banker Frank C. P. McGlinn, noted earlier; John C. Dorrance, Jr., of Campbell Soups; investment banker Howard W. Butcher III; George Bloom, for many years chairman of the Pennsylvania Utility Commission; Joseph T. Simpson of Harsco Steel (and an old Nixon friend); wealthy businessman Philip T. Sharples; and various members of the Pitcairn (Pittsburgh Plate Glass), Mellon and Scaife (oil, banking and aluminum), and Firestone (rubber products) families. Slightly to the right of center would be Philip Corson, a concrete-mix manufacturer, and Frank E. Masland, Jr., a carpet manufacturer from the central part of the state.

Even to the right of them is the Pew family, which made its money in the Sun Oil Company. It has dominated Republican finances in the state for a full half century. Every GOP candidate from governor to county clerk usually receives a contribution from a Pew. Sometimes the manner in which the money is given is bizarre indeed. One young state legislator, for instance, recalls receiving a contribution from the trustees of a Pew who turned out to be only eight months old at the time. Some Pews hold political views that even members of the family find conservative. During the 1952 GOP convention, for example, one Pew, a delegate, supported the candidacy of General Douglas MacArthur. When the delegation was polled on the convention floor, he became momentarily confused, forgetting which general he liked best, and mistakenly shouted "Grant!"

On the Democratic side, key men include John R. Bunting, president of the First Pennsylvania Banking and Trust Company; S. Harrison ("Sonny") Dogole, head of Globe Security Systems; James W. Greenlee, a lawyer and former head of the Philadelphia Housing Authority with considerable clout in Harrisburg; Frederic R. Mann, president of Industrial Container Corporation and a former ambassador to Barbados; and real estate developer Frank Binswanger.

The most interesting development regarding Pennsylvania's key men is that they seem to be dying out as a species. Key Republicans such as Richard King Mellon, Roger Firestone, J. Howard Pew and George D. Widener, the latter a horseracing enthusiast and son of P.A.B. Widener (who was a nineteenth-century key man with access), have all died within the last decade, and no one of similar stature and influence has come forward to take their place. In addition, McCabe, Gates and Sharples appear to have partially retired from the scene, and Bloom has reduced his efforts (partly because his boss, Governor Milton Shapp, is a Democrat).

The same is true with the Democrats: trucker Jim Clark, one of the best fund raisers Philadelphia Democrats ever had; Albert M. Greenfield, the realtor and longtime national Democratic contributor; Matthew McCloskey; and former Governor David Lawrence are all dead. The Kelly family (of Princess Grace fame) has retired or withdrawn from the scene. This leaves very few Democrats who are willing or able to raise large sums of money.

In fact, it can be said that only four men in the two parties—Butcher, Dogole, Greenlee and Bunting—are currently as active as their many former peers once were.

A similar situation exists in Michigan. The only remotely active key men with access are Republicans Walker L. Cisler of Detroit Edison (who contributed to both Humphrey and Nixon in 1968) and Max Fisher. The Democrats have had no comparable key man since the death of Walter Reuther. To be sure, most of the big Michigan names contribute—the Kresges (dime stores), Strohs (brewers), Williamses (soaps), Briggses (of Briggs & Stratton), Bagleys (tobacco), Algers (lumber), and Ketterings, Fords, Bugases, Motts, Coles, Knudsens, Fishers and Wilsons (automobiles)—but none of them play the key-man-with-access role. They are simply content to give and then retire from the arena. Although Stewart Mott is technically from Michigan, his base of operations is New York City. It is also questionable whether he qualifies as a key man with access, since he raises very little from others and carries almost no weight in political and fund-raising circles.

California has no such problems, probably because there is more new money there than in Pennsylvania and Michigan. The state abounds with key men with access, and only the more prominent ones not mentioned previously need be noted here. There are, for instance, those key men known as the "Checkbook Democrats"—hotelman Benjamin Swig, oilman Edwin Pauley, and businessmen Cyril Magnin, Robert M. Haynie and George Killion—so-called because they can be counted on to raise the necessary funds whenever a Democrat runs for state and national office.

There is also land developer Mark Boyar, who first began raising funds at the national level in 1948; Harold Willens and Martin Stone, both businessmen who raise money among liberal Democrats; and Harvey Aluminum heiress Carmen Warschaw, who also milks the liberal California community. Frank Sinatra raises funds for Democrats (and occasionally Republicans) among the Hollywood crowd. Van Nuys lawyer and state Democratic chairman Charles Manatt is also a key man; so, too, are Contra Costa County banker and freshman Congressman Fortney Stark, Marin County banker Byron Leydecker, lawyer Paul Ziffren and businessman Larry Lawrence, the latter two of whom have clout in the southern California Jewish community.

Jess Unruh, Speaker of the California House from 1961 to 1968, was once one of the state's most influential key men (see the following chapter); so were wealthy bankers Howard Ahmanson and Bart Lytton until their deaths in the late 1960's.

Republican key men include Leonard Firestone of the Firestone Tire & Rubber Company; Asa Call, a former president of the state Chamber of Commerce, who is skilled at raising money from California's powerful highway lobby; oilman Henry Salvatori, Los Angeles Ford dealer Holmes Tuttle, businessman Patrick Frawley, and actors Bob Hope and John Wayne, all of whom raise money for conservative candidates; and, until his death in 1967, Union Oil chairman A. C. ("Cy") Rubel.

Iowa, too, abounds in key men. The best known in the Democratic party are Joe Rosenfield, a retired Des Moines department-store executive, and Art Sanford of Sioux City. Both have been major fund raisers for Senator Harold Hughes. Sanford also raised funds for Adlai Stevenson in 1952 and 1956. Realtor Bill Knapp of Des Moines is another Hughes fund raiser–adviser, as are contractor Tom Mulgrew of Dubuque, lawyers Jim Bradley of Cedar Rapids and Emmet Tinley of Council Bluffs, and insurance agent Paul Ryan of Davenport.

Banker John Chrystol of Coon Rapids is another major Democratic mover in the state. He is a partner with Steve Garst in Garst & Thomas, a seed corn firm. Garst, also an influential Democrat, is the son of Roswell Garst, who hosted tourist Nikita Khrushchev in 1959. Other key Democratic moneymen include Abe Clayman of Des Moines, a big Humphrey backer; loan company executive Fred Moore of Spencer; and Ed Breen, president of station KVFV-TV in Fort Dodge. Clayman and Moore, while Democrats, accepted posts in the Republican administration of Governor Robert Ray, but they appear not to have lost any influence in Democratic financial circles as a result.

Key GOP Iowans include David Stanley of Muscatine, a member of the Stanley Tool Company family and unsuccessful candidate for the United States Senate (against Hughes in 1968); David Palmer of Davenport and the Palmer School of Chiropractic Medicine, and other interests; Dick Redman of Des Moines, who runs his own political fund-raising firm; Harold Goldman of Iowa Paint, who is good at tapping the local Jewish community; the Maytag (washing machines) and Vernon (novelty items) families of Newton; Jack Warren of Warren Truck Lines in Waterloo; Judge Herb Bennett of Fort Dodge; E. A. Hayes of Mt. Pleasant, a former state GOP finance chairman; lawyers Levi Call Dickinson of Des Moines and Robert Buckmaster of Waterloo; and the senior members of the MacNider family of Mason City, who own the local Portland Cement company, among other interests.

There are perhaps several hundred first-rank key men with political access in Texas, most of them nominal Democrats. Besides Lyndon Johnson, who stood in a class by himself and is discussed later in this chapter, and those mentioned previously, there is ex-Governor John Connally, who still retains his clout among Democrats despite his conversion to the GOP and service in the Nixon administration; Austin lawyer Frank Erwin, a Connally adviser and the chairman of the board of regents of the University of Texas; George R. Brown of the Brown & Root heavy construction company, and a longtime LBJ financial backer and adviser; independent oil producer Michael Halbouty of Houston; rancher-banker Alfred W. Negley of San Antonio; George Parr of Duval County, whose family has been a power in southern Texas for forty years; James A. Elkins, senior partner in the Houston law firm of Vincent, Elkins, Searls & Smith, one of the most powerful men in Texas because he is supposed to decide who gets the Establishment's money to run for governor; builder H. B. Zachry of San Antonio; and John Mitchell, president of the Jade Oil and Gas Company in Houston.

Crusty octogenarian Edward ("Mister Ed") Ball is the best-known key man with access in Florida. He runs the one-billion-dollar Alfred Du Pont empire which has heavy investments in Florida banks, railroads and real estate. He is supposed to have been primarily responsible for the "red scare" campaign of 1950 which drove Claude Pepper from the U.S. Senate. He was also one of the principal backers of Claude R. Kirk, Jr., who ran against Miami mayor Robert King High in the 1966 gubernatorial race, and Edward Gurney, who defeated LeRoy Collins in the 1968 senatorial race.

Other Florida movers are Arthur H. Courshon, a Miami savings and loan executive who backed Humphrey in 1968; Chester Ferguson of the Lykes shipping fortune; Ben Hill Griffin, Jr., a frozen-fruit-juice tycoon; the Davis family which built the giant Winn-Dixie grocery chain; Louis Wolfson (no relation to Louis E. Wolfson, the Miami financier who, among other things, was board chairman of Merritt-Chapman & Scott), who owns a string of Miami enterprises; bankers Harry Hood Bassett and Charles J. Zwick of the Southeast Banking Corporation; entrepreneur Maurice A. Ferré, a nephew of the former governor of Puerto Rico, Luis A. Ferré; Lewis S. Rosenstiel, founder of Schenley Distillers; Samuel Friedland of Food Fair stores; and Benjamin Novack, president of the Fontainebleau Hotel in Miami Beach. The latter three are influential fund raisers in Florida's Jewish community.

Among Republicans in Illinois there are ex-Treasury Secretary David Kennedy of the Continental Illinois National Bank, Robert S. Ingersoll of Borg-Warner, Charles Kellstadt of Sears-Roebuck, Ernest Marsh of the Santa Fe Railroad, and Robert Galvin of Motorola. In addition there are Clayton R. Gaylord, a Rockford industrialist who raised money for Goldwater in 1964; Charles

Barr, also a Goldwaterite and a former executive with Standard Oil of Indiana; Edmund B. Thornton, a wealthy downstate businessman; and wealthy multimillionaire insuranceman W. Clement Stone of Chicago.

It is currently fashionable to dismiss Stone simply as a big GOP contributor who likes to brag about it. But Stone is also very much a fund raiser. He views himself as a great inspirer of men and enjoys practicing his talent by raising funds. On occasion, he has raised vast sums by promising to match every dollar with two of his own, a tactic not many key men have the nerve or assets to try.

The Democrats have only one key man with access of any stature in the state: Richard J. Daley, mayor of Chicago. Daley looms so large over the state party fund-raising scene that, like Rockefeller in New York, he may end up demoralizing the party for years the moment he steps down from office. There is no one in the wings waiting to take up the fund-raising chores. Nor is there anyone save Daley himself with full access to the many financial levers and strings which, taken together, are the key to his efficient fund-raising machine. It can only be said that Daley, like any boss of such caliber, gets his campaign funds from three sources: downtown GOP businessmen (who support Daley locally but the Republican party nationally), his thousands of patronage employees, and individuals seeking favors or business contracts with the city, county or state.

In Ohio, lawyer H. Chapman Rose and entrepreneur Joseph E. Cole are, respectively, Republican and Democratic key men in the northern part of the state. In centrol Ohio the Wolfe family of Columbus, which has vast holdings in banks, newspapers, radio and television stations, and real estate is a major source of money for GOP candidates. Offsetting its influence somewhat is the Lazarus family, also of Columbus, owner of the Federated Department Store chain, which tends to give to and raise money for liberals and non-organizational Democratic candidates. In the southern part of the state, two Cincinnati families play key roles in GOP money matters: the Cox clan, which owns a string of newspapers and which tends to back moderate-to-conservative Republicans; and the Tafts, who tend to back moderate-to-liberal Republicans when they are not backing their own.

In Georgia, key men include Ovid Davis, a vice-president of Coca Cola, and Opie Lee Shelton, of the Georgia Chamber of Commerce. Between them, they recommend who will receive contributions from Coca Cola executives. Ex-Governor Carl Sanders, who knows every important mover and shaker in the state, is another key man; so, too, is lawyer Harley Langdale, Sr., of Valdosta, who has clout among timber company executives. Also influential in fund-raising circles are J. B. Fuqua, an Atlanta businessman and former state senator; Atlanta lawyer Irving K. Kaler; Mills B. Lane, Jr., president of the Citizens & Southern National Bank in Atlanta; and E. Smythe Gambrell, a former president of the American Bar Association and father of ex-U.S. Senator David Gambrell. The only Republican key man of note in the state is businessman Roy G. Foster, Jr., of Wadley, whose family for years has almost singlehandedly supported the Republican party in the state.

In Nevada, ex-Governor Paul Laxalt and Las Vegas banker Alexander K. Sample, Jr., are the top Republican key men. Ex-Governor Grant Sawyer is a key Democratic party fund raiser in the state. William Harrah of Harrah's Club in Reno collects from casino operators for preferred candidates (mostly Democratic).

For years the take from the gambling establishment was never less than $5,000 per casino. In fact, so much money was raised at election time that general fund-raising dinners fell into disuse. But after Howard Hughes moved into the state, subsequently buying up one sixth of the gaming industry, total contributions began to fall off. Hughes started the practice of writing one campaign contribution check for all his properties, the money being divided by his aides as he directed. The take per casino was subsequently smaller and, as a result, candidates for office were forced to revive the fund-raising dinner. Also hastening the decline in contributions from casinos was the fact that many gambling establishments have been bought up over the last decade by conglomerates whose corporate officers live far away and care little for contributing to Nevada candidates.

Every state, city and county in the nation, obviously, has its key men with access to political funds and influence. The purpose here is not to cite every individual, but to illustrate their variety.

To round out the picture, therefore, a few others must be mentioned.

In Missouri, the key Republican man with access is retired Major General Leif J. Sverdrup, an architect with the St. Louis planning firm of Sverdrup & Parcel. His Democratic counterpart is Sidney Salomon, Jr., a wealthy insuranceman and owner of the St. Louis Blues ice hockey team.

Key Republicans in Arizona include Harry Rosenzweig, a wealthy Phoenix jeweler who was one of Goldwater's original financial backers, and Stephen Shadegg, a professional campaign consultant and author. On the Democratic side, key men include former Governor Samuel P. Goddard, Jr.; Phoenix lawyer Herbert L. Ely, a power in the state party hierarchy; and businessman Guy Stillman (whose mother was a McCormick of reaper fame), a former national committeeman from Scottsdale.

The two most influential Republican moneymen in Indiana are Walter R. Beardsley, who runs Miles Laboratory in Elkhart, and Oliver Cromwell Carmichael, Jr., a South Bend businessman who is chairman of the board of at least three separate investment companies. On the Democratic side are Frank E. McKinney, a retired banker and former DNC chairman, and Robert Welch, a successful Indianapolis builder who is a relatively new key man with access on the scene.

In New Jersey, key GOP men to see are oilman Leon Hess; Gene Mori, who operates Garden State Race Track; and W. Paul Stillman, president of the First National State Bank in Newark. Most political professionals with whom I spoke in the state acknowledged privately that a minimum of one half of all Democratic party campaign contributions and perhaps as much as one quarter of GOP funds come from the Mafia. Usually the money is first laundered by passing it through the various state, county and local political committees.

Delaware is run by the Du Ponts, and entrée to family money can be obtained through State Senator Reynolds Du Pont, former Wilmington Mayor Harry G. Haskell, and former Governor Russell W. Peterson. Also influential in Delaware fund-raising circles are entrepreneur John Rollins and Thomas B. Evans, Jr., the latter a high official in the Republican National Committee.

The Weyerhaeuser family is a GOP power in both Minnesota and Washington state. The Coors family, with investments in breweries and a porcelain factory, among other things, is influential in Colorado. Robert O. Anderson, reputedly the largest private landowner in the United States, is a key GOP man in New Mexico when he is not traveling on behalf of Atlantic Richfield. Barry Bingham, editor and publisher of the *Louisville Courier-Journal* and son of a former ambassador to Great Britain, is a power among liberal Democrats in Kentucky.

At the state and local levels it is not unusual for government employees to raise campaign funds. In fact, one of the best ways to keep one's job from administration to administration, regardless of party label, is to prove oneself a good fund raiser. Insurance commissioners, for example, regularly tap insurance companies; Liquor Control Board members hit liquor dealers, nightclub owners and restaurateurs; the head of Properties and Supplies canvasses companies selling their goods and services to the state and/or local government; the secretary of mines collects from the extractive industry. Utilities, banks, architects and contractors are others regularly milked for funds by appropriate department heads.

These bureaucrats will even squeeze employees in their own departments. The standard practice is to ask for "voluntary" contributions to a "Flower Fund." Each contribution, usually from 2 to 7 percent of a person's yearly salary, is ostensibly used to pay for flowers at the funeral of fellow bureaucrats, but in reality is used to finance political campaigns. One of the jobs of a state's adjutant general, for instance, is periodically to shake down senior officers in the National Guard for campaign funds.

Such contributions actually amount to an assessment, since a refusal to pay is an invitation to be fired or to have one's job abolished. Most states, through the passage of "little Hatch Acts," have banned or severely restricted the soliciting of government employees, but the practice persists and is strongly entrenched in machine-prone states such as New York, Indiana, Pennsylvania, Illinois, New Jersey and Tennessee.

The late Paul Powell, who spent thirty-six years on the Illinois payroll as both an elected and appointed official, is considered by many observers to be a classic, if somewhat bizarre, example of a fund-raising state bureaucrat. While he was secretary of state, he regularly demanded contributions from anyone who wanted to do business with the state—from racetrack owners to food suppliers. He also demanded contributions from the 4,600 patronage employees under his control, many of whom wore Powell's name stitched to the back of their shirts, bowling-league fashion. Every year he threw a testimonial dinner for himself, tickets to which every lobbyist in Springfield somehow felt obliged to buy. His last such affair supposedly netted $100,000. He was so avaricious that, whenever he saw the possibility of a deal, he was wont to say, "I can smell the meat acookin'!"

But, in truth, Powell did not believe in giving. Of all the money he collected over the years, very little of it was passed along to others. After his death in 1970, over $800,000 in cash stuffed in shoeboxes was found in his apartment, and his estate was valued in excess of $3 million—all this for a lifelong state employee who began his career penniless and never made more than $30,000 a year. Powell, in fact, was not a key man with access, but a man with sticky fingers who assumed the key man role only if it satisfied his greed.

A more common example of a state-employee fund raiser would be William O. Cowger, who, when he was mayor of Louisville, Kentucky, said that his administration collected "voluntary" contributions from patronage appointees. They were told to chip in 2 percent of their monthly salary. Cowger said that he raised so much money that he found it difficult to spend it intelligently in his campaigns. Some of it, he said, once went to pay for a victory party.

In New York City, to cite another example, city planning commissioner Abraham ("Bunny") Lindenbaum once openly sought political contributions for Mayor Wagner at a luncheon held for that purpose. When the luncheon became public knowledge, Lindenbaum was forced to resign.

Despite the Hatch Acts, federal employees are regularly asked to contribute. Some agencies are more political than others, among them the Government Services Administration and the Federal Trade Commission. At the latter, for instance, everyone down to grade GS-13 is dunned for political contributions. Former commissioner Paul Rand Dixon was supposedly proud of his fund-raising prowess within the department.

Wealthy noncareer ambassadors and other high-ranking appointees are also solicited. In 1968, for example, Congressman John J. Rooney of Brooklyn, New York, chairman of the House Appropriations subcommittee which passes on the State Department budget, received large donations to his reelection campaign from, among others, AID director William C. Foster, Ambassador Angier Biddle Duke, Deputy Assistant Secretary of State Katie S. Louchheim, and at least twelve other high-ranking State Department officials.

Sometimes the bureaucracy is used to shake down others. One big-city Pennsylvania congressman, for example, regularly raised money by arranging with an Internal Revenue Service employee to inspect a potential contributor's tax return; when the individual called for help, the congressman arranged to call off the inspector in return for a fat contribution.

As head of his party, a President or a nominee for the job is a fund raiser. No recent President or serious contender has been a poor fund raiser for, indeed, being a success in politics and being a good fund raiser cannot be separated. However, each takes to the task with a different degree of enthusiasm. Eisenhower and Stevenson, for instance, did not relish fund raising, and were used primarily as ornaments in the money-raising process to loosen wallets. They preferred to leave the arm-twisting to others. The same has since been true of Eugene McCarthy and George McGovern.

Roosevelt, Truman and both John and Robert Kennedy were judicious mixtures of ornaments and arm-twister: all loved the rough and tumble of fund raising, but not to the point where it obsessed or distracted them. Goldwater, Reagan, George Wallace, Muskie and Humphrey have been similarly inclined.

By contrast, the careers of Nixon and Johnson have been marked by intense personal arm-twisting, although each developed his own particular style. Nixon's has been cool, corporate and controlled while Johnson's was emotional, physical and erratic.

Like any good corporate manager, Nixon delegated nearly all his arm-twisting to others. At the top of the fund-raising chart, before the Watergate scandal broke, were Maurice Stans, Herbert Kalmbach, John Mitchell and perhaps a score more topflight national fund raisers, with Stans clearly *primus inter pares.* (Stans, Kalmbach, and Mitchell have subsequently fallen from grace as a result of their associations with Watergate, and no new group of fund raisers has emerged to fill the void; however, it is unlikely that Nixon needs active arm-twisters anymore, since his fund-raising days, at least in his own behalf, appear to be over.) Below them were the Republican National Committee and the House and Senate campaign committees, in addition to 50 state fund-raising organizations. These, in turn, had subsidiary offices collecting down to the local level.

This well-organized juggernaut has left no stones unturned. In both the 1968 and 1972 elections, it not only systematically milked every major business in the country but went so far as to set up fund-raising units in Europe to extract the odd franc, mark, shilling, pound and lire from Americans living abroad. In the 1972 election, contributions were methodically extracted from all black antipoverty consultants holding federal contracts, and from all minority businessmen on the approval list to receive Small Business Administration loans.

In anticipation of his reelection campaign, Nixon sent Vice-President Agnew around the country to raise money from state organizations. Even in the best of times a state fund-raising organization has difficulty meeting its own money needs; and a popular national figure, realizing this, usually takes only a token percentage of the proceeds for the national campaign. This is particularly true in off years. But Agnew was so popular a speaker that the RNC would agree to no speaking engagement unless the state organization guaranteed a certain return to the national party. Sometimes it was a flat figure (which could leave the state group profitless if the turnout were light), and sometimes it was a percentage figure (on occasion as high as 50 percent of gross receipts).

Nixon's fund raisers also squeezed patronage appointees and special interests. In 1970, for instance, they set up a back room fund-raising unit which, in the best Harding style, operated out of a Washington townhouse basement. It was run by Jack A. Gleason, Charles W. Colson and Harry S. Dent, all White House aides, to raise money for preferred congressional candidates. Most of the money came from Fat Cat ambassadors and the dairy lobby.

Johnson's fund-raising style lent itself to no particular historical comparison, for in many ways it was unique. His ability to attract serious money was based partly on his shrewd understanding of human nature, partly on an earthy, backslapping, elbow-pinching manner, and partly on an all-consuming ambition.

He realized early in his career that no one went places in Texas politics without the backing of oil money, even though in his early political years he himself was not Big Oil's favorite candidate. While he was still a young congressman he was asked by FDR to raise and disburse campaign funds for various Democratic candidates for the House. In a few short weeks he had collected about $100,000, which in prewar days was big money. Some of the funds came from Fat Cat oilmen, who were subsequently to become the base of Johnson's political finance empire.

During his entire Senate career, Johnson jealously guarded the Finance Committee, the bastion of the tax loophole. He would not allow anyone unfriendly to oil to be appointed to the committee. He also used the Majority Leader's position, by controlling the type and flow of legislation, to extract large sums from Fat Cats. Added to Johnson's native abilities, it gave him extraordinary leverage over wealthy contributors, which he never hesitated to use.

His usual method of raising money was to call a potential contributor into his office and tell him exactly how much he was to give, and to whom. If there were any hesitation, he would remind the Fat Cat of pending bills affecting him or his business. Occasionally he would take a potential contributor into the Senate gallery and begin comparing the good Democratic senators with some of the Republican mossbacks. Sometimes, if the contrast were not sufficiently evident, he would signal Senators Robert Kerr, George Smathers, Earle Clements or Allen Frear on the floor—all of whom were part of his fund-raising clique—who would then rise and goad the Republicans into fits of anger. Usually such a display was sufficient to elicit a contribution.

Johnson carried this intensely personal, old-fashioned manner of fund raising with him into the White House. Arms were squeezed and sometimes twisted, sums were demanded and usually given unquestioningly, hostile legislation was threatened for recalcitrants, and jobs and favors were given in return for promised contributions. Johnson was so much in the center of fund-raising affairs during his years in the White House that other Democratic fund-raising groups, most notably the Democratic National Committee, became shriveled appendices to the key man in the White House. As a result, he ended up destroying the party's nationwide fund-raising network, which even in the best of times could hardly be called a cohesive group. The 1968 party debt is a reflection of the extent of the destruction.

The man who taught Johnson most of what he knew about fund raising was Senator Robert Kerr of Oklahoma. "When people talk about big contributors to political campaigns," said one political pro, "I always think of Kerr." Kerr built a reputation that he was not a man to cross. He was not above asking for specific amounts and could be vindictive if the contributor failed to come through as expected.

His immense personal wealth and his clout in the oil industry allowed him to influence many congressional races. He became a funnel for oil money and, later in his Senate career, other interest money as well. The manner in which he dispensed the money was unusual. One story is illustrative. On January 31, 1962, James B. Pearson, a Republican from Kansas, was appointed to the Senate to fill the vacancy caused by the death of Senator Andrew Schoeppel. Pearson then ran in the general election that year and won the seat in his own right.

Sometime between January 31 and election day, 1962, Pearson received a message that Senator Kerr wanted to see him in a certain room in the Capitol. Pearson went to the room and waited. Suddenly Kerr swept in, sat down at the opposite end of a long table and said, "I've been watching you. I like you. I understand you have an election coming up. Do you need any financial help?"

Pearson said, yes, he did need help. Kerr then slapped the top of the table with the palms of his hands and without another word left the room. That was the last time Pearson saw Kerr, but according to one observer, the money came pouring in.

The mantle of key man with access on Capitol Hill has since

passed to Senator Russell Long of Louisiana, who became chairman of the Senate Finance Committee in 1966. Long has admitted candidly that he funnels oil industry contributions to needy senators in return for their votes on certain issues. Senator Thomas Dodd was one recipient of oil money from Long.

In 1969, it was revealed that Harold M. McClure, president of the Independent Petroleum Association of America, an oil lobby organization, had consulted occasionally with key staffers in Long's office about "who is good and who is bad" before deciding on oil industry contributions. McClure once gave $2,000 to be distributed to candidates of Long's choosing. A federal grand jury in Baltimore found that the money had gone to Maryland Senator Daniel B. Brewster, having first passed the Maryland Democratic Central Committee, which was financing Brewster's unsuccessful reelection bid.

For years the Republican key man with access on the Hill was Senator Everett Dirksen. He was a channel for many special interests, among them oil and gas, timber, utilities, mining, insurance, savings and loan, and banking groups. His 1962 reelection campaign was financed in large part by pharmaceutical company executives out of gratitude for his fight against drug industry control legislation. In fact, Dirksen's office was often used to promote drug industry views on the Hill, part of which included the distribution of campaign funds to sympathetic legislators.

Dirksen was also the beneficiary of a fund, held in a special bank account, which was used to pay some of the senator's television, radio, advertisement, benefit ticket and other expenses. The donors, most of them officials of the interests he served, supposedly contributed "from the heart." Mrs. Dirksen kept the books on the fund, which produced $10,000 to $12,000 per year and on which no taxes were paid.

The heirs to Johnson, Kerr and Dirksen no longer have the power they once had over political finances. Their "buying power" has diminished because of more intense scrutiny by the press, because of the 1971 law, but most of all because of the "Class of 1958," a large group of senators elected that year who have refused to play the old political games. This new breed began taking over the reins of Senate power by 1964. One veteran Hill staffer recalls Senator William Proxmire (Class of 1958) proclaiming to

LBJ what an extraordinary group had just been elected to the Senate that year by both parties. Senator Kerr, who overheard the conversation, is supposed to have added, "Yes, and who the hell can make any deals with this kind of people!"

Key men with access are also found among the various national Republican and Democratic campaign committees. In the GOP, for instance, the chairman of the RNC has traditionally been a good fund raiser among the party faithful. Ray Bliss, Rogers C. B. Morton and Senator Robert Dole would be typical. The chairman of the Republican National Finance Committee, which is the heart and soul of the parent RNC, has also traditionally been a well-known businessman noted for his ability to raise money. Typical examples are J. Clifford Folger, Ralph Cordiner, Lucius D. Clay and Jeremiah Milbank, Jr.

In the National Republican Congressional Committee and the National Republican Senatorial Committee, the key men currently are, respectively, Jack Calkins and Congressmen Robert H. Michel and Bob Wilson, and Buehl Berentson and Senator Peter H. Dominick. Calkins is a professional fund raiser and Berentson is a former director of the GOP's Governors' Association. Michel, Wilson and Dominick are influential legislators whose power stems in part from their power to dispense campaign funds.

In the Democratic party, the chairman and treasurer of the DNC are usually both picked because they are key people with access. Robert Strauss and Matthew McCloskey are typical examples. Virtually all 110 national committeemen and committeewomen in the party are also selected for the job because of their money-raising abilities.

The key men in the Democratic Senatorial Campaign Committee are Frank ("Nordy") Hoffmann and Senator Daniel Inouye, and in the Democratic National Congressional Committee, Congressman Thomas P. ("Tip") O'Neill, Jr., and, until recently, Kenneth Harding. Harding is the son of Victor Hunt ("Cap") Harding, who, like his son, served many years as the committee's executive director. Both father and son worked for one of the Hill's most venerable key men with access, Congressman Michael Kirwan of Ohio.

For many years, Kirwan, who died in 1970, was chairman of

both the House Appropriations Subcommittee on Public Works, known as the "Pork Barrel," and the Democratic National Campaign Committee. The combination gave him extraordinary power and leverage over candidates in need of campaign funds.

Kirwan was the last of the old-time, Harding-style politicians. He believed that all money as a matter of course came and went with a quid pro quo attached to it. A casual glance, for instance, at the guest list of the DNCC annual dinner would give a good indication of what kind of legislation was coming out of his committee that year. He came from the political school that barely recognized Republicans at all and divided Democrats into five or six categories, ranging from a high of friendly cronies to a low of eastern liberal intellectuals.

He was very much a part of the old Sam Rayburn–John McCormack House leadership clique, sometimes known as "The Board of Education." Nearly every day, immediately after the House adjourned, all these politicians, plus assorted lobbyists and a few other cronies, would climb into the Speaker's Cadillac and repair to a downtown Washington hotel for an evening of high-stakes poker. The air was blue with cigar smoke, and it was understood that the lobbyists were supposed to lose. It was in this atmosphere that many critical legislative decisions were made.

Kirwan was not above reinforcing his prejudices, which grew in strength around the poker table, by giving or withholding campaign funds. He once denied campaign funds to Congressman John Foley of Maryland because Foley had the effrontery to introduce a bill seeking to preserve the Chesapeake and Ohio Canal as a national monument without first going through his subcommittee. In another instance, he short-counted campaign funds to Congressman Joseph Vigorito of Pennsylvania because Vigorito made the mistake of demonstrating that a Kirwan-backed canal and reservoir scheme in eastern Ohio was a colossal waste of money.

Congressman Thomas L. Ashley once asked Kirwan to include in his legislation a project favorable to Ashley's district. But Kirwan appeared not to be interested. All he talked about was the annual DNCC $100-a-plate dinner. Kirwan thought Ashley should sell several tables' worth of tickets back in his district, but Ashley missed the point because, although a Democrat, his district was full of Republicans.

Later, after the dinner had been held and as public works legislation was about to be considered, Ashley went back to Kirwan because he saw that his project was omitted. Kirwan again began talking about the recently completed dinner.

Ashley: "But you're not talking about my project."

Kirwan: "We *are* talking about your project."

He then handed Ashley a bunch of tickets to the dinner just past. Ashley got the point, sold the tickets back in his district, and his project was included in the legislation.

Kirwan never failed to support his friends, even if he had to bend the rules a bit. Traditionally, congressional committees stay out of primary fights; they usually distribute their funds only as the general election is getting under way. But Kirwan had the habit of giving campaign funds to those friends of his who had tough primary fights (but no general election fights) the day after the primary.

The style in which the national and congressional committees operate varies considerably. The Republicans, for instance, have developed a smoothly efficient fund-raising machine that regularly produces enough funds to cover both off-year party overheads and election-year needs. All the GOP campaign committees operate with a minimum of friction between them. Indeed, they live within yards of each other on Capitol Hill. The RNC, including the Finance Committee, concentrates on the national election; the Boosters raise money for nonincumbents; and the House and Senate campaign committees worry about reelecting those already in office. On entering any one of these offices, one is struck by the similarity in decor, dress, hair styles, noise level and accent to a branch office of, say, Union Carbide or Bethlehem Steel.

The Democratic party committees, on the other hand, operate in an atmosphere of chaos and anarchy. There always seems to be a sense of crisis among them, and while the decor and dress are like their GOP counterparts, the hair styles, noise level and accent are more that of a Woodstock nation or a union meeting hall.

For years the Democratic National Committee has fought with the two congressional campaign committees over jurisdiction, areas of authority and how much one or the other should get from a joint fund-raising effort. The breach was at its worst during the Johnson years because the President's men were siphoning off all the money they could for the 1968 reelection campaign. The quarrel has been patched up somewhat but a residue of suspicion still exists—epitomized by the fact that the two congressional committees are located on Capitol Hill, but that the DNC (long housed in the Watergate complex in Foggy Bottom) is located in downtown Washington several miles away.

Most of the money for all these committees comes in from fund-raising dinners. The Democratic congressional committees hold a joint $500-a-plate dinner in May or June each year, and the proceeds are split 55 percent to the House committee and 45 percent to the Senate committee. The dinner is usually well attended by lobbyists and federal employees.

In addition to seeking individual gifts from Fat Cats, the DNC raises funds through both a "Sponsors' Club," a descendant of the President's Club, and "Participating Memberships," which is designed to appeal to middle-income contributors.

Mass mailings are also a good source of funds, now that the names, form letters and the inflow and outflow are all computerized. The DNC often buys subscription lists for approximately $100 per 1,000 names, and if the return is greater than 1 percent, then a profit is realized. Each contributor's name goes onto a master list which, if not used too often, will produce a 35 to 50 percent response. Typical lists include those of Marboro Books, Brentano's and UNICEF, the *Bulletin of Atomic Scientists, American Scholar, House Beautiful, Progressive* and *Ramparts* magazines. Two of the most lucrative sources for Democratic funds, the National Committee for an Effective Congress and the Americans for Democratic Action, do not share their lists with the DNC.

The Republican committees hold one $1,000-a-plate fund-raising dinner a year, the proceeds of which are divided equally between the national, House and Senate committees. In a good year (which usually means a Republican in the White House) $2 million can be cleared from it. The Boosters have another affair, run jointly by the House and Senate committees, which raises another $1.5 million. One third of it goes to help elect new GOP senators, and two thirds to help elect new GOP congressmen.

RN Associates, through various Fat Cat functions, raises another $2 million or so each year. The Sustaining Fund, a kind of subscription for the party faithful designed to underwrite over-heads, brings in an astonishingly good $3.2 million or so a year. Even more extraordinary, the party's *Newsletter,* a partisan and often bloody-minded weekly for the truly committed, brings in over $2.5 million from subscriptions.

When a party holds the White House it is relatively easy for any of its campaign committees to raise funds; when out, it is quite difficult indeed. All the national and congressional GOP commit-tees, for instance, could raise only $3.3 million and $6.5 million in 1962 and 1966, respectively, years when the party was out of power. But in 1970 they could raise nearly $11 million, mostly because of White House pull. The Democrats were exceedingly fat until 1966–67 but went $9 million or so into debt in 1968. In 1970 the national and congressional Democratic committees could raise only $3.5 million, the poverty level of national political finance.

Oddly enough, both parties between 1968 and 1972 used Nixon and Agnew as their favorite selling theme. A standard fund-raising letter sent out by the DNC during this period, for instance, gave two reasons why good Democrats should give to the party:

One is President Nixon
The other is Vice-President Agnew.

Nick Kostopulos, a DNC fund raiser, believes that Agnew cannot tone down because, he says, if he does "some contributors will feel they aren't getting their money's worth." Ted Henshaw, research director of the DNCC, said with slight envy in his voice, "He's a helluva hatchet man!"

The Republicans, quite obviously, see their leaders in a different light. Lee Nunn of the NRSC exclaimed to me in 1970: "It takes something good to sell and we've got Agnew now. He's the best!" After a moment of thought, he added, "Hell, he's tops!"

Since the House and Senate campaign committees of both parties are located in government-owned buildings, all the fund raising, claim the committee leaders, actually takes place down-town in public hotels, since to solicit funds on government prop-erty is against the law. To be sure, the attention-gathering fund-raising dinners are held on neutral ground, but in truth the wooing of individual contributors, whether Fat Cat or union official, mostly takes place in the government buildings on Capitol Hill.

Nordy Hoffmann tells the story of an elderly couple who walked into the DSCC offices in the Old Senate Office Building and asked if each could contribute to the committee. Hoffmann did not know the couple but said yes, figuring each would be good for $100 or so. In fact, each gave $5,000, much to Hoffmann's surprise. He told the story to illustrate that there is never a dull moment in his job, but unintentionally it was an admission that he, and no doubt his counterparts as well, raise their money in the offices in which they work.

Each committee dispenses its funds in a different manner. The national committee of the party in control of the White House is used as the personal tool of the President—to engineer his own reelection, to help elect favorites to office, or to help defeat those he dislikes. RNC funds in 1970, for example, went to help defeat Democratic Senator Albert Gore of Tennessee and Republican Senator Charles Goodell of New York, two particularly prickly administration critics.

The National Republican Congressional Committee has devised a complicated formula to determine how much a nominee for office receives after the primary. In 1970, incumbents in non-marginal districts (55 percent or more of the vote) received $4,000, while freshmen congressmen and those in marginal districts received $7,000. In addition to this money, the committee also underwrote some of the television, radio and newsletter costs.

In the Democratic National Congressional Committee, contributions are based on political need only. A maximum of $5,000 is given for close races and nothing for safe seats. Henshaw believes that $5,000 in the right campaign can mean the difference between winning and losing. In the 1969 special elections, Congressmen John Melcher of Montana won by approximately 2,100 votes, David Obey of Wisconsin by 4,055, Robert Roe of New Jersey by less than 1,000, and Michael Harrington of Massachusetts by approximately 5,000. Henshaw is convinced that his committee's contributions made the difference.

In the National Republican Senatorial Committee, certain seats are "targeted," usually about half of those being contested. The rest are abandoned as safe Democratic, and the Republican challenger gets nothing, perhaps a token amount. A safe GOP incumbent can count on $10,000 from the committee, while most nonincumbents receive between $25,000 and $30,000. In 1970, however, Senator John Tower, who was distributing the funds, was accused of favoring conservative Republican candidates over liberal Republicans. For instance, through the committee he gave over $72,000 to George Bush, unsuccessful candidate for senator from Texas. In contrast, liberal incumbent Charles Goodell received only $5,000. Josiah Spaulding, the liberal and personable kamikaze GOP challenger to Senator Edward Kennedy the same year, received only $1,500.

The Democratic Senatorial Campaign Committee is particularly vague about the distribution of its money, but it appears from what records are available that an incumbent Democratic senator up for reelection receives about $10,000, of which $9,000 is a drawing account, the remainder of which is specifically to be used for travel. This sum is invariably augmented by labor union funds, sometimes contributed directly to the candidate, sometimes earmarked through the committee.

These committees are the ones in which earmarked money is often seen. The favorite reason to earmark the contributions is still the desire for anonymity. When I brought the subject up to Nordy Hoffmann, he replied, "We know that. Hell, we're not stupid!"

But to some campaign-committee fund raisers earmarking is beginning to look less and less attractive. Every earmarked dollar detracts that amount from the power of the committee to exercise its own discretion and wisdom in apportioning the money. Also, more and more earmarked money comes with strings attached to it. Sometimes it smacks of bribery. Hoffmann tells the story of a man who came into his office with a suitcase filled with $20,000 in cash. The man was willing to contribute the money to a certain senator if the senator would push a particular piece of legislation. Hoffmann threw the man out of his office—doubtless a painful experience to a conscientious moneyman.

VIII

Lobby Money

The nature of lobbying has undergone a change over the years, and no better illustration is possible than comparing the individualistic styles of two once-prominent lobbyists in California politics: Arthur H. Samish and Jess Unruh.

For years lobbyists have been such a powerful force in California's legislative process that they have come to be known collectively as the "Third House." From 1932 until 1949 the dean of Sacramento's business lobbyists was Arthur Samish, who represented at one time or another a variety of special interests: brewers, liquor dealers, racetracks, cigarette manufacturers, restaurants, bus companies, railroads, banks, taxicab companies and chemical firms.

Senator Estes Kefauver once described Samish as "a combination of Falstaff, Little Boy Blue and Machiavelli, crossed with an eel." Physically, Samish was enormous, standing over six feet two inches, and weighing close to 300 pounds. He had the bland look of an *enfant terrible* about to play a prank on his nurse. Samish's cynicism and arrogance were legendary. He often boasted that he could tell on first meeting whether a man preferred "a baked potato, a girl or money." One of the best ways to test the latter, he once mused, would be to scatter a handful of coins on the Capitol rotunda, speculating that "two bucks" might "start a riot." On another occasion, when his power to influence the lawmakers was challenged by the governor, he declared, "I am the governor of the legislature! To hell with the governor of the state!"

Samish's major client during these years was the California State

Brewers Institute, a trade association comprising eleven of the fourteen breweries in the state, and accounting for 86 percent of the production there. The members of the association paid, among other assessments, five cents per barrel into a special bank account over which Samish had complete control. Between 1932 and 1938, more than $935,000 was raised from this assessment.

Most of the money went to elect the "right guys," in Samish's words, men who were "honest, outstanding officials that subscribe to the temperate use of beer, wine, spirits and other things." In his testimony before the Kefauver Committee hearings in 1951, Samish admitted that 95 percent of his campaign contributions were made in cash and that he kept no records either of how much money the institute made available to him or who received the contributions. "I take the recapitulation, the bank statement and the canceled checks," he said, "and I throw them in the waste-basket."

There was no doubt, however, about Samish's influence. The five-cent assessment brought in an average $150,000 per year which, in prewar days, represented a significant percentage of the total campaign costs of electing the entire California legislature. In some districts a $500 contribution might represent as much as half of a candidate's costs of running for the Assembly, or perhaps one fifth the average cost of a state senate campaign. With the total number of legislators in both houses never exceeding 140, $150,000 in contributions could almost buy the lot. Samish became so powerful that he was known at various times as either "the million-dollar lobbyist" or the "secret boss of California" who held the legislature in the palm of his hand.

In 1938, there was an investigation of the California legislature and the results were incorporated into a report prepared by ex-FBI man Howard R. Philbrick. The report was so devastating that it was almost immediately suppressed, and copies of it soon became a collector's item. Among many of its charges, the report found:

> The principal source of corruption [in the legislature] has been money pressure. The principal offender among the lobbyists has been Arthur H. Samish. . . . Lobbying of the type represented by Mr. Samish, as distinguished from open legislative representation, has been a major corrupting influence.

Somehow Samish survived this charge and continued to dominate California's legislature for another decade. His decline can be dated from 1949 when he allowed himself to be photographed by a national magazine with a small puppet on his knee. The caption had Samish saying, "How are you today, Mr. Legislature?" Californians were sufficiently provoked by this to demand that the state government pass, as it subsequently did, several laws curbing the behavior of lobbyists, particularly their enthusiasm for not reporting expenditures. Several years later Samish became embroiled with the IRS and eventually went to jail for income tax law violations.

He was to be succeeded by Jesse Unruh, a Democratic member of the California Assembly from 1955 and its Speaker from 1961 to 1968. Unruh was of a different stripe than Samish. Technically he was not even a lobbyist but a powerful wheeler-dealer legislator who acted as a focal point for lobby money. Furthermore, despite his reputation for ruthlessness and brutal political maneuvering, Unruh unquestionably left the system better than he found it.

Unruh was always ambivalent in his attitude toward the Third House. He recognized that, in the absence of any strong statewide party system, lobbyists exercised far more influence than their size and economic power warranted. Yet, while he took their money out of necessity, he seldom produced more than a fraction of the rewards they expected.

He developed his "tangled thicket theory" in dealing with lobbyists: a small group of legislators, he believed, sold out to the lobbyists while another group, the moralists, took another path; both courses, he thought, were ineffectual. But the great majority of legislators of which he was a part, the pragmatists who wanted to accomplish something while still retaining their principles, hacked out their own tortuous path through the thicket of lobbyist pressures, constituents' needs and legislative limitations. Others call this route "muddying the waters," but whatever it was called Unruh never lost his skepticism of lobbyists. "If you can't eat their food, drink their booze, screw their women and then vote against them, you have no business being up here," he was once quoted as saying. Nor did he ever lose his appreciation of adequate campaign funds. "Money," he once said, "is the mother's milk of politics."

Unruh's political skill at controlling the course of events in the

Assembly soon attracted the attention of Fat Cat contributors. They began directing their contributions to him for distribution among other legislators, knowing on the one hand that Unruh could direct the funds to better effect, and hoping on the other hand that their money tied this most astute politician to them.

Among those who contributed heavily to Unruh in this manner were millionaire Beverly Hills Volkswagen dealer Manning J. Post, Howard Ahmanson, Benjamin Swig, Edwin Pauley, Bart Lytton, Louis Warschaw of Harvey Aluminum, and executives of oil and insurance companies.

The arrangement worked well for both parties: Unruh had money for the candidates of his choice, and thus soon acquired a near stranglehold over the Assembly, while the Fat Cats found themselves with a relatively sympathetic legislature and occasional business from the state. Ahmanson's National American Fire Insurance Company, for instance, was awarded an exclusive five-year $3.5 million contract to write fire policies on all Cal-Vet homes in the state, despite cries of anguish from 238 small insurance companies that had previously shared the business.

After becoming Speaker of the Assembly, Unruh refined his money-gathering efforts by setting up a secret slush fund for Fat Cat contributors. This fund subsequently drew so much criticism that Unruh abolished it in 1964. In its place, however, he created the California Committee for Better Government, which was simply a less secret slush fund with a high-sounding name. Through this committee and various Unruh Dinner Committees, the Speaker was able to continue his fund raising and dispensing activities unimpeded by the glare of significant disclosure. By his own reckoning, Unruh was doling out as much as $365,000 per year at the height of his powers. This kind of money at the state level can buy a lifetime of loyalty from struggling politicians.

Like Samish, Unruh was reluctant to account for his political financing activities. He was once asked what he planned to do with funds raised at a political dinner, and he replied, "Spend it."

"How?" he was asked.

"That's my business," replied the Speaker.

Despite his political gyrations, Unruh ended up improving the system by weakening the power of the Third House. The lobbyists would have preferred to continue contributing directly to candidates, but Unruh's power was such that he would not allow it. Thus, by having lobby funds channeled through him, he took the credit rather than the special interests. Furthermore, there were so many lobbyists funneling their money through the Speaker that, even had he wished, Unruh could not possibly have satisfied their legislative desires. As a result, the implied political debt to the Fat Cat contributors was reduced significantly. The legislators, in turn, found themselves indebted to Unruh, not the lobbyists, and most cast their votes as the Speaker instructed them to. But that was not always in the best interests of the lobbyists.

He also improved the system by creating a large professional class of legislative assistants. These experts, similar to those in the Legislative Reference Service in the Library of Congress, answer only to the Assembly and Senate. Their breadth of knowledge and lack of vested interests cut the ground from under the lobbyists who for years had flattered themselves into thinking that they were an indispensable source of wisdom and technical information for the state legislature.

Business money is the lifeblood of American campaign finance for Republicans and Democrats alike. Historically most of this money has come from individual Fat Cats in the business community. Within the past two decades, however, an increasing amount of business money has been coming from "political action committees." These committees, which are usually organized to represent the political interests of a specific industry, raise their campaign war chests from senior executives in the various businesses within a particular industry. This money is then contributed in the name of the committee (rather than an individual) to candidates who are or might be sympathetic to that industry's points of view or problems.

These committees appeared on the scene in response to several political developments. One was the formation of the labor-oriented Committee on Political Education in 1955, whose contributions of both money and manpower to prolabor candidates, many businessmen believed, were undercutting the voice of industry in the halls of Congress and state legislatures. Many of these same businessmen, furthermore, were disturbed by what they believed to be the willingness of postwar governments, both federal and state, to move into spheres of action such as health, welfare and commerce, which had previously been the private preserve of "free enterprise."

One of the first groups to organize politically was doctors. Serious pressure for some form of national health insurance began in Truman's administration; the proposed legislation, however, was decisively defeated with the help of massive lobbying by the American Medical Association. By the 1960's the pressure had once again built up for some form of government-backed medical plan for the aged. Since it was and still is against the law for a tax-exempt group such as the AMA to contribute campaign funds to candidates, the association's leaders in 1961 set up the American Medical Political Action Committee (or AMPAC) which is technically independent of the AMA, in the same manner that COPE is technically independent of the AFL-CIO.

AMPAC had two major objectives: one, to educate the public to its point of view, and the other to provide direct financial aid to candidates for public office. Its money comes from several sources: contributions from individuals, called "hard dollars," and corporate support from the AMA or medical supply firms, known as "soft dollars." The committee claims that for every dollar spent at the federal level, at least five dollars more is raised and spent at the state level. In one election, for instance, former Republican Senator Thruston B. Morton of Kentucky was supposed to have received $5,000 from AMPAC and another $80,000 from state and local medical PAC's.

Exactly how much a candidate gets is not divulged because AMPAC will often route its contribution first through a state medical committee, which follows laws that usually do not require complete disclosure. Prior to 1972, some of the money was routed through the Physicians Committee for Good Government, a non-reporting D.C. committee which used the money to pay for dinner tickets, speaking honoraria, and a wide range of lobbying activities. Generally, AMPAC contributions have gone to "pro free-enterprise medicine" candidates at the federal and state levels, particularly those who have some control over the passage of legislation.

Between 1962 and 1965 AMPAC spent about $850,000 at the federal level, and perhaps another $3 million at the state and local levels, to fight Medicare legislation. All this money went for naught with the passage of the Medicare bill in 1965. But AMPAC is far from powerless. It had sufficient strength to defeat the nomination of Dr. John Knowles in 1969 as the number-two man in the Department of Health, Education and Welfare.

Part of its growing power lies in the amount of money it now dispenses at the federal level—from $400,000 in 1964 to nearly $700,000 in 1968, with another $3.5 million from state and local medical PAC's. For 1972 AMPAC's expenditures in federal elections topped $1 million dollars.

In 1963 another business lobby joined the fray: the Business-Industry Political Action Committee, or BIPAC. This committee owes its existence to the success of COPE. It was founded by senior executives of the National Association of Manufacturers in the belief that Congress governs best when controlled by probusiness lawmakers. Unlike AMPAC, BIPAC does not have state or local affiliates; it limits its gift-giving exclusively to congressional candidates. It is quite conservative in its viewpoint and tends to concentrate its funds on old-guard Republican and Democratic incumbents in both the House and Senate who have marginal seats (less than 55 percent of the vote).

In 1968, $2,000 donations went to such conservative Republican congressmen as Ben Blackburn of Georgia, Earl Landgrebe of Indiana, Jerry Pettis of California and Chalmers Wylie of Ohio. Democratic Congressmen William Jennings Bryan Dorn of South Carolina, G. V. ("Sonny") Montgomery of Mississippi and David Satterfield of Virginia also received the same amount. Senators Bellmon of Oklahoma, Cotton of New Hampshire, Dominick of Colorado, Goldwater of Arizona and Packwood of Oregon received $5,000 apiece. Altogether, BIPAC spent nearly $500,000 in 1968, up from $200,000 spent in 1964.

Because of the relatively high cost of campaigning, BIPAC finds that it is besieged with requests from many other candidates for funds. A review board in the committee's head office in New York City decides who shall get money and how much. A check is then forwarded "on behalf of the businessmen of the state and nation." Lest the recipient begin making antibusiness remarks, BIPAC requires that the check be acknowledged in writing. Sometimes the decision-making process can be excruciatingly painful. For instance, in 1968, BIPAC contributed to Republican liberal Richard Schweiker, who had a 91 percent COPE rating, because he was preferable to the incumbent, and very liberal, Democratic senator, Joseph S. Clark.

In addition to the medical profession and the business world in general, a third group has made its power felt in American political finance, namely the banking industry. While technically it is against the law for any national bank to make a contribution in a federal election, many bankers have skirted the intent of the law by establishing committees that are supposed to be independent and nonpartisan.

The "League for Good Government" in Seattle, Washington, for instance, is a front for banking contributions. In April, 1970, it circulated a memo suggesting that all bank officers in the area making between $12,000 and $30,000 kick in between $56 and $210 per year. The memo suggested that all contributions be mailed to a post office box which turned out to be the same address as the National Bank of Commerce of Seattle.

In October, 1970, Congressman Patman wrote to the Attorney General stating among other things that the Manufacturers Hanover Trust Company of New York required its top officers to contribute a percentage of their salaries into a special account run by the bank's controller; from there the money is contributed to friendly candidates. In Texas, a number of bankers have set up a political fund in which the contributing formula is based on the dollar reserve of each bank. The fund tries to disassociate itself from the tax-exempt Texas Bankers Association, but its literature states that "funds will not be expended contrary to any official position of the Association." In Ohio, key executives in the Central National Bank of Cleveland have set up a "Good Government Program" in which political contributions are handled, at least in part, on a payroll deduction basis.

In November, 1969, officers of the Marine Midland Trust Company of Western New York held a meeting in Toronto, Canada, to explore ways of setting up a political fund. A memo from the bank's senior vice-president to the president during the meeting stated:

Those bankers who have successful programs all state that [collecting funds] cannot be done on a voluntary basis. A certain degree of persuasion has to occur. I think this could be accomplished successfully if our officers at all levels were made aware of the legal problems involved, as well as the significant impact upon our earnings of the level of our public funds.

The reference to "the legal problems involved" apparently referred to federal legislation pending at the time which proposed closing certain loopholes in the Bank Holding Company Act of 1956; and the reference to "level of public funds" apparently referred to the bank's ability to attract deposits of public monies as a direct result of what it contributed politically.

In 1970, a nationwide fund-raising effort by commercial banks was organized under the name of Bankers Political Action Committee, or BankPAC. Its purpose, according to one draft solicitation letter, is "to support financially the campaigns for the U.S. Congress [which] have demonstrated and expressed a real understanding of the proper function and structure of our banking system and its necessary part and contribution to our society and its economy." More specifically, BankPAC opposes the hyperactive chairman of the House Banking and Currency Committee, Wright Patman, who harbors well-developed suspicions of all bankers and their motives. It was Patman, for instance, who introduced the loophole-closing legislation to the Bank Holding Company Act of 1956 that so upset the nation's commercial bankers.

BankPAC's organizers were familiar with the ways of operating within the letter, if not the spirit, of the then existing campaign finance reporting laws. Its solicitation letter suggested, for instance, that checks of $99 or less be written ("to avoid Federal reporting requirements"). It also expressed the view that such contributions, while "peanuts" to the individual, would collectively carry great influence in legislative circles.

In the 1970 Congressional elections BankPAC rifled its contributions of $35,000 to twenty-one of the thirty-five members of the House Banking and Currency Committee. An additional $46,050 went to six of the ten Democratic, and three of the five Republican, members of the House Rules Committee which decides if and when legislation is to be cleared for floor action; some of the funds also went to influential members of the House Ways and Means

Committee, which writes tax legislation. BankPAC delayed disbursal of these funds long enough to prevent them from becoming a matter of public record until after the November 3 election. In fact, in the three-way Virginia senatorial race, it waited until it was clear that Independent Harry F. Byrd, Jr., was the victor before it mailed him a $5,000 check.

When eyebrows were raised over these contributions, thirteen recipients decided to return the money to BankPAC. As a result, the committee found itself with a larger nest egg than anticipated for the 1972 election. This time the money was spent with more sophistication.

The oil lobby is such a large source of campaign contributions that there is no one major spigot through which the money flows to candidates. Some of the funds are directed to candidates by executives of the American Petroleum Institute and the Independent Petroleum Association of America. A former president of the latter claims that he, alone, contributed $90,000 to various campaigns in 1968. Some oil money, as previously noted, flows through the likes of Senator Russell Long, as it did through Senators Johnson and Kerr and Speaker Sam Rayburn in the past. Most oil money is concentrated on federal elections. No President of recent memory has been anti-oil; about one third of the Senate and House are hard-core pro-oil, so most of the money is spent to keep friends happy and win over enough fence-sitters to gain a majority.

At the heart of the industry's power is its reputation as having unlimited campaign cash available. In 1956, officials of the top twenty-nine oil companies gave a recorded $345,000 to Republicans and nearly $15,000 to Democrats in the general election. This does not include the nearly half-million dollars given by three oil families—the Mellons, Pews and Rockefellers. By 1968, the industry's contribution had risen to nearly $800,000. Yet, many observers consider these figures to be only the tip of the iceberg.

On occasion oil money can be brutally frank. In 1956, for example, an oil lobbyist tried to bribe Senator Francis Case of South Dakota with a $2,500 cash contribution in return for his vote on natural gas legislation. Case was outraged and the ensuing scandal forced President Eisenhower to veto the legislation, a move he very much wished to avoid.

The behavior of three politicians illustrates the oil lobby's power. First John F. Kennedy, long a critic of oil's privileged position and one who voted to reduce the depletion allowance, equivocated on the subject in 1960 because he needed campaign funds from the oil lobby.

Then Eugene McCarthy voted consistently against oil industry privileges during most of his first term in the Senate; but in 1964 he cast his first vote in favor of depletion, and from then on until he left the Senate in 1970 he generally favored the oil industry's position. He is supposed to have raised about $40,000 for his 1968 Presidential campaign in one day at the Petroleum Club in Houston.

Finally, Edmund Muskie was long in favor of the Machiasport development which would bring cheaper fuel into New England— a move opposed by most of the oil industry. When election time 1972 rolled around, however, his criticism of the oil industry and support for Machiasport dropped off to a whisper.

The oil lobby is the most powerful part of an even larger pressure group known as the highway lobby. The combined power of the highway builders and the oil, rubber and automobile industries account for no less than 16 percent of the nation's Gross National Product. The power of this lobby is formidable. For instance, in 1968, legislation permitting wider, heavier and longer trucks on the nation's interstate highway system was under consideration in Congress. To the bill's backers, mostly trucking interests, its passage would mean that the cost of handling goods would be reduced, that consumer costs would be lowered, and that highway revenues would be increased. To opponents, the passage of the "big truck bill," as it was (and still is) called, would reduce safety clearances on all roads (thus rendering them obsolescent), increase hazards to cars, and pour more money into the Highway Trust Fund when the revenue could be better used on alternate methods of transportation.

To ensure the passage of this legislation, the Truck Operators Nonpartisan Committee, or TONC, an arm of the American Trucking Association, which represents most of the nation's long- and short-haul trucking firms, began shooting large contributions to key legislators as far back as two years before the bill came

under active consideration. Eleven of the thirteen ranking Democrats on the House Public Works Committee received contributions ranging from $500 to $3,000. Five high-ranking Republicans
on the committee also received comparable contributions.

Committee chairman George Fallon of Maryland, according to
TONC's report filed with the Clerk of the House, received $1,000
at a testimonial dinner, but nowhere did Fallon's report reflect the
same fact. He listed in his report $6,000 received from the same
dinner but did not break down the sum into specifics. He simply
stated that "No tickets were sold for more than $25." If true, then
TONC bought at least 40 tickets.

In addition, TONC rifled campaign contributions to key men on
the House Rules Committee, which approved the bill for floor
action after a very brief hearing. Also receiving contributions were
members of the House Ways and Means Committee and Senate
Finance Committee (both of which have jurisdiction over highway
use tax rates), the Senate Public Works Committee, the House
Interior and Foreign Commerce Committee, the Senate Commerce
Committee, and the House and Senate Appropriations Committees. Four powerful legislators who received large contributions
from TONC, it was later revealed, were unopposed for reelection
that year.

One of the leaders of the opposition to the bill was Republican
Congressman Fred Schwengel of Iowa. Schwengel, among other
things, is a well-known Lincoln buff and, at the time, was president
of the Capitol Historical Society. In February, 1968, recalls
Schwengel, several trucking executives mentioned during a ban-
quet that the Brooks Brothers suit in which President Lincoln was
assassinated was up for sale. One of the executives suggested that
the truckers' might put up the money so that the suit would come
into the possession of the government rather than another private
owner. Shortly thereafter, the Capitol Historical Society was presented with a $25,000 check which it used to purchase the suit.
Schwengel then presented the items to the Interior Department for
placement among Lincoln memorabilia in Ford's Theatre.

Four months later an executive of the Iowa Truckers Association, in the course of a conversation with Schwengel, brought up
the subject of Lincoln. The truckers, he said, "did all right by you
on that Lincoln suit." Schwengel replied that, if the truckers

believed that buying the Lincoln suit was part of a quid pro quo for his vote in favor of the bill truck bill, they were quite mistaken.

Schwengel continued to oppose the legislation and was instrumental in its eventual defeat. But the truckers have not given up. Several years later they came up with a "big bus bill" which they hoped and still hope to have passed with the help of more large contributions to the right legislators. Schwengel believes that it is nothing more than a stalking horse for another big truck bill.

The second example of the highway lobby's power concerns the defeat of Proposition 18 in California in 1970. Proposition 18 was an amendment to the California constitution which would have allowed a city or county to devote up to 25 percent of its share of highway money, derived from vehicle or gas tax revenues, for mass transit systems or pollution control caused by motor vehicles. It was supported by every major conservation group, both gubernatorial candidates (Reagan and Unruh), the California League of Women Voters, the League of California Cities, the Los Angeles Chamber of Commerce, and every influential newspaper in the state. An indication of the support it enjoyed is reflected in the enthusiasm with which it passed the legislature: to get on the ballot requires a two-thirds vote in both the state Senate and Assembly; both houses, in fact, approved the measure overwhelmingly.

The highway lobby, however, was against Proposition 18, and it marshalled its forces under an organization entitled "Californians Against Street & Road Tax Trap." The thrust of the highway lobby's argument against the measure was that it was actually a tax-raising measure.

In its reports to the California Secretary of State, CASRTT listed its contributors, which were a good cross-section of the state's highway lobby: automobile clubs, oil companies, road contractors, rock, sand and asphalt suppliers, land development companies (The Irvine Company, Boise Cascade), paving companies, tire manufacturers, heavy equipment dealers, taxicab fleet owners, and construction unions. One of the reports listed four "anonymous" donors of $20,000, $30,000, $25,000 and $20,000, respectively. It was later revealed that the money had come from four big oil companies: Standard of California, Mobil, Gulf, and Union. Standard alone reported giving $75,000.

Altogether, CASRTT reported spending nearly $350,000 to defeat Proposition 18, and some observers believe the true figure, if indirect costs are taken into account, would be in excess of $1 million. In comparison, "Californians Against Smog," the major group supporting the proposition, raised $15,000 and spent $23,000. Its two biggest contributors were Kaiser Industries ($2,500) and the Tuberculosis and Respiratory Disease Association of California ($500).

Another powerful business group which spreads its money around is the milk producers' lobby, composed mostly of dairymen, milk cooperatives and milk processing companies. Their income, for the most part, is directly dependent on federal and state price support and marketing programs administered by various executive agencies.

Like BankPAC, this lobby has only been active in campaign financing since the 1970 election. In that year the Missouri-based Agriculture and Dairy Education Political Trust (ADEPT) and the Agricultural Cooperative Trust (ACT) raised $10,000 each from milk producers around the country for distribution among congressional candidates. The contributions of the San Antonio–based Trust for Agricultural Political Education (TAPE) and the Kentucky-based Trust for Special Political Agricultural Community Education (SPACE), however, dwarfed the other gifts. They raised over $535,000 and $100,000, respectively, for the 1970 campaign, most of the money coming from a voluntary one percent levy on milk sales.

Like the other business lobbies, the milk producer groups rifled their contributions to House and Senate members who they believed could help them best. TAPE, for instance, contributed $5,000 to Congressman W. R. Poage, chairman of the House Agriculture Committee, even though Poage had no opposition in either the primary or general election campaigns. Four other Democrats on the committee, two of whom had no opposition, also received large contributions as did the ranking Republican, Page Belcher. Several senators received as much as $10,000 apiece, among them Scott of Pennsylvania, Brock of Tennessee, Humphrey of Minnesota, Proxmire of Wisconsin and Muskie of

Maine. Altogether, no fewer than 96 House and 37 Senate candidates received contributions from the dairy producers.

In several instances the dairymen hedged their bets by giving to both sides. Lloyd Bentsen, Democratic candidate for U.S. senator from Texas, received a large contribution, as did his Republican opponent, George Bush. While the milk producers were giving $5,000 to Congressman Belcher, they were also contributing the same amount to his Democratic challenger. Milk money also went to both sides in the Indiana and Wyoming Senate races. The treasurer of TAPE at the time, Robert O. Isham, explained why his organization hedged its bets: "We hope to have a friend no matter which one is up there in Washington," he said.

In 1971, newsmen checking campaign financial reports filed with the Clerk of the House found that more than $200,000 from dairy groups had been funneled into at least 60 secret D.C. committees over the year. Many of the committees appear to have been organized in some haste; the address of one, for instance, turned out to be the location of a downtown Washington nightclub. Typical of the names used were "League of Dedicated Voters," "Supporters of the American Dream Committee," and "Volunteers Against Citizen Apathy." This money is believed to have found its way into the Republican party's 1972 campaign war chest.

The manner in which this money and other contributions were given raised speculation that a quid pro quo had been reached with the Nixon administration: that in return for a fat contribution the government would increase the milk price support level. Whether or not such an agreement was ever reached has never been proved, but the fact is the support level was raised in 1971, and the events leading up to that action indicate that it was, at best, a remarkable coincidence.

On March 22, 1971, TAPE contributed a total of $10,000 to four Republican campaign accounts. The next day, President Nixon and his Secretary of Agriculture, Clifford Hardin, met at the White House with a group of dairy industry leaders. They urged President Nixon and Secretary Hardin to reconsider the increase in the milk support price which Hardin had turned down two weeks previously. Hardin's original decision had been based on the belief that an increase would lead to overproduction and excessive government stockpiles.

The following day, March 24, SPACE contributed a total of $25,000 to four Republican committees. On March 25, Secretary Hardin announced that the milk price support level would be raised after all, from $4.66 per hundred pounds of fluid manufacturing milk to $4.93 per hundred.

Following this decision, the three big dairy lobbies, TAPE, SPACE and ADEPT, contributed another $287,000 to various secret committees which in turn funneled the money to the Republican party. ADEPT, whose announced purpose is "education," gave an additional $45,000 to nine GOP finance committees. All told, some $322,000 in dairymen contributions ended up in the Republican campaign coffers in 1971, in anticipation of the 1972 Presidential campaign.

The number of business lobbies does not end with AMPAC, BIPAC, BankPAC, the highway lobby and dairymen. In fact, there are so many business groups contributing money in such large quantities in American political campaigns that they now represent a major source of campaign funds for both parties. Fat Cats have long been the largest single source of funds for both Republican and Democratic parties at the federal and, to some extent, the state level. Mass mailings have long been the second most lucrative source, with business solicitations a distant third. Now organized business threatens to replace mass mailings as the second most important source of funds.

Thus, some of the other business groups deserve mention if for no other reason than to illustrate their size, power, tactics and idiosyncrasies.

Executives within Union Carbide Corporation, for example, have a program designed to encourage contributions into a central fund located in the firm's New York City head office. A small group of key company men then decides which candidates should receive contributions. A check is then mailed or hand-carried to the candidate along with a list of the names and addresses of the Carbide executives involved in the contribution. The list does not reflect any of the individuals' connections with the company, and it is left to the candidate how he should report the contribution.

The Union Carbide group tends to concentrate its funds on congressmen or senators who might be helpful. Representative

John Slack of West Virginia, for one, received $1,025 from twenty-five Carbide executives living in five different states in 1970. He represents a district in which Union Carbide is the largest employer. Carbide's contribution was Slack's third largest after the $1,500 he received from both COPE and Hughes Aircraft Corporation executives. Slack, it should be recalled, not only serves on the House Appropriations Committee but on the subcommittee that handles the Defense Department budget—of interest to both Union Carbide and Hughes Aircraft.

Surprisingly, while the Corrupt Practices Act of 1925 required that groups raising and disbursing funds in two or more states had to file reports regularly with the Clerk of the House, Union Carbide seemingly qualified for inclusion under the rules but never filed any reports at all. The existence of the Carbide fund was revealed only after extensive work undertaken by researchers supported by a grant from the Fund for Investigative Journalism.

Aerojet-General has raised large amounts of campaign funds over the past two decades although its program currently appears to have fallen on indifferent times. At the height of its activities in the 1964 election, Aerojet-General raised and spent around $136,-000. Part of the firm's activity was due to the fact that Aerojet-General's president, Dan Kimball, was also a leading Democratic party fund raiser at the time.

The General Tire division of the Aerojet-General complex still raises money from executives through its Good Citizenship Fund. In 1970 it reported acquiring over $21,000 from just thirty-one executives—an average of almost $700 per person.

In 1967, the Western States Meat Packers Association attempted to raise from $25 to $99 apiece from the executives of the 600 or so meat packing firms in western states. The fund-raising effort came at a time when Congress was considering two meat inspection bills. One of them, the weaker of the two and supported by the packers, offered federal aid to states willing to improve their inspection systems; the other, called the Smith-Foley Bill, which the industry opposed, sought to expand federal inspection to 6,000 plants now exempt because they do not sell across state lines.

The meat packers' funds, according to L. Blaine Lilijenquist, president and general manager of the association, were to be used in the 1968 campaign for the purpose of reelecting friendly congressmen and senators. When House Agriculture Committee chairman Poage heard of the fund-raising effort, he sent a strongly worded letter to Lilijenquist saying that such effort, no matter how well intentioned, would harm the passage of a good meat inspection bill. The association subsequently stopped its solicitation, but not before Congress passed the weaker of the two bills.

In September, 1966, Iowa Senator Jack Miller, of the Senate Select Committee on the Aging, introduced an amendment on nursing home reimbursement which would have benefited the owners of private nursing homes by giving them several billion dollars a year in federal subsidies under the Medicare program. Miller's amendment was modified in a House-Senate Conference Committee, but the nursing home lobby was still so pleased with the senator's effort that, three weeks after the original amendment was passed, a check for $2,500 was sent to Miller's reelection campaign committee. The check was drawn against the American Nursing Home Education and Political Action Committee, located in Alexandria, Virginia.

Over the years this lobby has contributed to other well-known legislators. It gave to Wayne Morse in 1968 because, in the words of one nursing home lobbyist, "if the Senate goes Democratic, he will be the chairman of a very powerful committee" (referring to the Senate Labor and Public Welfare Committee which handles legislation concerning nursing homes). The Senate went Democratic as expected in 1968 but, unfortunately for the nursing home lobby, Morse lost. Two years previously, ANHEPAC contributed $3,000 to Congressman Hale Boggs and smaller sums to eleven other members of the House Ways and Means Committee who had jurisdiction over Medicare and Medicaid legislation.

The Action Committee for Rural Electrification, or ACRE, supported by dues from rural electric cooperative employees, has been contributing funds to federal and state candidates since 1968. In that year it gave away over $88,000, mostly to candidates on the House and Senate Agriculture, Appropriations, Interior and Public Works Committees where rural electrification legislation is processed.

The Forest Products Political Education Committee, the contributing arm of America's timber lobby, also has rifled its money to good effect. It reported giving $500 in 1968 to Congressman

John McMillan, second in command at the time of the House Agriculture Committee and a leader in pro-timber lobby legislation. McMillan, however, failed to show the contribution on his report. Other recipients of the lobby's "education" money were members of the House Interior and Insular Affairs Committee and Ways and Means Committee, both vital to the passage of any lumber legislation.

In 1972, the Restaurateurs Political Action Committee, an arm of the National Restaurant Association, spread $23,000 around Capitol Hill during the summer months of the campaign. It gave $1,000 each to at least two congressmen who had no opponents in the November general election (and only one of whom had token opposition in the primary election). The contributions came at a time when Congress was considering a minimum wage bill, which restaurateurs generally oppose.

Some business lobbies contribute through committees which, on their face, do not reflect the true source of funds. General Electric, for instance, has its Effective Citizens Association. Textile manufacturers contribute through an organization named the Committee on American Principles. Merrill Lynch, Pierce, Fenner & Smith, Inc., the huge brokerage house, contributes through its Effective Government Association. The Government Improvement Group raises its money in sums of $100 or less, so no clear picture of who it represents has emerged. At one time GIG's treasurer was the registered lobbyist for the Rolled Zinc Manufacturers Association; another source claims GIG is a front for candy manufacturers who seek legislation allowing nonnutritive substances in their products.

Other businesses with similar campaign organizations, some of which have obscure names and some of which do not, include Procter & Gamble, The Ethyl Corporation, Republic Steel, Bethlehem Steel, U.S. Steel, Martin Marietta, Libby-Owens-Ford, Pittsburgh Plate Glass, Hughes Aircraft, McDonnell Douglas, Northrop, The Olin Corporation, Union Oil, Sterling Drug, Thiokol Chemical and Dow Chemical. As is readily evident, many of these companies are heavily dependent on the federal government for contracts.

For years the Cleveland-based firm of TRW, Inc., a company with many federal contracts, ran a Good Government Fund which contributed heavily to influential lawmakers. It differed from other funds in that it encouraged employees to have their contributions automatically deducted from their paychecks. In late 1971, Common Cause, the citizens' lobby, initiated a lawsuit against the firm, claiming that the Federal Election Campaign Act (which was actually not signed into law until early 1972) precluded such activity by both corporations and unions doing business with the government. TRW eventually agreed to dissolve its fund, return unspent contributions and stop soliciting political contributions from its employees.

This action appears to have had little effect on other corporate or union funds of this nature, for none were voluntarily closed down prior to the 1972 election. However, it did frighten opponents of reform sufficiently for them to rush legislation through the House of Representatives a month before election day designed to exempt corporations and labor unions from a ban on political contributions by government contractors. No hearings on the measure were held and debate on the floor of the House took up only five and one-half pages of the *Congressional Record*. Congress adjourned *sine die* before the Senate could consider the bill.

Business lobbies are also a major source of campaign funds at the state and local levels. Highly paid representatives of the liquor, insurance, banking, manufacturing and construction industries, as well as utilities, real estate, racetrack and highway interests, among others, can be found well entrenched in most state capitals, county court houses and city halls. In some 17 states it is not against the law for corporations to contribute to state and local campaigns; 46 states allow unions to make direct contributions. Furthermore, with the exception of perhaps half a dozen states, campaign finance laws at the state level are far more permissive than the federal law. Thus, there is seldom a need for front groups—"political action committees," "education associations" and so on—which are so numerous at the federal level.

The ties between business and politicians at the state and local levels are much more direct. It is not surprising when one considers that it is at these levels of American politics where most contracts are let, concessions granted, rates set and licenses issued.

Any state or local fund-raising effort will reflect the business-political tie. Examples are many but one will suffice. In April,

1970, a fund-raising "birthday celebration" was announced to honor Governor Marvin Mandel of Maryland. In reality, the event was held to eliminate Mandel's past campaign debts and to provide funds for his reelection race. Those attending represented typical businesses that support the thousands of such functions which are held every year throughout the country.

Contributing the maximum allowable $2,500 were such firms as Raymond-Dravco-Langenfelder, the prime contractor for the parallel Chesapeake Bay Bridge; Potts & Callahan, a large Baltimore paving firm; the Cherry Hill Sand & Gravel Company; Regal Construction Company of Upper Marlboro; Equitable Service Plan, Inc., a suburban Washington, D.C., finance company, one of whose stockholders was an unsuccessful candidate for state banking commissioner; Milton Pollinger and Morris Perlmutter, both real estate developers; the Rosecroft Trotting and Pacing Association; the Maryland Jockey Club of Baltimore; two engineering firms, a manufacturing firm and two labor unions. Each of the organizations was doing business with the state. Altogether, this "birthday party" raised over $187,000.

If one were to believe the average lobbyist, one might become convinced that they were simply "legislative advisers," as they like to style themselves, and spokesmen for their clients' various points of view. Critics, on the other hand, see lobbyists at the state and local levels as corrupters of the public weal with their large reserves of cash and their apparent willingness to satisfy the weaknesses of all the legislators. The truth of the matter is that these lobbyists fall somewhere in between these two archetypes. They are not the manipulators of the Sam Ward type, the corrupt "king of the lobbyists" in Washington during the Civil War, nor the wheeler-dealers of the Arthur Samish stripe. On the other hand, they are not the saints they would like us to believe they are.

In many ways a corporation is like a feudal state. It has its kings, barons, dukes, knights and heirs to the throne; it makes its own internal laws and sets its own restrictions; it has allies, enemies, ambassadors and a home guard; and its employees live in a state of voteless dependence.

As with any state, it must maintain relations with other states. For large domestic corporations the most important embassy post is in Washington, D.C. Since a lobbyist's (or ambassador's) job is to protect the interests and possessions of the corporation (or state) and augment its wealth, contributions are often viewed by the corporation as a payment (or bribe) in pursuit of these goals, little different than, say, a company contribution to the employees' health insurance program.

Quite clearly business and government, like many nations, are dependent upon each other, one for maintaining a healthy business climate, and the other for providing the taxes to fuel the government machine. As a consequence the pressure for campaign contributions has never been onesided, with wealthy lobbyists hovering over impoverished candidates, checkbooks at the ready. On the contrary, there has long existed a counter pressure wherein candidates have sought to bleed reluctant lobbyists for funds.

The leeching methods are quite simple, particularly for an incumbent legislator. A bill is introduced to, say, regulate an industry. The industry's lobbyist then rushes into the fray with "campaign contributions" to ensure the bill's defeat. Sometimes the sponsor of the legislation is even hired by the industry affected for a large fee to kill the proposal. These bills go by a variety of names: "milker," "cinch," "squeeze" or "pinch" bills. In Oklahoma they are known as "margarine" bills because, in a butter-and-eggs state, the margarine manufacturers are always vulnerable.

In Alabama they have a quaint custom in the legislature called "Baseball Day" during which any legislator can introduce a bill of his own choosing. The measure is then voted up or down without its having to go through the long committee and reading processes. Usually the galleries are packed with lobbyists; whenever a bill hostile to a particular industry is introduced, the appropriate lobbyist races to the bar of the House and offers sufficient campaign contributions to ensure the bill's demise.

In other states "Kill Day" is the custom where all legislation still pending in committee at the end of the session is brought up for a vote, ostensibly to be voted down, or killed. However, some legislation is deliberately introduced early in the session simply to squeeze the lobbyist later when the money is needed the most.

A typical pinch bill might demand, for instance, strict American medical educational standards. In all probability such a bill would result in funds flowing in from nonestablishmentarian medical groups such as herbalists, chiropractors and osteopaths. For years legislators from dry states introduced bills which would legalize the manufacture and sale of liquor, the purpose being to shake loose campaign funds from bootleggers and church groups. The introduction of such legislation became so routine that the resultant contributions came to represent a form of taxation. Currently it is now fashionable in many states to shake down lobbyists who represent high-pollution industries. A common refrain heard among politicians discussing such tactics is that "your enemies end up contributing as much as your friends."

At the federal level milking the lobbyists is only slightly less obvious. When Mrs. Helen D. Bentley, head of the Federal Maritime Commission, told a group of shipping company executives in 1970 that Vice-President Agnew was interested in seeing Republican C. Stanley Blair become governor of Maryland, the shippers caught the hint and kicked in heavily to his campaign.

In 1970, to cite another example, a fund-raising dinner was held in Chicago for Senator Vance Hartke of Indiana who was up for reelection. The senator provided a tickle list of those he thought should buy tickets. When he saw that the drug industry was not coming through as expected, he modified a speech to suggest that he had shifted his attitude slightly toward the industry. The drug companies got the message and bought their quota of tickets.

If ever there was a trend among politically active businesses and their lobbyists, it is their willingness to absorb certain campaign costs, which in effect amounts to a business contribution. It is becoming increasingly more common for corporations to sluice campaign mail through the company postage meter, to underwrite some printing, advertising and public relations expenses, to assign company employees temporarily to campaign duty, and to pay other campaign workers by corporate check. Businesses are also willing to donate their credit cards, airplanes, cars, hotel suites and billboard space to favored candidates. One of the most valuable assets in recent campaigns has been the hundreds of hours of computer time donated by friendly corporations.

Examples are legion and only a few not previously noted need be mentioned. In the 1966 Pennsylvania gubernatorial election, for instance, Harsco Steel offered to put certain GOP campaign employees temporarily on its payroll; the offer was seriously considered but, for a variety of reasons, was eventually turned down. In 1968 PepsiCo was supposed to have provided free Pepsis in all the major Republican campaign offices. In the 1972 election, a Boeing employee, using travelers checks issued by the company, worked in the Wisconsin primary on behalf of Senator Henry Jackson. Bristol-Myers' jet airplane was available to John Lindsay during the early months of his try for the Presidency in 1972. A Philadelphia investment banking house, to cite a final example, maintains a suite in New York City which is available to any influential Pennsylvania politician.

All too often companies that absorb campaign expenses compound the felony by attempting to write them off as business expenses. This practice is known in the trade as "double billing" because the donation is recorded by the campaign finance manager as a contribution from an individual and by the firm as a deductible expense. For years no corporations were prosecuted for breaking the law in this manner, partly because of the relative ease with which such "expenses" could and still can be hidden in company records, and partly because of a general reluctance by Congress and the Justice Department to track down the offenders.

But following the 1968 election, a rash of indictments were handed down on several firms accused of making illegal contributions. It was the first concerted effort by the federal government to enforce the campaign financing laws as they then existed.

The National Brewing Company of Baltimore, Maryland, for instance, was accused of contributing $5,000 to the Pierre Salinger primary campaign for the Democratic nomination for U.S. senator from California in 1964. The money was supposed to have been routed through the Walter Leftwich Organization, a Beverly Hills, California, advertising and public relations firm that ran the Salinger campaign, including the fund-raising efforts. In return, the brewery was supposedly sent a receipt from the Leftwich Organization for $5,000 worth of advertising and public relations "services rendered," which are tax-deductible items for business firms. The company was indicted by a grand jury in Baltimore for making illegal contributions; it pleaded guilty and was fined $7,500.

The Rossmoor Corporation, a California "leisure world" firm, was also accused in 1969 of making an illegal contribution of $5,000.32 to the same Salinger campaign. After lengthy pretrial hearings, the company decided to plead guilty and was fined $3,500. In another 1969 indictment the Clougherty Packing Company of Varnon, California, was also charged with making an illegal $13,750 contribution to the Salinger campaign. The president of the firm was indicted on an additional charge of consenting to the illegal contribution. Both pleaded guilty and were fined $5,000 and $1,000, respectively.

In the same year, Howard F. Ahmanson's Home Savings & Loan Association was accused of, among other charges, making an illegal contribution of over $41,000 to the 1964 Lyndon Johnson campaign. Two other indictments charged Home Savings & Loan with disguising contributions it had made to several state campaigns as advertising expenses on its 1964 and 1965 federal tax returns. (Corporate contributions are legal in California state campaigns but cannot be deducted on federal income tax returns.) The company pleaded guilty and paid a total of $15,000 in fines.

Several other Ahmanson firms, an advertising agency and two other savings and loan companies, were also indicted on charges of making illegal contributions to the Johnson campaign. They pleaded guilty, like their sister company, and were fined $25,000.

The Fluor Corporation of Los Angeles, an international construction firm, was likewise indicted in 1969 for making illegal contributions of $25,000 to the 1964 GOP Presidential campaign, $1,500 to Senator Richard B. Russell's 1966 campaign for reelection (in which he had no opposition in either the primary or general election), and three other illegal contributions in 1966 to campaigns in Texas and California. The company pleaded guilty on all five counts and was fined $10,000.

The International Latex Corporation of New York City was charged in 1969 with making an illegal $8,000 campaign contribution in 1964 to Senator Thomas H. Dodd of Connecticut. The contribution was made, according to Dodd's former administrative assistant, on the understanding that Dodd would find an ambassadorship for International Latex's board chairman, Abe Spanel. Spanel has yet to be appointed ambassador, and the company pleaded no contest and was fined $5,000.

Finally, two shipping firms, American President Lines and

Pacific Far East Lines, were charged in 1970 with contributing illegally nearly $6,000 to twenty key federal legislators in the 1966 and 1968 elections. The largest sum, $1,500, supposedly went to Congressman Edward A. Garmatz of Maryland, then chairman of the House Merchant Marine Committee. Senator Warren Magnuson of Washington State, chairman of the Senate Commerce Committee and its Subcommittee on Merchant Marine and Fisheries, supposedly received $1,000. Both men oversee legislation establishing federal subsidies for the lines. The money purportedly was channeled from the two firms through a San Francisco public relations man. A federal grand jury handed down indictments on the two lines; both pleaded guilty and were fined a whopping $50,000 apiece.

These examples represent only a fraction of the number of companies willfully breaking the campaign finance laws. The IRS, for instance, had 130 other cases pending on the 1964 election alone before the five-year statute of limitations expired. The true number of corporations flouting the law today probably runs to several thousand in any election year—and that includes the reforms incorporated into the Federal Election Campaign Act of 1971.

In 1969, three years before the Watergate Affair broke, IRS Commissioner Randolph Thrower told a group of tax consultants that "we have found creeping into some of the fund-raising practices in political campaigns, an element of conspiracy reflecting a great deal of cynicism and disrespect for the tax law and other laws on the part of some of the very people on whom we would normally rely heavily to establish a high standard of compliance." He went on to say that the IRS had "even found conspiracies of this sort where cynicism and disregard for the law are so flagrant that businessmen were invited to a group meeting, as a breakfast or a luncheon, and openly briefed upon the plan for concealing the true nature of the contribution."

The 1971 reforms, as will be pointed out in the last chapter, have done very little to change this attitude.

With over 18 million members, or 9 percent of the population, and a net worth exceeding $4 billion, American labor unions constitute perhaps the most powerful lobby in the country. No single group can match the combination of money it dispenses to candidates and the vast army of election workers it fields. In 1968, labor unions contributed a reported $7 million to federal and state campaigns and over $10 million in 1972. If a monetary value could be put on the free time union members devoted to political activities in either election, it would amount to an absolute minimum of $10 million more. Any group that can offer $20 million for starters in campaign cash and services definitely has clout in our political arena.

The Federal Election Campaign Act, like the Corrupt Practices Act before it, forbids labor unions from using dues or general union funds to support candidates for federal office. But the law does not rule out voluntary contributions from individual members. Many unions have set up special organizations to collect and disburse this money.

The largest and most powerful of these organizations is the AFL-CIO's Committee on Political Education, which spends about $2 million in election years in congressional, senatorial and the Presidential races. COPE claims it keeps records of donations so that it can prove the gifts were voluntary, although such records are ordinarily not made public. To raise its funds, the committee sets a quota for its national and international unions, asking each to collect a minimum of $12.50 per year for every hundred members. Some unions, such as the Steelworkers and Rubber Workers, regularly exceed their targets while others, particularly the high-skill craft unions, provide little or no funds at all.

In some unions, such as the Steamfitters, every new member of the union receives a political fund check-off card along with his medical forms and other necessary documents. Most find themselves "volunteering" a certain amount each payday. The union collected an average of $50 per union member in 1968. Generally, the job steward collects from the men under him, the shop foremen collect from the job stewards, the general foreman collects from the shop foremen, and so on up the line until the money is deposited in the union's political fund. Ordinarily, union brass are not asked to contribute at all, and few do.

On the surface most of the twoscore or so unions active in political finance raise their funds in this manner. In practice, however, some unions use other means, most of which are quite illegal.

Since 1936, when unions first began contributing funds in a significant way, a large portion of the money donated has come from union treasuries rather than a political fund. When John L. Lewis was asked where the nearly $500,000 came from for the 1936 Roosevelt campaign, he replied, "I'll tell you where it came from. Right here, from the coffers of the United Mine Workers of America. It came by request of the President of the United States through one of his trusted aides."

Lewis's tapping of general union funds for political purposes was legal in 1936 and was not to be banned until the passage of the Smith-Connally Act of 1943. But the practice has persisted despite that and subsequent laws designed to bring unions under the same restraints as business.

During the McClellan hearings in the 1950's investigating improper activities in the labor-management field, for instance, it was revealed that unions were still dipping into general funds to finance their favorite candidates. Carmine S. Bellino, an ex-FBI man knowledgeable in the ways of union finance and an investigator for the Senate Permanent Investigating Committee, testified that two Teamsters unions had contributed $15,000 from their general funds to a candidate for the Democratic nomination for U.S. senator from Michigan in 1954:

> *The Chairman.* What was that paid out of?
> *Mr. Bellino.* That was paid out of dues of the Teamsters money.
> *The Chairman.* Out of union treasury?
> *Mr. Bellino.* Yes, sir.
> *The Chairman.* Regular union dues?
> *Mr. Bellino.* Yes, sir. . . .

Another $17,000, testified Bellino, came out of welfare funds:

> *The Chairman.* You mean money was contributed to [the] political campaign out of welfare funds?
> *Mr. Bellino.* The good and welfare fund [a special fund used to support families of union members in jail].
> *The Chairman.* . . . How did the money get in there, and what is the source of that money?

Mr. Bellino. It would be contributions from other locals which would be members' dues.

The practice continues to this day. The Seafarers' International Union was indicted in 1970 for violating the federal statutes which prohibit the use of general union funds for political contributions. It had allegedly contributed as much as $750,000 from general union funds through its Seafarers' Political Action Donation, or SPAD, committee between 1964 and 1968. In May, 1972, a federal judge dismissed the suit because the Justice Department failed to press the case for two years. Subsequently, the Justice Department decided not to appeal. Interestingly enough, exactly one week before the Presidential election the SIU contributed $100,000 to the Nixon campaign.

Along the way, the Seafarers developed a new technique to fatten their union's political fund, namely extracting large sums from foreign seamen signed aboard American ships through SIU hiring halls abroad. While American nationals have chipped in a token $5 or $10 per person to the SIU fund in recent years, the foreigners apparently have developed such an enthusiasm for American political traditions that most of them have contributed between $100 and $500 a year each. No such enthusiasm, however, has seized Paul Hall, the SIU's president. He has not been recorded of late even contributing as much as $100 to the fund, despite his $40,000 salary. He much prefers doling out the $990,000 or so his 80,000 fellow unionists kick in every Presidential election year.

In 1972, to cite another example, W. A. ("Tony") Boyle of the United Mine Workers was convicted, among other counts, of diverting general union dues for political purposes. At this writing, the case is still under appeal.

The manner in which unions distribute their money is quite similar to the way business lobbies distribute it. Like AMPAC, for instance, COPE channels about half of all its funds collected at the national level through state and local COPE's, which has the advantage of muddying the source somewhat and enhancing the influence of the state and local donors with the recipient. Unions also tend to concentrate on marginal races where $2,500 to $10,000 might be the difference between victory and defeat for a prolabor candidate. Seldom is money wasted on prolabor kamikazes.

Rifling contributions to friends such as Senators Harrison Williams, Gore and Yarborough (the latter two of whom were defeated in 1970) is also a common practice. The Seafarers regularly give heavily to House and Senate committee chairmen who control maritime legislation. The Steamfitters contributed $60,000 to the 1964 Johnson-Humphrey campaign supposedly in return for a Presidential commutation enabling the union's business manager and boss to resume union activity following a six-year prison term for extortion.

When they feel it necessary, unions, like businesses, will back both sides. During the McClellan hearings, one senator asked a Teamster official: "But if you pick losers, then you also contribute to the winners. Is that the point?"

"That is right," replied the Teamster.

The United Mine Workers supposedly contributed to both Presidential candidates in 1968. In 1972, the Teamsters supposedly gave $250,000 in cash to the Nixon campaign (some say as part of a deal to release James Hoffa from jail), while many local Teamster unions donated their money to the McGovern-Shriver ticket.

Like businesses, unions also give support in kind as well as cash. Union mimeographs, printing presses, telephones, loudspeakers and trucks are often put at the disposal of candidates. During the McClellan hearings it was revealed in one instance that the Teamsters had contributed money to underwrite the costs of a thirteen-week television series on trucking. The last two weeks of the show, however, turned out to be devoted to the reelection campaign of a judge. The judge was a vice-president of the advertising company handling the show and he received $1,300 for bringing in the account.

Unions have also used secret D.C. committees in the past as channels for campaign funds. They usually had innocuous-sounding names so that no one would have any idea what their sources of money were. The Democratic, Republican, Independent Voter Education Committee, or DRIVE, the Teamsters counterpart to COPE, for example, contributed money in 1964 to "Citizens Committee, P.O. Box 1658, Washington, D.C." DRIVE officials claimed they knew neither the purpose of the committee nor to whom the funds eventually went. In the same year COPE contributed large sums to the Inter-Regional Civil Association which listed its address as 1725 I Street, N.W., Washington, D.C. Upon inspection, however, no such association was listed in the building's directory, although the building did house a number of law firms, one of which was probably the true home of the association.

Buying tickets to testimonial dinners is another favorite way for unions to contribute to candidates. For a while, following the censure of Senator Thomas Dodd in 1967, unions (and other fund raisers) shunned the practice, but now they are back in style. The value of a testimonial, as opposed to a fund-raising, dinner is that the money does not have to be reported as long as the recipient refrains from stating that he intends (as he usually does) to use the gifts for campaign purposes.

Another preferred method is to extend an invitation to an influential legislator to speak before a union group. To sweeten the arrangement, a large fee, usually no less than $1,000, is offered. In some cases the speech is ghostwritten by union flacks, and the dining room or hall is packed with union members, many of whom are coerced to attend. Several union regulars claim they have memorized by heart certain of the speeches they have been forced to hear each week.

The 1971 reforms ostensibly brought many of these practices to an end. But, in fact, they continue along other avenues. While secret committees have been outlawed, unions still hide the source of their funds by earmarking it, like Fat Cat businessmen, either through the many congressional and national campaign committees or through the large union political committees. Testimonial dinners and large speakers' fees have not been outlawed. Nor has there been anything written into the new law that effectively allows union political books to be inspected by the public. Thus, the wall of secrecy that surrounds union contributions remains largely intact.

Ideological money plays a small but significant role in the American political process. This money is not to be confused with, say, liberal Democratic money from California that curses the day it was not born poor and black, or conservative Republican money that prays for the restoration of pure laissez-faire capitalism. True ideological money does not feel at home within either of the two big parties, even though most of the money ends up going to Republican or Democratic candidates.

The most influential money group on the liberal end of the political spectrum is the National Committee for an Effective Congress. It has been around since 1948 endorsing candidates, working behind the scenes and contributing money. It has only been since the mid-1960's, however, that the committee became a power to be reckoned with.

It is one of the few organizations that has successfully raised money from direct mail solicitation. About half of NCEC funds come from a list of 100,000 names which is guarded jealously. The rest of the money comes from liberal Fat Cats such as Gordon Sherman of Midas Muffler, GM heir Stewart Mott, wealthy New Jersey businessman Fairleigh Dickinson, Jr., and investment banker Orin Lehman.

As its name implies, the NCEC concentrates on electing liberal, ADA- or New Deal-oriented candidates to the House and Senate. It prefers to concentrate on marginal races in which its $10,000 to $15,000 contribution might be crucial. It never contributes to shoo-ins or kamikazes. According to Russell D. Hemenway, the committee's national director, a potential beneficiary of NCEC funds must meet three criteria: there must be a chance of winning, there must be clear philosophical differences with the opponent, and there must be some indication that NCEC money will make a difference.

Races in low-population and low-budget states such as Oregon, Montana and Colorado are preferred, although the committee is willing to plunge into other contests in high-population, high-budget campaigns if the arithmetic is right. It has, for instance, contributed to Senate candidates Paul Douglas of Illinois, Clifford Case of New Jersey and Hugh Scott of Pennsylvania.

Most of the money spent by the NCEC in election years goes to Democratic candidates, helping rectify the apparent financial imbalance between the two parties. In 1968, during which it spent nearly $500,000, the committee endorsed, and presumably supported financially to some degree, 11 Democratic and 2 GOP senatorial candidates, and 50 Democratic, 10 Republican and 1 Independent House candidates. An extraordinary 70 percent of them won their contests, and the NCEC believes that its funds made the difference in most cases.

The secret of success, according to Susan King, who runs the committee's Washington, D.C., office, "is to know how to interpret an urgent cry for help from a candidate who says just a little bit more money for this or that additional exposure will win him the election." Political experience, she went on, "is crucial. I suppose the key to our success has been and will continue to be how finely tuned our ears are to the political requirements."

In the years ahead, if any trend is visible at all, the NCEC will probably concentrate more money on fewer candidates because it believes that fewer contests will be marginal. It will no doubt continue to play a significant role in pushing for further campaign finance reform, as it did in the passage of the Federal Election Campaign Act of 1971.

Collectively, right-wing money is far more available than liberal and left-wing money. This is particularly true when a "liberal" occupies the White House. But even when a relatively conservative President such as Nixon is in office, the outside right can still come up with some impressive sums. In 1968, it spent around $1.7 million directly in the political arena, and in 1970, another million dollars. Some of this money is spent indirectly on general right-wing propaganda, but still the total exceeds anything liberal and left-wing groups can offer.

The United Republicans of America, which is not associated with the GOP, raised nearly half a million dollars in the 1968 election. About $42,000 of that was contributed in the form of cash and another $238,000 was offered in campaign services. It cost an extraordinary $140,000 to raise the half million, and another $71,000 went for office expenses. Such high administrative costs have led some observers to the conclusion that the URA is more interested in perpetuating itself than electing conservatives to office.

The URA supported thirty-eight conservatives in the 1968 general election. Only thirteen were successful and all but five of them came from safe districts. On the surface, therefore, it would appear that the URA has a weakness for kamikazes. Some of those it supported in the primaries that year include William J. Mullaney, a member of New Jersey's right-wing "ratfink" faction which had fallen out with the state's GOP regulars, and G. Gordon Liddy, a New York Conservative party member who unsuccessfully challenged Congressman Hamilton Fish and who was later to become involved in the Watergate affair.

The United Congressional Appeal is much smaller than the URA, contributing annually in the neighborhood of $100,000 to $150,000, but its influence on the right is nearly as great. UCA raises its funds partly through mass mailings and partly from Fat Cats, among them some of the country's wealthiest bankers, brewers, pharmaceutical manufacturers and industrialists. In 1968, the year UCA was organized, campaign funds went to such bedrock right-wingers as Congressmen Walter S. Baring of Nevada, Benjamin Blackburn of Georgia, John R. Rarick of Louisiana and Albert W. Watson of South Carolina. The organization also backed Max Rafferty in his unsuccessful race for the Democratic nomination as U.S. senator from California, and Archie Gubbrud, a conservative who ran against Senator Mc-Govern in South Dakota.

Some of the more sophisticated conservatives, such as Congressman John Ashbrook, stiffarm UCA support. This caution stems from the fact that UCA's founder and guiding light is Willis A. Carto, a secretive figure who has been active in "Liberty and Property" and its publication, *Western Destiny,* the Noontide Press, the Yockey Movement and Liberty Lobby, all of which have clear racist overtones. He was also believed by many to be close to the John Birch Society and Billy James Hargis's Christian Crusade.

Carto organized the appeal with the idea of eventually controlling a large bloc of right-wing votes in Congress. To this end he began compiling a file on legislators so that he might better understand what motivated them on the great issues. The file is supposed to have been called "Kosher Konservative Kongressmen"—or the KKK file.

So far, Carto's efforts have been unavailing. While some right-wing candidates accept his money, none so far have admitted following their benefactor's legislative desires.

A third group that pumps money into the political process is

Americans for Constitutional Action. It was founded in 1958 originally to publish a congressional voting index to counter the influence of the liberal ADA's well-known index. Since then it has branched out into organizing and financing political campaigns. In 1962, ACA provided field men for 11 senatorial and 35 congressional candidates. A total of $28,000 was spent in 16 states, 2 of the 46 candidates receiving direct contributions. By 1970, it was helping 223 candidates in 43 states and spending $150,000 on 105 candidates.

Many of ACA's funds come from right-wing Fat Cats. Wealthy trustees of the organization include Patrick J. Frawley, one of the right's biggest bankrollers and the man who put Senator George Murphy on the payroll of Technicolor, Inc., at $20,000; actors Walter Brennan and John Wayne; retired Admiral Ben Moreell, former chairman of the board of Jones & Laughlin Steel Corporation; and William Loeb, publisher of the *Manchester* (New Hampshire) *Union Leader* and other newspapers. In the past ACA has accepted funds from E. Ainsworth Eyre and Mrs. Seth Milliken, both of New York and both Endorsers of the John Birch Society. Other contributors have been Helen Clay Frick, DeWitt Wallace and various members of the Pew family.

Underworld money plays a role in American political finance but no one is prepared to say precisely how large. Authorities on organized crime such as Charles Rogovin—a member of the President's Commission on Law Enforcement and Administration of Justice, especially involved with its Task Force on Organized Crime, and a past president of the Police Foundation—will say that the amount of money it contributes in a campaign depends on how one defines the underworld. But even then, he adds, it is not possible to pick an accurate figure.

If a strict definition of the underworld is used—that it is composed of individuals engaged in illegal activities such as selling narcotics, bootlegging, loan sharking, labor racketeering, running prostitution rings and illegal gambling games, and the like—then the amount of money spent as "campaign contributions" would no doubt run into the millions each year. However, if a broader definition is used, to include individuals who occasionally or even frequently, but with knowledge aforethought, seek the goods and services offered by the underworld, then the yearly amount of "campaign contributions" would run into the tens of millions.

No more precise estimation can be made because, in a field already obfuscated, virtually all underworld contributions are made in cash, no vouchers are kept, no names are put on lists, and no reports of such contributions ever reach the Clerk of the House, Secretary of the Senate, or state and local reporting authorities, except by mistake.

Underworld money thrives in American political finance because politicians have a chronic need for campaign funds and the mob is willing to give them. When Senator Charles W. Tobey of New Hampshire asked New York City Mayor William O'Dwyer during the Kefauver Hearings on Organized Crime what he considered the basis of Mafia chieftain Frank Costello's appeal to politicians, O'Dwyer replied, "It doesn't matter whether it is a banker, a businessman or a gangster, his pocketbook is always attractive." Costello, on the other hand, when asked the same question, was far more circumspect. "I know them, know them well, and maybe they got a little confidence in me," he said with some understatement.

While politicians need campaign funds, the underworld needs protection and friends in high places. In the 1949 New Jersey gubernatorial campaign, for instance, Newark racketeer Abner ("Longie") Zwillman, through an intermediary, offered the Democratic nominee $300,000 in return for the right to approve the man appointed attorney general in the state. The offer was turned down flat, and the Democrat was subsequently defeated, in large measure by a heavy vote from Hudson County, Zwillman's stronghold.

This alliance between mutual possessors of power is often an uneasy one in which the participants exhibit a common hatred toward one another along with a grudging realization that they must work together. In Mount Vernon, New York, one political party in the mid-1960's reluctantly turned to gambling figures for campaign funds because it claimed it was too poor to raise the money elsewhere. The mayor of Elizabeth, New Jersey, admitted accepting $100 or $200 contribution from Simone ("Sam the Plumber") DeCavalcante during the 1964 election but insisted he knew nothing of DeCavalcante's Mafia connections.

The proximity of gangsters and politicians does not necessarily make anyone guilty, but it has been going on for so long that it has given many people pause to wonder. At the 1950 marriage of Mafia leader Anthony ("Tony Boy") Boiardo, for instance, among the several thousand guests were Congressman Peter R. Rodino; Willie Moretti, a gambler who was shot to death the following year; Congressman Hugh Addonizio, later mayor of Newark who was convicted in 1970 on numerous counts of extortion and conspiracy; Gerardo ("Jerry") Catena, who is now supposed to be one of the top Mafia leaders in New Jersey; and Ralph Villani, a former mayor of Newark and later president of its city council.

The underworld raises its campaign funds in a variety of ways. Sharks will often call in some of their loans. Narcotics peddlers and numbers runners are usually given a dollar figure by their bosses and told to "get it up." Businesses are sometimes shaken down and gambling establishments skim profits off the day's take before figuring the mob's percentage. When possible the underworld prefers loans, which they insist be paid back (sometimes with interest), because it ties the politician more securely to his underworld benefactor.

In the Addonizio extortion-conspiracy trial, it was alleged that the mob had extorted money from several businesses to finance Addonizio's political campaigns. Fifteen thousand dollars was also extorted from Newark contractors, it was reported, for use in the 1965 New York Democratic mayoralty campaign.

The numbers racket has long been a potential source of campaign funds. In 1958, for instance, a group of Ohio politicians wanted to curry favor with the Democratic candidate for governor, Michael V. DiSalle, by making a large contribution to his campaign. The best way to raise the money, they decided, was to rig a day's play of the numbers, which they believed would bring in $50,000. Cleveland's numbers play, where they planned to place the bet, was then based on the last three digits of the day's total transactions on the New York Stock Exchange. The idea was to have a confederate flash the number to Cleveland the moment it was announced in New York, put in a large, last-minute bet, and collect the $50,000. Unfortunately for them the plan fell through because Cleveland bookies closed their accounts for the day well before the Stock Exchange stopped trading.

In 1967, the President's Commission on Law Enforcement and Administration of Justice published its Task Force Report on Organized Crime. Part of the report included a study of "Wincanton," a fictitious name for Reading, Pennsylvania, and the empire of underworld boss Abe Minker. The report covers many aspects of the town's and Minker's corruption—from illegal gambling and numbers running to bootlegging and prostitution—but what it has to say about campaign contributions is revealing in that it describes the true cynicism of the underworld. Minker is referred to in the report by the fictitious name "Irving Stern." Stern, said the report:

> was a major (if undisclosed) contributor during political campaigns —sometimes giving money to all candidates, not caring who won, sometimes supporting a "regular" to defeat a possible reformer, sometimes paying a candidate not to oppose a preferred man. Since there were few legitimate sources of large contributions for Democratic candidates, Stern's money was frequently regarded as essential for victory, for the costs of buying radio and television time and paying pollwatchers was high. When popular sentiment was running strongly in favor of reform, however, even Stern's contributions could not guarantee victory. Bob Walasek [a fictitious name], later to be as corrupt as any Wincanton mayor, ran as a reform candidate in the Democratic primary and defeated Stern-financed incumbent Gene Donnelly [also a fictitious name]. Never a man to bear grudges, Stern financed Walasek in the general election that year and put him on the "payroll" when he took office.

Contributing money, the report went on to point out, was one basic way Minker sought protection, and it ensured that complacent mayors, councilmen, district attorneys and judges were elected.

Like the business, labor and ideological lobbies, underworld contributors tend to rifle their offerings to individuals who can do them the most good. Sometimes they will concentrate on powerful public servants such as the chairman of the liquor control or pardon boards, or on law enforcement officials. But more often than not they will zero in on candidates for office who, if elected, can pull the right strings.

There are very few big-city congressmen, district attorneys, mayors or aldermen in office today who, if they received any outside campaign finance support at all, have not been funded in part by the underworld. This would be true of governors, senators and state legislators in at least seventeen states where the mob is unusually active. There have been at least half a dozen congressmen in office over the past two decades who were or are still considered "owned" by the Mafia. In the same period at least a dozen other officeholders—U.S. senators, governors, mayors and judges—in hock to the Mafia come readily to mind. Most candidates in areas where the underworld is strong will acknowledge the existence of such funds, but few of them in all fairness are aware of either the true source of the money or the nature of any quid pro quos arranged by their campaign aides.

Invariably underworld contributions are laundered beforehand by being channeled through respectable or semirespectable fronts. It is also common practice for the underworld to back both candidates in any significant race in which the outcome is in doubt.

Sometimes underworld contributions can be quite crude. New England Mafia boss Raymond Patriarca, for instance, allegedly tried to bribe Massachusetts' ex-Lieutenant Governor Francis X. Bellotti with a $100,000 campaign contribution in both his races for governor in 1964 and attorney general in 1966. Bellotti rebuffed both offers but his honesty went unrewarded. The mob soon spread the word that he had actually taken the money, and the rumor became a factor in Bellotti's defeat in both elections.

In Nevada, the Mafia gambling interests regularly gather together to fix the amount of their contributions. Usually a candidate for governor will get $20,000, and lesser state offices are scaled down accordingly—to an estimated $200 for justice of the peace candidates. The Nevada underworld will also join with legitimate gambling interests and contribute heavily to "law and order" candidates, particularly sheriffs, in southern California. By helping these men win office, they know it keeps down the competition and drives the bettors over the border to the Nevada tables.

In one New Jersey town the story is told of a visitor who

dropped by the mayor's office several years ago, bragging of the help he gave to the mayor in his campaign. He said he was interested in winning a contract for certain special, heavy-duty vehicles such as street sweepers and dump trucks. The mayor offered to find a set of specifications but the visitor broke in: "No, no, that's not what I'm interested in. I mean specials. How much off the top?"

The mayor played it innocent and the visitor continued: "It's simple business," he said, "and you're protected all the way. We negotiate a price that includes something for you. You get yours as a contribution to your campaign fund, but of course you don't have to explain how you spend it." The mayor paused for a moment and then remarked that he thought the offer smacked of a bribe.

"What are you," replied the visitor, "a Boy Scout?"

IX

The Money Trough

Half of all campaign spending, it has often been said, is wasted, but the trouble is no one knows which half. In a Presidential campaign, for example, it would not be unusual for one party to spend between $600,000 and $800,000 on buttons and bumper stickers alone, even when it is clear that neither item will win over many votes. But is it a waste? There are those who argue that money spent on such gimcracks—including balloons, plastic skimmers, paper dresses, sashes, jewelry, and so on—is necessary to rally the loyal party troops; while there are others who hold that a candidate with a good track record and the ability to deliver a few well-chosen speeches should be sufficient to fire up the faithful. Since both arguments have merit, who is to say where the waste may be found?

Even though waste is endemic to most political campaigns, it is kept in check somewhat by the shifting of financial priorities as the political realities dictate. Such was the case between 1932 and 1950, when radio time commanded some of the campaign funds that had previously gone to torchlight parades and public rallies. In the 1950's and 1960's the realities required that more money be spent on television, air travel, polling and computer services, and less on radio (although it is now staging somewhat of a comeback) and whistle-stop tours. Today, the realities in any federal or major state campaign dictate that money be concentrated in three areas: organizational overhead, media and consulting.

Organizational overheads can sometimes run as high as 25 to 30 percent of a campaign's entire budget. It is no secret, today, that campaign salaries are vastly inflated. John N. Mitchell, before he resigned as Nixon's 1972 campaign manager, was paid at a rate of $60,000 per year by the Committee to Re-Elect the President. He was also entitled to all the perquisites of office such as a car and driver, an unlimited expense account and free use of campaign credit cards. Some speechwriters demand and get $500 and up per speech. Press aides may make between $1,000 and $2,000 per month, plus expenses.

Even at the state level salaries run high. In the 1970 Pennsylvania gubernatorial race, for example, the Republican campaign manager was paid $3,000 per month, the traveling press secretary $1,250 per month, the research director $2,000 per month, and the chief of field men $900 per month. The total campaign payroll for four months alone came to $140,800.

Telephone costs also run up the overheads. Until recently there was no way to discover what kind of a bite they took out of a campaign budget because the Corrupt Practices Act exempted them from reporting requirements. The 1971 reforms now require that certain, but not all, telephone expenses be reported, which has cleared the murk somewhat.

An indication of how large telephone expenses can be occasionally surfaces. In 1972, the American Telephone & Telegraph Company threatened to sue the Democratic National Committee for nonpayment of $1.5 million in telephone bills left over from the 1968 election. It must be remembered that this sum represents only the *unpaid* portion of what was spent altogether in the campaign. Another example: in the 1960 election the phone bill for election night alone at the Kennedy Hyannisport compound was supposedly $10,000.

Mailings also constitute a major investment in any campaign, and as constituencies grow so do the costs of communicating with voters by mail. In an average congressional district it would cost between $16,000 and $20,000 to send one first-class letter (at the eight-cent rate) to every household in the district. This is for stamps alone and does not include the costs of the paper, printing, typing and envelope stuffing. "If you don't go first class," says Senator Alan Cranston, "your literature is all too apt to land unopened in the wastebasket." In his first try for the Senate in 1964, Cranston spent over $204,000 on mailings—and that was at the five-cent rate.

These mailing costs place a particular hardship on challengers because they do not have access to as many money sources as the incumbents, nor the benefit of the free franking privilege (which technically cannot be used for partisan political purposes but often is). Even at the third-class bulk rate of 4.8 cents per piece, a challenger in a congressional race would still have to spend a minimum of $9,645 on postage alone to reach every household one time.

Most mailings at the national level are appeals for money. Historically these appeals have not been successful, except for minor party candidates, because of the poor quality of the lists and because such appeals tend to be directed to everyone in general and no one in particular.

One story is illustrative. In 1960 Edward Brooke ran for secretary of state of Massachusetts. He was the first black to be nominated for statewide office since Reconstruction and was held in high regard by Republicans, blacks and many other voters. Following the Republican convention a "Dollars for Decency" program was organized to raise money for Brooke nationwide from blacks. The enthusiasm was enormous but the appeal was too general and the effort flopped. "If it raised *one* dollar I'd be surprised," one liberal member of the Nixon administration told me.

Mass solicitations of this nature are most successful when they are tailored to a particular audience. This is why Eugene McCarthy, George Wallace and George McGovern have been so successful in their mass mailings: they have specific grievances which they detail in their letters, and it strikes a response with the reader.

Computers, also a major overhead item, are now being used successfully by the two national parties to make mass mail appeals pay off. The extraordinary success of the various GOP campaign committees in raising sufficient money is due to the intelligent use of computers. They enable the dunning letters to be more specific, with the reader's name interspersed throughout the letter, and the responses have sometimes been as high as 10 percent, which is over three times the break-even point.

Travel costs are another heavy overhead item. Again, the old law did not require precise accounting of travel expenses, and the 1971 reforms are still too new for any conclusions to be drawn; thus, one is left to make educated guesses about how much was spent by a candidate to meet the voters. The 1968 Nixon campaign reported spending $1.8 million on what it called the "tour," minus $492,000 reimbursed by the media. But this total does not include staff travel, the truth squad, surrogate travel and advance work. Still, it is a lot of money for a three-month campaign.

Election-day expenses can also be heavy. In machine-prone cities and states they can sometimes amount to as much as 80 percent of all overhead expenses. Most state laws allow political parties to name two pollwatchers each in every election district. For this work they can be paid, the money usually coming from the state or municipal committee. But beyond that, few states allow additional election-day expenses. Over the years, however, a wide range of unofficial expenses have been condoned to the point where they are now considered almost legitimate. Ward leaders and precinct captains, for instance, receive "walking around money," sometimes as much as $1,000, which is supposed to be passed on down the line to help get out the vote. Committeemen and committeewomen are also paid to get out the vote, and most of them believe that the $20 to $30 they receive is part of the perquisites of office. Cash is also passed out to babysitters, car drivers, and providers of snacks, refreshments and dinners. Sometimes money is distributed to individuals called "agents" and "club leaders," and for such vague work as "municipal aid" and "defrayed expenses."

Occasionally money can be saved by the clever manipulation of human impulses. In 1964, for instance, Harlem numbers operators offered a special inducement to their customers: in return for registering and voting they would be given a one-dollar free play on the numbers. The controllers and runners policed the agreement by driving voters to the polls and assigning babysitters when necessary. The heavy anti-Goldwater vote in Harlem that year was ascribed in part to the charisma of Robert Kennedy, who was running for the Senate. But insiders knew better.

Inevitably, some campaign funds "go astray," as politicians like to say. Senator Thomas Dodd, for one, used campaign contributions collected at "testimonial dinners" to pay some of his household expenses. He was subsequently censured by his Senate colleagues for his behavior. After he announced his intention of running for reelection in 1970, Dodd was sent a $10,000 contribution by the Democratic Senatorial Campaign Committee. Later Dodd withdrew, but because of his death in 1971, there is still a question whether the money was ever returned.

Congressman James Utt once used $9,000 in contributions to wage a libel suit against the Columbia Broadcasting System. In 1970, one Republican governor was accused of transferring campaign funds to his personal account and investing them in the stock market. In 1971, over $50,000 in unspent campaign contributions were found in the estate of Senator Everett Dirksen. A similar amount was found the same year in the estate of Senator Richard Russell; the money had originally been raised in 1952 to finance Russell's bid for the Presidency.

The media are another trough for campaign funds. Ten seconds of television time in Los Angeles during prime time in 1966 cost around $800. Twenty seconds on each of Arizona's ten commercial TV stations the same year cost a total of $1,000—at first glance a bargain until one considers the relatively small size of the audience (an estimated 1.5 million, half the population of greater Los Angeles). Sixty seconds of time on *Gunsmoke* in 1968 cost $50,000 (the ad would have been seen by 19 million people of voting age). Thirty seconds at the end of the *CBS Evening News* with Walter Cronkite in 1970 cost $1,500. A quarter hour of prime-time television cost approximately $35,000 in 1970, and an hour cost around $165,000. None of these amounts include the costs of production or compensation for the talent on the preempted shows.

Radio time can run from $20 to several hundred dollars, depending on the length of message, size of listening audience and time of day. A full-page advertisement in a weekday edition of the *Los Angeles Times* costs over $5,800; a three-color, full-page ad in a Sunday edition of the *Chicago Tribune* costs over $9,600; and a full-page ad in *The New York Times* daily edition costs over $9,300. Billboards rent for as little as $75 per month in rural areas and as much as several hundred dollars per month in urban areas, depending on size and location. In the 1965 New Jersey gubernatorial race, the GOP paid $27,000, which included production costs, for 215 twenty-four-sheet billboards, 122 of which were illuminated, for the six weeks prior to election day, which averages less than $100 each on a monthly basis. Congressman James Wright of Ft. Worth, Texas, claims one billboard once cost him $550 per month in rent. In New York City, a strategically placed billboard can rent for several thousand dollars per month.

The trend in political advertising over the past two decades, as observers of the political scene are aware, is toward the use of more and more spots. In 1962, spots represented 74 percent of all television time bought by candidates. By 1970 the amount had risen to 95 percent. The argument in favor of spots is that a message can be presented to the viewer or listener before he can reach over and switch the dial. A five-, fifteen- or thirty-minute segment, replacing, say, *All in the Family* or *Marcus Welby,* claim the experts, simply antagonizes the viewers.

Radio spots are also increasing in popularity because they can be bought on as little as four hours notice, and thus are a natural outlet for "late" money; additionally, they can reach certain groups such as commuters, blacks and classical music lovers more readily than TV spots; and they can carry stronger messages that might backfire if presented visually.

Billboards, in a sense, have always been spot advertisements since they must produce an impact within the limits of four or five words. Like posters and placards, they are declining slightly in use because the public tends to associate them with litter and urban blight.

For all the money spent on the media, what is gained? For the most part it buys a message that, while technically well produced, is of relatively low quality, like headache remedy advertisements. In the past twenty years of the political hard sell, not one memorable political advertisement has been produced which has not been either vicious or fatuous in the extreme. Perusing a library of past political television spots, according to lawyer Paul Porter, who has been involved in Presidential elections since 1936, is like "spending an afternoon in the snakehouse of the zoo or riding through a sewer in a glass-bottomed boat."

One of the most poisonous was the anti-Goldwater spot run by the Democratic party in 1964 showing a little girl plucking petals from a daisy and happily counting from one to ten, followed by a countdown from ten to one, with the picture then fading to a mushroom cloud billowing up from an atomic explosion. The President's voice is then heard saying, "These are high stakes. To make a world in which all of God's children can live or go into the dark. We must love each other or we must die." There was another one in the same election which showed a young girl licking an ice cream cone while a voice in the background cited the dangers of fallout from cesium-138 and strontium-90.

Another vicious advertisement reportedly used in the 1966 California gubernatorial race had a voice that identified Ronald Reagan as an actor and then added, ". . . and, of course, you know who shot Lincoln, don't you?"

In his unsuccessful race for the Senate against Vance Hartke in 1970, Richard Roudebush ran a spot on Indiana television stations which showed an actor dressed as a Vietcong guerrilla loading a rifle and pointing it at the viewer. A voice then intoned: "The weapons the Vietcong use to kill American servicemen are given to them by Communist countries. Senator Vance Hartke voted for the bill to permit trade with these Communist countries. Isn't that like putting a loaded gun in the hands of our enemies? Vote for Dick Roudebush. Roudebush thinks the way you do."

But for the most part political spots are either in mildly poor taste or a bore. John Tunney, for instance, when he ran for the Senate in 1970, approved a series of television spots which made him and his family look and act like John F. Kennedy and his family. Senator Ralph T. Smith in his Senate race against Adlai E. Stevenson III carried on a campaign of innuendo by asking such wife-beating questions as: "What has Ad-a-lay got against the FBI and the Chicago police?" Albert Gore, in his unsuccessful bid for reelection to the Senate in 1970, was shown in one TV spot riding a white horse. (In the face of criticism, his supporters pointed out that Gore actually owned the horse, but failed to add that that was not the purpose of the ad.) Congressman Morris Udall claims that the principal TV advertisement for a recent candidate for the House showed the man in an apron taking cookies out of the oven.

A typical example of a spot advertisement which says nothing was the 60-second TV spot run by Senator Howard Cannon of Nevada in his successful 1970 reelection campaign. The script ran as follows:

VIDEO	AUDIO (voiceover)
CANNON AT LAKE TAHOE—ALONE AND SEATED ON A ROCK.	He cares about the things that matter. . . .
CLOSE ON BIRD.	He's been our Senator for 12 years now. . . .
CLOSE ON CANNON OFFERING FOOD.	His name is Howard Cannon. . . .
CANNON AND CHIPMUNK.	Persistent, patient but deter-
CLOSE ON CHIPMUNK.	mined. He's deeply concerned
EASE UP CAMERA TO CANNON	about the kind of world we're making for our children now. He's deeply involved in preserving the environment of man— its natural beauty that makes living in Nevada great!
LONG-SHOT VIEW OF TAHOE.	Let's keep it that way– Reelect the man who cares! Vote for Howard Cannon on November 3.

Radio also produces its own quota of pejorative political advertising. Consider, for example, the series of attacks by the Republican party of Pennsylvania on Milton Shapp during the 1970 governor's race. Each commercial began with an announcer saying: "Another question from the people for Milton Shapp." Then a folksy voice asked a question over a telephone line, such as:

> Yeh, I remember reading in the papers that back at the Democratic Convention in Chicago in 1968—you know, where they had all the demonstrations and the Chicago Seven—I remember reading that Milton Shapp not only marched with the demonstrators in the streets, but Shapp actually put up the bail money for the protesters. What does he say about that now?

The announcer then asked: "How about it, Mr. Shapp?"

A Chicago playboy ran unsuccessfully in a congressional primary on the slogan "A Man Who Drinks Champagne and Plays Polo Can't Be All Bad." Another neophyte politician, Pat Milli-

gan, won election to the California State Senate simply by renting
billboard space and distributing handbills carrying only the slogan
"Three Cheers for Pat Milligan." During the 1961 municipal elections in New York City, campaign funds were actually invested in
a 45-rpm record of a song entitled "Lefkowitz, Fino and Gil-
hooley," candidates that year for various offices.

Political advertising over the past decade has clearly reached the
saturation point. In some instances during the last weeks of a
campaign all the available advertising spots on a metropolitan
television or radio station are filled with messages of candidates
seeking office. These wall-to-wall ads, like their deodorant and
soapflake counterparts, tend to cancel each other out. Since most
political advertisements are directed to no more than 20 percent of
the population, representing the swing, or undecided vote, they
also tend to irritate the rest of the audience that has already made
up its mind. Unquestionably, part of the 30 to 45 percent of the
eligible voters who refuse to exercise their franchise is made up of
those people who are repelled by what they see and hear in political advertisements.

The benefits of media advertising are also vastly overrated. It
may be true, of course, during a primary election (many of which
are not truly competitive) that television and radio can propel an
unknown into serious contention. Such was the case for Richard
Ottinger and Howard Metzenbaum. But for many candidates, no
amount of media expenditures will change the voter's minds. In
the 1972 Florida primary, in fact, some of the campaigns flour-
ished in inverse proportion to the amount spent on the media. John
Lindsay, the "media candidate," spent $170,000 and won 7 per-
cent of the vote; Muskie spent $130,000 and won 9 percent;
Humphrey spent around $75,000 and won 18 percent; and George
Wallace also spent $75,000 and won 42 percent of the vote.

It is difficult to recall one campaign in the last quarter century in
which political advertising clearly made the difference between
winning and losing in a general election. This does not include, of
course, political debates, which are technically not political advertising in the sense used here and which definitely have had an
impact upon occasion on the outcome of some elections. Every
campaign has its own set of media imperatives, some of which
require that a large amount of money be poured into the trough,

others that require that less money be spent, and some that require that no money be spent. In the past, whenever there was a question of which route to take, the tendency was to opt for the first course. Often the result was a colossal waste of money, an intolerable imposition on the patience of the audience, and no guarantee that the expenditure would ever elect the candidate.

The secret appears to be in the choosing: relying on free network coverage in the manner of George Wallace; using minimum TV exposure to complement other efforts in the manner of Humphrey; finding a gimmick such as walking from one end of the state to the other in the manner of Senator Lawton Chiles; laying low lest you expose your flanks in the manner of Richard Nixon; or trying to turn a defensive posture into an attack on limited funds in the manner of McGovern.

The source of much of the discontent with the manner in which candidates seek to sell themselves can be found among the "technicians" or "hired guns" of American politics: the campaign consultants. The techniques of airbrushing out all of a candidate's spiritual, intellectual and physical warts so that only the "best" characteristics are emphasized are as old as politics itself. They did not originate with the consultants but have instead simply been adapted to meet the requirements of the electronic age.

Political consulting as we know it today was born in 1936 when the California public relations firm of Whitaker & Baxter began to accept accounts for candidates and ballot issues. Since that year the demand for packaged professional political expertise has increased rapidly. Today, nearly 300 firms offer their specialized campaign talents to candidates, mostly as a sideline to their regular commercial business. Only about 30 of these firms, however, classify themselves as full-time professional campaign management firms.

Among the better known consultants and their firms are Roger E. Ailes, of REA Productions, and Harry W. Treleaven, Jr., of Treleaven Associates, both of New York City. Both played a leading role in the 1968 Nixon campaign. Ailes also worked in the 1970 campaigns of Governor Francis W. Sargent of Massachusetts; Robert A. Taft, Jr.'s Senate campaign in Ohio; and in Donald E. ("Buz") Lukens's unsuccessful bid for the GOP nomination for governor of Ohio. In the same year, Treleaven ran the media campaigns of GOP senatorial candidates William E. Brock of Tennessee, George Bush of Texas and William C. Cramer of Florida.

Although both men maintained close ties to the White House and Republican National Committee following the 1968 election, neither took a leading part in the 1972 Presidential campaign. In their place, the Nixon managers organized the "November Group," an ad hoc collection of advertising executives on leave from their agencies. Most of them had little previous political experience.

Robert Squier is another political consultant who burst out of obscurity in 1968 when he ran Hubert Humphrey's media campaign. He has since worked for John Burns of Hawaii, Marvin Mandel of Maryland, Howard J. Samuels of New York, and Larry Carr of Alaska in their respective campaigns for governor. He also directed the Muskie prenomination media effort in 1972 until the campaign began to fall apart following the Wisconsin primary, as well as the losing gubernatorial effort of Hargrove ("Skipper") Bowles, Jr., in North Carolina.

Joseph Napolitan is one of the best-known consultants. He has been active in nearly sixty campaigns since 1961, among them Shapp's campaign for governor of Pennsylvania in 1966, Mike Gravel's campaign for the U.S. Senate in 1968, Humphrey's Presidential bid the same year, Fred Pollard's gubernatorial race in Virginia in 1969, and the 1972 Puerto Rican gubernatorial race. Napolitan is also one of the few consultants who advises foreign politicians, among them Pierre Trudeau of Canada in 1968 and Ferdinand Marcos of the Philippines in 1969. He is also the founder of the American Association of Political Consultants, an organization that seeks to establish an ethical code of behavior for the industry.

Three other well-known firms are Garth Associates, Guggenheim Productions, and Bailey, Deardourff & Bowen. David Garth is one of the few consultants who offers his talents to both Republicans and Democrats, but in either case prefers liberals. He handled Lindsay's media campaigns in both 1965 and 1969, as well as his abortive try for the Presidency in 1972. He has also worked for Arlen Specter, Republican candidate for mayor of

Philadelphia in 1968, Governor John Gilligan of Ohio, Richard Ottinger, Adlai E. Stevenson III and New York Congressman Ogden Reid, the last three in 1970.

Charles Guggenheim, who runs his firm from Washington, D.C., built a reputation as a documentary filmmaker before he turned his talents to political consulting. He won an Oscar for his film "Nine from Little Rock" and also directed the film on Robert F. Kennedy for the 1968 Democratic Convention. Like Napolitan and Squier, Guggenheim prefers to work for liberal Democrats such as Shapp in 1966, Robert B. Meyner in 1969, Senators Hart, Moss and Stevenson in 1970, and candidates Metzenbaum and Walinsky the same year. The 1972 McGovern media campaign was directed by Guggenheim who made an effort to portray his client in warm and human terms. McGovern, he realized, does not come across well in mob scenes so he showed him in one-to-one exchanges with different types of voters. "For McGovern," said Guggenheim, "TV's not really an audience of 1,000, but 1,000 audiences of one."

The firm run by Douglas Bailey, John Deardourff and John Bowen caters exclusively to candidates "on the moderate, progressive or liberal end of the Republican spectrum." Among some of its clients have been Senator Richard Schweiker (in 1968), Governors William Cahill of New Jersey (in 1969) and William Milliken of Michigan (in 1970), Congressman Pierre S. DuPont IV (in 1970 and 1972), and Governor Christopher ("Kit") Bond of Missouri, Senators Brooke and Percy, and unsuccessful candidate for the House William Weeks of Massachusetts (all in 1972).

Yet another well-known campaign consultant is Jerry Bruno, who built his reputation as an alert advanceman for Democratic candidates. He worked with John F. Kennedy in 1960 and Robert F. Kennedy in 1968, and other clients have included Senator Proxmire, Nassau County Executive Eugene Nickerson, Sargent Shriver and wealthy New York City Councilman Carter Burden.

F. Clifton White and Stephen Shadegg both run firms that cater exclusively to conservative Republican candidates. White operates out of New York City and Shadegg out of Phoenix, Arizona. White has been active in Republican strategy at the national level since 1948 and was the man chiefly responsible for bringing the 1964 GOP nomination to Barry Goldwater. His most recent major victory was winning one of North Carolina's Senate seats for Jesse Helms. Shadegg, very much a key man in Arizona as noted in Chapter VII, has been the brains behind various campaigns of Senators Goldwater and Fannin of his home state, and John Tower of Texas.

On the West Coast there are two well-known political consulting firms: Whitaker & Baxter and Spencer-Roberts & Associates. Whitaker & Baxter works exclusively for Republicans, among the more recent being Senator Robert P. Griffin of Michigan and Samuel P. King, candidate for governor of Hawaii in 1970. One of its most celebrated efforts of the past was the campaign it conducted on behalf of Senator Everett Dirksen in support of a constitutional amendment which would allow states to apportion certain elective offices on some formula other than population.

Spencer-Roberts is one of the best-known political consulting firms in the country. In any election year it may be involved in 25 to 30 campaigns, most of them in California. Until recently, it worked exclusively with Republicans, but in 1972 welcomed clients from either of the two major parties. Its first Democratic client was Jess Unruh, who hired Spencer-Roberts to run his campaign for mayor of Los Angeles in 1973. In recent years the firm has suffered from an earlier decision to go national: it not only decided to accept Democratic candidates as clients, but actively sought them out in other regions of the country. The policy has not been a success so far, and as a result many good people have left the firm because they disagreed with the course the company was following.

One of the most unusual political consultants is Matt Reese of Washington, D.C., who concentrates solely on creating, from scratch, grass-roots organizations on short notice to get out the vote. He is an unabashed admirer of the old big-city machines as organizations, particularly their ability to create and maintain almost routinely a block-by-block network of organizers. Over the years, as these big-city machines and their organizations began to break down, many candidates turned to the likes of Matt Reese to provide them with the instant machine they needed to get out the votes. His success has been phenomenal: of the 72 contests in which he was involved between 1966 and 1972, he won 58 of them.

In 1967, he was hired by Mayor James H. J. Tate of Philadelphia, whose reelection campaign was imperiled because the city Democratic machine had turned against him. Reese simply substituted his own organization of 10,000 block captains and a battery of telephone operators capable of making 18,000 calls a day. Tate won renomination by a 2 to 1 margin and went on to win the general election.

Reese believes that the mass media have been overemphasized in American politics, and spurns their use in most of his campaigns. Perhaps out of reaction to mass media, he is the inventor of the walking candidate, among them Senator Lawton Chiles of Florida and Governor Daniel Walker of Illinois.

Like food caterers, most full-time political consulting firms, Matt Reese's notwithstanding, will provide a candidate with a complete range of services—from the soup of a press release announcing his availability to the salted nuts of a victory party. Although financing is usually the preserve of either the party organization or the candidate himself, consultants will often advise what money-raising efforts would be most effective, draw up budgets and determine the most productive allocation of funds. Press and public relations, volunteer recruitment, scheduling, research work and speechwriting are all offered by political consultants.

But their three major areas of expertise are polling, computer work and media campaigns.

President Johnson's love of polls has subsequently left the impression with many people that polltaking is limited to determining an individual's personal popularity among the voters. On the contrary, polling is so expensive that few can afford such a luxury. Most polls today are designed to find out, for the purposes of campaign planning, such things as the issues uppermost in the minds of the voters and how deeply they feel about them, and what the voters know about a candidate's position on the issues and whether it adds up to a plus or a minus.

Often the first large expense of a prospective candidate for major office is for a poll to determine how much the voters know about him (called "voter identification"), what they think of him, and whether or not this would be a good time to run. The Sesler case is typical. Early in 1970, Market Opinion Research of Detroit conducted a "Pennsylvania Statewide Study" to determine if William G. Sesler, a relatively unknown state senator from Erie, should run for the U.S. Senate against Minority Leader Hugh Scott. The study concluded in part: "With a large undecided vote of 43 percent the Senate contest at this point appears somewhat open and a large expenditure of money by Sesler to increase his awareness among voters might well decrease Scott's margin significantly." This kind of advice is not cheap. It is supposed to have cost Sesler $17,000. He followed the advice but lost.

No polling, in fact, is bought at discount prices. The basic personal-interview poll, in which between 300 and 1,500 voters (depending on the size of the state) are interviewed face-to-face, would rang frm $5,000 to $20,000. Ordinary telephone polls cost about 50 to 60 percent the price of personal-interview polls, and follow-up calls to the same individuals cost from $750 to $5,000. Congressional and metropolitan personal-interview polls, in which between 200 and 400 voters are queried, cost from $3,000 to $6,000.

Scout studies, which are quick polls on a particular question among a certain group of voters, cost between $250 and $1,500, depending on the type of voter sampled. These prices may vary upward by as much as 15 percent among the better-known firms such as Oliver Quayle & Company of Bronxville, New York; Opinion Research of Princeton, New Jersey; Decision Making Information of Los Angeles; and The Roper Organization of New York City. The most up-to-date poll, it must be remembered, is a minimum of one week old by the time it is published. Telephone polls take three or four weeks to complete, and personal-interview polls five weeks or longer.

Computers, like polls, are also expensive to use. An hour of computer time costs a minimum of $600, and the price can rise sharply depending on the complexity and type of question that needs answering. It would not be unusual for a statewide campaign to spend $200,000 in one year on computer information, including that which is gathered by the polling firms. For this kind of money, a candidate can find out the names and addresses of all his supporters, those who lean his way and those who oppose him. He can be told what the problems are that bother the swing voters and the stand he must take on an issue to please them.

Computers offer other services as well. For instance, a candidate can use a computer to record a variety of telephone messages which are geared to specific voting groups. In the 1972 Florida primary, Humphrey's campaign, which spent more on computers than television, sent out letters that had been programmed by computer to appeal specifically to teachers, pharmacists, "space-oriented counties," Jews, senior citizens and blacks. The Nixon campaign in 1968 spent $250,000 on a computer whose memory bank held Nixon's position on 67 issues. A voter could ask it questions via a tape recorder in local campaign offices, and the answer was spewed out on a piece of paper. The computer was programmed to give slightly different answers to the same question in order to appear individual.

The biggest benefit computers offer, however, is their ability to make profitable the solicitation of the small-sum contributor. Except for fringe candidates, it has never previously paid the two major parties to solicit givers of less than $100 because of the paperwork involved. Now computers can do all the letterwriting, sorting, cataloguing and bookkeeping with such efficiency that many candidates find themselves less and less dependent on Fat Cats for their campaign funds. Ironically, it may be that the technology which made fortunes for many Fat Cat contributors will soon be brought to bear on a wide scale to lessen their influence on political finance matters.

Computers will no doubt increase in popularity in the years ahead, particularly for candidates for federal office, because of the ten cents per voter media limit imposed by the 1971 reforms. No such limit applies to the use of computers. The weakness of computers, of course, lies in their lack of individuality, their propensity for breaking down and their immense cost. But to most the advantages outweigh the disadvantages, which means that computers will doubtless remain for some years to come a major expense item in a candidate's campaign budget.

The media campaign is the basic service provided by political consulting firms. How much they charge for their expertise is a closely guarded secret, but some indication of the amount of money spent on them can be determined from the few facts that are available. The head of a consulting firm will usually charge no less than $500 per day for his own services and $100 to $200 per day for each of his staff assigned to the job. This means that a candidate for the House of Representatives might spend as much as $20,000 on consultant advice alone (not counting the cost of services they provide), that a candidate for the Senate or a governorship might spend as much as $50,000 on fees, and that a candidate for President might spend as much as $200,000.

Some consultants also take a 15 percent commission on the cost of all advertisements placed for the candidate, a standard Madison Avenue practice. Thus it pays for some consultants to buy as much TV and radio time, and newspaper and billboard space, as the campaign budget will allow, since it means more profits for the consultant and his firm. This practice leads to the needless inflating of campaign costs and is one of the primary sources of financial waste in American political campaigns.

In nearly every well-run race, a consultant will begin his work by drawing up a "Campaign Plan," which is usually a thick document, complete with appendices, describing in some detail the overall campaign strategy and rationale; the type and size of campaign organizations that need to be established; research, press and public relations requirements; voter contact schemes such as mailings and phone banks; and the projected campaign budget. Central to the study, of course, is the media campaign. The cost of compiling such a plan often runs as high as $20,000.

These plans are closely guarded and circulate only among the candidate and his inner circle of advisers. The reluctance to give these plans widespread circulation is well-founded, because most of them speak in the frank terms of *realpolitik*. Many of them will stress the need to pit business against labor, town versus county, whites against blacks, Protestants against Catholics, and rich against poor, all in the hopes of forging a simple majority of voters on election day. Prejudices that may help or hinder a candidate are examined in detail, and what emerges for all the money spent is often a document that reflects the truly divisive aspects of American life.

To cite one example: in the 1970 Pennsylvania gubernatorial race, Bailey, Deardourff & Bowen drew up a plan for the Republican candidate, Raymond J. Broderick, and his running mate,

Ralph Scalera, which spoke of the critical swing vote in the following manner:

> Our analysis for preparation of an appropriate formula for allocation of campaign emphasis among the 201 districts has gone beyond a normal ticket-splitter search. The split-ticket voter of the 1960's, which was instrumental in the Kennedy, Scranton, Johnson, Scott, Humphrey (and to some degree Schweiker) victories in Pennsylvania is probably not available in large quantities to Broderick-Scalera in 1970. To the degree that these voters compulsively split their ticket between the top two races, they are likely to vote for Scott and, therefore, for Shapp. This pattern is made all the more likely by the ethnic make-up of large segments of the traditional ticket splitter segment of the voting public (e.g., a set percentage of Negros [sic]; a high percentage of Jewish voters, etc.).
>
> On the other hand, a separate swing vote, in many respects entirely separate from the first, is likely to appear in the Governor's race. Its component parts, loosely described, are as follows:
> —Irish voters responding to Broderick.
> —Italian voters responding to Scalera.
> —Catholic voters responding to both of them.
> —Anti-Jewish voters.
> —Disappointed Casey supporters, including Scranton voters and sportsmen.
> —Urban Catholic, blue collar vote, fed up with reflex liberal theories, stressing law enforcement, etc.
> —Middle income tax payers against the [state] income tax.
> This kind of swing vote should respond to an Irish/Italian urban Catholic ticket with liberal credentials talking the right issues rather than what sounds like an all Jewish ticket which can be painted as "reflex liberal" and supports an income tax.

The phrase "what sounds like an all Jewish ticket" refers to the fact that Milton Shapp is Jewish and that his running mate, Ernest P. Kline, who is Catholic, has a name that sounds Jewish.

The advertising, suggested BD&B, should among other things put "emphasis on Judge Scalera for [the] Italian vote" and identify "both candidates, and particularly Broderick, as Roman Catholic."

First, the opening newspaper ad in September should be basically biographical on both men—emphasizing those things which indicate Catholicism, such as education record and family pictures. Second, use of big family picture in closing ad. Third, heavy use of Catholic diocesan papers for advertising, including treatment of parochial school issue in last week.

As for Shapp, suggested BD&B:

Negative advertising is complicated but even more likely to be productive than positive advertising. We strongly suggest sandwiching such an ad campaign between positive issue thrusts. . . .

Among other thoughts offered by BD&B was that the press should be "spoon-fed."

Bailey, Deardourff & Bowen's suggested timetable for media advertising is of interest because it not only reflects how consultants think but indicates where all the money goes, week by week:

Phase I	Pre-Primary: No media advertising.
Phase II	Post-Primary Blitz (May 20–June 10): Outdoor, radio, TV name identification.
Phase III	June 11–August 1: Low profile; no media advertising.
Phase IV	August 2–September 6:
	Radio: For two weeks, August 24–September 7, name identification, music. ($50,000).
Phase V	September 7–September 27:
	Outdoor: Start of two month showing (September 3–November 3), all metro markets, concentrated paint boards in all urban centers. ($103,000).
	Daily Newspapers: One 1800 line ad, positioned, all dailies, ID—biographical. ($63,000).
	Weekly Newspapers: Ca. September 20, one 1200 line ad, ID—biographical. ($24,000).
	Television: Broderick and Scalera on issues; 10 60-second spots daytime, 10 60-second spots fringe, 10 30-second spots daytime, 10 30-second spots fringe each station. ($214,000).

Phase VI September 28–October 11:
Outdoor: Boards continue.
Daily Newspaper: Five 1000 line ads, positioned, every daily, negative factual advertising on opposition. ($175,000).
Radio: 36 60-second spots per week for 2 weeks, major metro stations, humorous anti-opposition spots. ($68,000).

Phase VII October 12–October 25:
Outdoor: Boards continue.
Transit: 100 showing, two weeks, bus sides and bus rear, 15 metro markets, to start October 19. ($37,100).
Weekly Newspapers: Week of October 19, 1000 line ad, tax issue; family picture ads in Catholic weeklies, weeks of October 12 and 19, on drug and personal safety issues. ($20,000).
Radio: Subdued profile, 18 60-second spots per week for two weeks, major metro stations, music and issues. ($44,000).
Television: Subdued profile, 10 20-second spots fringe, 10 20-second spots prime, each station, three issues (taxes, drugs and one to be chosen). ($158,-600).

Phase VIII October 26–November 3:
Outdoor: Boards continue.
Transit: Showing doubled for last week. ($26,-500).
Weekly Newspapers: Week of October 26, 1500 line ad, family picture, with final message, to include tax copy; final Catholic weekly ad with family picture, with personal message on parochial school aid. ($30,000).
Daily Newspapers: 1500 line ad, positioned, all dailies, on October 28, covering taxes; 2100 line ad, positioned, all dailies; on November 2, family picture with personal message covering tax issue. ($126,-000).
Magazine: Full page, four color regional editions of Time, Newsweek, Look, Life, straightforward general argument on issues, including taxes. ($22,000).
Radio: High profile, 36 30-second spots per week,

all stations, music and taxes, momentum frequency.
($60,000).

Television: High profile, 8 10-second spots prime,
8 10-second spots fringe, 8 10-second spots daytime,
4 20-second spots prime, every station, three issues
(taxes, primarily, drugs, and one to be chosen).
($125,000).

BD&B's view of what it takes to win elections is not unique.
Oliver Quayle & Company, for instance, undertook a study in
1971 for its Republican client, John Heinz, of the 18th Congressional District of Pennsylvania and an heir to the H. J. Heinz
Company fortune, in which it examined what name style Heinz
might use to win the most votes in the upcoming special election.
Quayle found that:

> Using "John Heinz," the Republican's margin is but 2 points
> with 66 percent undecided. The margin increases to 8 points when
> "H. J. (John) Heinz III" is used but here the undecided explodes
> to 70 percent. Finally, however, when we described the Repub-
> lican as "H. John Heinz III," his margin widens dramatically to
> 16 points as he attracts 30 percent of the voters leaving a much
> smaller group (56 percent) undecided. . . .
> The findings of this survey emphatically show that the best
> name to be used is "H. John Heinz III" probably because it re-
> minds voters of the family and company name.

The study goes on to suggest that "the more that John Heinz
can identify with the company and the more the company can be
shown as a good neighbor, the more John Heinz will benefit as a
candidate." Lest the association be lost, all Heinz's bumper
stickers were printed in either pickle green or catsup red.

This attitude extends to spot advertisements. Most consultants
shoot millions of feet of film, all but several hundred of which are
discarded as unrepresentative of the candidate. Charles Guggenheim, for instance, shot 200 hours (which is over eight full days of
time) of film in 1970 showing Senator Philip Hart of Michigan at
work. Only several minutes of this vast footage, however, was
selected for the final 30- and 60-second spot advertisements.
Guggenheim's greatest talent lies in his *cinéma vérité* techniques;

but considering that several minutes of film taken from 200 hours of raw footage cannot possibly show the candidate as he normally is, Guggenheim has been accused, as have other consultants, of using more *cinéma* than *vérité*.

While many voters have expressed their displeasure with consultants selling candidates like soap, more and more candidates as well have also become disillusioned with some of the ideas offered by political consultants. Undoubtedly these experts have increased the efficiency of campaigns, bringing some order to the usual chaos and providing the contemporary tools with which more rational decisions can be made. But when two competing candidates both use the services of experts, these assets, like competing TV advertisements, tend to cancel each other out. The result is that the costs of each campaign rise steeply while at the same time neither side gains any particular advantage.

While many politicians have an extraordinary capacity for self-destruction, even they balk at the price some consultants ask them to pay. Consider the words of Robert MacNeil, author of *The People Machine:*

> It is the ruthless world that the politician invades at election time, perhaps innocently believing he is welcome there. . . . It is essential, if . . . the politician . . . is to reach the mind of anyone in this world, that he make himself competitive, that he sufficiently resemble the other goods sold in this market. . . . [F]or the politician it means the willingness to be sold like Geritol.

Most disturbing of all to thoughtful politicans is that these consultants are speeding up the process of replacing the candidates with the tools used to attract the voters' attention—a situation akin to Mortimer Snerd or Howdy Doody becoming more real than their creators. Writes David Adamany, author of *Financing Politics:*

> While politicians in all ages have employed entertainment as a campaign device, in the 1960's the process has been carried to its logical conclusion—the displacement of some politicians in elective office by the entertainers they formerly used as campaign attractions. Such a practice has its logic for both the public and the celebrities: it eliminates the middleman.

When consultants first appeared on the political scene in quantity in the mid-1960's, their record of success was extraordinary. For a Napolitan or a Spencer-Roberts to lose an election was considered a freak accident. Today, of course, this is no longer true, particularly since many campaigns feature head-to-head competition between consulting firms in which one must lose. Charles Guggenheim, for instance, won 20 of 33 races between 1954 and 1969 for a win average of 61 percent. In 1970 he won four races and lost three for an average of 57 percent. Other consultants have done about the same. In 1970 Joseph Napolitan won three and lost one; Roger Ailes won two and lost two; David Garth won three and lost three; and Harry Treleaven won one and lost four. The 1972 election saw very few net winners—BD&B, Reese, White and perhaps half a dozen other firms. The remainder had either indifferent-to-dismal records, such as Garth, Squier and Spencer-Roberts, or were operating at such a reduced level of effort that no comparison with the past is possible.

In many respects the years 1968 to 1972 were a period of transition for consulting firms. It was a shake-out time for the fly-by-night firms, a period that saw the end of easy victories, a time for wide experimentation in techniques (which has still not ended), and a period in which consultants were first subjected to the glare of public scrutiny. The acid test of survival in those years, according to John Deardourff, "was when you found that your original customers were coming back for seconds." BD&B is one of the few firms today that can make that boast.

The industry, despite Napolitan's efforts, is still plagued by a lack of any ethical standards. Typical of the behavior is the time Spencer-Roberts was paid an estimated $150,000 to soften Ronald Reagan's right-wing image in the 1966 California governor's race only two years after accepting a similarly high fee from Nelson Rockefeller in the California primary to label Reagan an arch-conservative.

Whitaker & Baxter, to cite another case, was once hired to promote a water project submitted for referendum. The voters supported the project over the strong opposition of the utilities—who promptly hired Whitaker & Baxter to handle their campaigns in future public controversies.

Unlike commercial firms, whose advertisements must adhere to some thread of truth, no matter how tenuous, under threat of FTC and FCC harassment, political consultants operate under no such constraints. They promote many advertisements that do not meet the minimum standards of decency and honesty that the politicians for whom they work require others to follow. Bill Roberts of Spencer-Roberts, who is one of the most respected political consultants in the business, expressed the industry's attitude best when he was quoted as saying: "I think I ought to have the right to lie to you if I think it'll help me win. I think you have the responsibility to detect my lie and vote no when you go in the polling booth."

PART THREE

THE
FUTURE

X

Toward a Healthy Money Tree

American campaign financing practices are surrounded by rhetorical smoke. *Time* magazine, among others, calls them a "national disgrace," the *National Observer* a "scandal." The *Washington Post* favors such headlines as "Campaign Cost Rise May Bar All But Wealthy," or "Campaign Cost Deters Able Men," and speaks of recent reform efforts as "the same old flimflam." A regular columnist for *Newsweek* writes about "Elections for Sale," Roscoe Drummond in the *Christian Science Monitor* speaks of the "stench" of campaign costs, political observer Richard Harris refers to the entire subject as "A Fundamental Hoax," and John Gardner of Common Cause refers to money in American politics as "The Dirty Little Secret That Everyone Knows." On the opposite side of the ledger, those in favor of present practices argue with equal vigor that more and tighter laws will lead to a drying up of campaign money at its source, an impoverishment of the entire political process, and ultimately and inevitably to the abridgement of our freedoms of association and speech.

One way to cut through this rhetorical smoke is by examining the myriad myths and truths that appear to cling in unusual numbers to the subject. Only then might we glimpse ways in which we could provide long-lasting health and strength to our political money tree.

Perhaps the premier myth is the belief that we spend too much money on our party and elective politics. In some ways this is so. The amount of money needed to run for any of the top 1,500 elective offices in the United States is invariably quite high. Unless very wealthy, an individual cannot seriously consider running for the offices of President, senator, representative, governor or mayor of a city over 200,000 in population without the help of many financial angels. Usually more money has to be spent to win one of these offices than the job itself pays over the entire term of office. Hundreds of candidates go broke each year seeking these jobs. Many of them have to spend years paying off their indebtedness.

The intangible costs are just as high. They rise beyond the bounds of reason whenever a candidate, no matter how honest or high-minded, is forced to beg or bargain for the necessary funds; whenever he becomes beholden, either directly or indirectly, to his financial backers; and whenever he promotes the special interests of his angels to the detriment of the general public welfare. The cost is also too high whenever it stifles political competition, entrenches the old guard in power, encourages frivolous behavior, hinders any significant change in the status quo, distorts the legislative process, discourages talented men of average means from entering the arena, or promotes a widespread cynicism among the people. Since these conditions exist today, quite clearly some of the costs are too high.

But it can also be argued that we do not spend enough on our elective process. The estimated $175 million spent in 1960 at all levels of American politics represents only 0.0003 percent of that year's Gross National Product, only 75 percent of what we spent to clean and repair our shoes, and only twice the amount spent by the Red Cross. The estimated $35 million spent on the 1964 Presidential race is less than one-tenth what was spent that year on spectator sports; and the total campaign bill of $200 million is only one-fifth the sum we spent that year on movie tickets. The estimated $12.5 million spent in 1968 to advertise Richard Nixon is less than what was spent that year promoting deodorants. The $58.9 million spent on television at all levels (not including production costs) is slightly less than the cost of one Lockheed C5-A military transport plane. The $300 million total campaign spending in 1968 is 25 percent less than what the top two corporate advertisers, General Motors and Procter & Gamble, spent flogging their wares, 16 percent less than what tobacco manufacturers spent advertising their products.

Presumably the purpose of long and expensive campaigns, in

addition to allowing voters an opportunity of choosing their leaders, is to sharpen issues and to rekindle interest in and deepen our understanding of democratic themes and processes. If that is the case then an even stronger argument can be made that, despite the fact that we misdirect much of what we do spend, we are not spending enough. For all the money spent in our political campaigns over the last quarter century, 30 to 45 percent of all eligible voters still refuse to exercise their franchise in Presidential election years. The percentage is even higher in off years. For all the money spent we have still not been able to create an atmosphere in which issues can be debated fully and rationally. Too many candidates for high office, for instance, still find it profitable to hide behind 20-, 30- and 60-second spots where no issues can be discussed in any depth. Nor has all this money even made the arena physically safe for those who wish to journey through it. Those Presidential candidates who have not yet been gunned down, for instance, find it wise to shield themselves from the people with a phalanx of bodyguards. Nor has all this money, judging from our behavior, given us uniformly good legislators and leaders; nor has it increased our collective wisdom and overall political stability.

The question is: if we believe that democracy flourishes half on the free exchange of ideas and half on human effort, how much should we be spending on both in our electoral process as part of our entire effort throughout society to nurture the growth of democracy? Is it $200 million? $300 million? $400 million? Or should we perhaps begin thinking in terms of spending on the order of $3 or $4 billion on our electoral process every four years, and appropriate sums for the off years? Considering what all the millions we have spent in the last quarter century have brought us, the question clearly deserves some deep thought.

The myth of excessive spending is in reality a clouding of the truth that much of the money we spend in politics is wasted and misdirected. Contributions from special interest groups to House and Senate candidates who are running without opposition are clearly a misdirection of campaign funds. Television spots that sell candidates like soap are wasteful and add virtually nothing to the sum of our political knowledge. It is areas such as these where excesses exist, and where reform is necessary, not in the general realm of total money spent.

Many Americans also labor under the false belief that spending is rising at a profligate rate. On the contrary, only recently have certain expenses increased steeply, and they have tended to distort the overall picture. Prices have been driven up, as they have been in other sectors of the economy, by inflation, by a continuously expanding constituency and by the costs of new techniques.

Consider the ravages of inflation alone. A conservative 3 percent compounded yearly inflation rate applied to the estimated $144 million spent on elective and party politics at all levels in 1952 equals $162 million in 1956, $183 million in 1960, $205 million in 1964 and $230 million in 1968. Since less money was actually spent on American politics in 1956, 1960 and 1964 than the above totals, an argument can be made that there was a *decrease* in real spending in those years. Only in 1968 were the actual costs of $300 million greater than the inflation rate of $230 million. Even then, the difference is only 25 percent, which cannot be called a spending spree.

The 1972 total costs of $400 million exceed the compounded inflation rate total for that year ($260 million) by 35 percent; but to put these figures in perspective, it must be recalled that actual inflation between 1968 and 1972 was far in excess of the 3 percent calculation used here. In fact, the true lack of spectacular growth in campaign spending over the years, including 1972, would be further emphasized if other factors besides inflation, such as the needs of servicing larger constituencies and the costs of new techniques, were taken into account.

Another persistent myth in American politics is that "poor but deserving" individuals, as they are usually described, are blocked from higher office because of the heavy costs of American politics. On reflection, it is difficult to recall one single person in the United States who deserves to be in office but was denied it for lack of money. The truth of the matter is that Americans have never wanted such individuals as their leaders. To them, "poor but deserving" is a badge of failure. The men and women we elect to office may well be poor *and* deserving, but invariably they also have other, more important qualities such as leadership ability, a vision of tomorrow, a driving ambition and a knack for success which strikes a responsive chord in the voters. None of our leaders have been held back because of a lack of money or the need to raise it, any more than a poor but deserving entrepreneur with similar qualities has been held back from raising the money needed to start his own business.

A number of politicians complain that lack of money denied them the opportunity of running for higher office. Of the hundreds who use this excuse each year, Stanley Mosk in 1964 (when he failed to win the Democratic nomination for the U.S. Senate in California), Eugene Nickerson in 1970 and Senators Vance Hartke and Edmund Muskie in 1972 come most readily to mind. What these men are saying, in effect, is that their track records will carry them only so far but no farther, that for the moment they do not have what it takes to win higher office. They use the issue of money as an excuse because it salves the ego. Politicians are like everyone else in this respect: they, too, do not like to be known as losers.

None of these individuals during the time they are making excuses recall that money was forthcoming in sufficient quantity during their past campaigns, nor do they cite the fact that their more successful competitors for higher office, for the most part individuals like themselves with no funds of their own, have little or no trouble raising the needed money. For instance, when Eugene Nickerson complained that lack of money prevented him from winning the Democratic nomination for governor of New York in 1970, he failed to mention that Arthur Goldberg, the party's eventual nominee, entered the race with no more funds at his disposal than Nickerson had. If anything, Goldberg had less.

Money in American politics, as in commerce, finance, philanthropy, and other endeavors, is attracted to winners. No one likes to back losers, not even the small contributor. The ability to attract money, therefore, is an indication of how far an individual might go in politics. How far he goes depends in large measure on his financial "slack," that is to say, money that is attracted to him but is not needed for a particular campaign. During the course of raising, say, $50,000 for a congressional campaign, a candidate might find that he can attract another $300,000 or more around the state. This is his slack and is based largely on his ability to win. Its existence also convinces him, and others, that he could run for higher office. If indeed he then runs successfully for higher office, and he still has a promising future, his financial slack will increase not only in the state but around the country. This, in turn, will encourage him to run for even higher office. At any time along the political trail that this slack disappears, it virtually spells the end of any advancement for the candidate. Measuring a politician's slack, therefore, is the most accurate way of gauging his political future.

There is a body of opinion in this country that seriously contends that political office is limited to rich men, but there are too many individuals of ordinary means involved for the statement to be true. A cursory review of the financial status of Presidents, congressmen, senators, governors and various mayors over the past quarter century would reveal that the vast majority of them have not been rich at all. Most of them, in fact, entered the arena relatively impoverished and left it, or will leave it, years later in the same modest financial position.

Consider, for example, Presidential candidates since the end of World War II. Only three—John and Robert Kennedy and Nelson Rockefeller—could be called truly rich, wealthy enough to finance a Presidential campaign out of their own or family's funds without at the same time destroying their fortunes. Several others—Taft, Eisenhower, Stevenson, Johnson, Reagan, Romney and Goldwater —were or are wealthy, but not so rich that they would not have had to depend upon others for financial support. The majority— Truman, Dewey, Stassen, Vandenberg, MacArthur, Richard Russell, Henry Wallace, Thurmond, Kefauver, Eugene McCarthy, Humphrey, Muskie, McGovern, George Wallace and Nixon—were and/or are relatively poor.

The same holds true for other major elective offices. The United States Senate, for instance, is not the "millionaires' club" it is so often termed. Of the current crop of senators, no more than 20 could be called very wealthy. What can be said of nearly all of them, however, is that they are prosperous and successful people, qualities that are admired by the average voter. But this is not the same thing as being rich.

It is true, of course, that rich men have advantages. They can drive up the costs of campaigning, thus making it more difficult for less wealthy opponents to compete. They have access to others with wealth which can heighten their advantage. Their names have visibility and, superficially, they seem not to need the job. Many of them have name identification among the voters—a politician's most treasured asset—and appear to be more trustworthy and to hold higher ideals. They also can afford to maintain large staffs between campaigns. But it can be argued as well that rich men having the advantage is a condition of life in American society which must be overcome by less wealthy individuals in whatever endeavors they pursue if they wish to succeed. Therefore, to assign a special evil to the advantages rich men have in politics is to give them a worth they do not deserve. To be sure, there are even drawbacks to being rich. Wealthy men often give the impression they do not need others to help them, and everyone active in politics wants to feel needed. Rich men also seem to speak for interests rather than the people as a whole. Both tend to drive away support and votes.

Another myth is that the side with the most money usually wins. If it were true, the Republicans would have held national power virtually uninterrupted since the Civil War, which of course they have not. Those who promote this myth do not appreciate the fact that campaign funds are used primarily to buy goods and services that are not volunteered. Historically, the Democrats have been far more adept than the Republicans at corralling volunteer help, mostly through the labor unions. As a result, Democratic party spending totals often appear lower than GOP totals because fewer goods and services have to be bought.

Nor does it follow that the Democrats are the party of the poor and the GOP the party of the rich. This may be true according to broad voting patterns, but it is certainly not true when it comes to where both get their money. Fat Cats are permanent fixtures in both parties, and on occasion those contributing to Democrats outnumber those contributing to Republicans.

Nor is it true that the Democrats are perennially strapped and that the GOP is awash in campaign money. Both parties have their fat and lean years. Periodically they sink into the red out of either design, last-minute zeal or inept financial management. Whatever the case, a downturn in a party's financial fortune is not necessarily an unhealthy development because it encourages the promotion of new ideas and new leaders. Neither major party has a vested right to remain on the scene indefinitely, and if one (or both) fails to have anything relevant to say at least to a near majority of voters, it should fade into history. The wealth or poverty of a party's bank account is thus an indication of the general nationwide support it is receiving at any given moment.

It is also a myth that the process of campaign financing is essentially dirty or immoral; that everyone who gives gets something, thus diminishing the democratic process; that those who give are elitists representing special interests; and that those who receive the contributions and run the political process are greedy and cynical.

Of course, part of the process is unsavory; there are, it is true, those who are rewarded for their gifts; some of the contributors undoubtedly harbor undemocratic attitudes; and there is little question that the arena abounds in crooked and cynical souls.

But in the main it is not true. The manner in which we finance our political campaigns is no more dirty, cynical or immoral than other endeavors in American life. It only appears that way because our politics are subjected to so much public scrutiny. If the same amount of light were cast upon the behind-the-scenes behavior of businessmen, union leaders, lawyers, professional athletes, doctors, philanthropists and clergymen as is currently directed on American campaign financing practices, a similar amount of unsavory information would no doubt be unearthed.

Despite the large number of jobs given to Fat Cat contributors, many contributors give with no specific favors in mind, as noted previously. In fact, the number of Fat Cats who are rewarded with jobs is miniscule compared with the total number of Fat Cats giving. Over 13,000 individuals reported giving $500 or more in 1968 to a Presidential candidate, although the true number is probably closer to 30,000. Assuming half of the 13,000 gave to Nixon, it would mean that 6,500 Fat Cats expected jobs. In fact, Nixon appointed less than 200 Fat Cats to jobs, many of them of the honorary, nonpaying variety. Only 34 Fat Cats were appointed to prestigious jobs such as ambassadorships or departmental and cabinet secretaryships.

The fact that warts exist on the face of our campaign financing practices does not mean that they should be condoned. On the contrary, because politics so influences our lives, and because the financial aspect is so crucial to the manner in which it functions, our political process should be free of blemishes, clean, open, healthy and vital. But then so should business, unions, the legal profession, athletic contests, the medical profession, philanthropy and the church, among other institutions. By spreading the falsehood that the character of American politics, and its financial sector, is fundamentally different from the character of American society at large is doing a gross injustice to the cause of reform, for one will not be changed without the other being changed.

Which brings us to some of the truths of American political finance. One fundamental truth is that the way we raise and spend money in politics is little different from the way we handle money in all our other pursuits. If they happen to be dirty, underhanded and immoral, then our entire financial system is of the same order. In the case of our campaign financing practices, it is clear that only certain rules and practices need to be changed. The warts must be excised, not the head chopped off.

To give an example of the similarities between politicians and others who must raise money: a man of moderate means who wishes to start a business, for instance, would have to go into the economic marketplace for his money; if his pitch is good and the moneymen like his credit, or track record, he would be advanced all or part of the money on which he would pay interest. Likewise, if a man of modest means wants to run for office, he would have to go into the political marketplace for his money; he would make his pitch and if the moneymen like his track record, or credit, he would be given all or part of the needed money. The candidate pays off his debt not in interest as such but by being a good legislator. What constitutes "good," of course, is subject to some interpretation but, except in a relatively few instances, has no unsavory meaning at all.

In either case the man whose past performance is superior to others will be able to raise more money. He is welcome in the market, people will shower him with funds (to one as loans, the other as contributions), and his horizons will expand accordingly. But if the entrepreneur begins to lose money, or fails to pay back his loan, or the politician begins to shirk his duties, then money will be tighter next time around. The respective moneymen will tend to advance it to more reliable people. If future funds are withheld entirely, it may spell the end of the entrepreneur's business and the defeat of the politician.

Another truth is that, in campaigns for the most powerful elective offices, costs are exceedingly high. The amount of money spent per voter over the years to elect a President tells the story. Between 1912 and 1952 the cost per voter, despite expensive years here and there, averaged about 20 cents. By 1960, however, the cost had risen to 29 cents, by 1964 to 35 cents, by 1968 to an estimated 60 cents. Costs for 1972, not all of which are in, indicate the per voter cost will approach one dollar.

The big jump since 1960 can be attributed to new techniques such as television, extensive jet travel, polling, computer time and consultants which have only recently come into widespread use. It is the cost of these items that has tended to distort the overall picture of campaign spending, and it is they, not all campaign costs, which need to be brought under control.

It is also a truth that money has always been easier, cheaper and more rewarding to raise in large sums from the wealthy few than in small sums from the electorate at large. The reasons are obvious: to collect $50,000 from one Fat Cat takes a great deal of planning but costs virtually no money, while to raise an equal amount from a computerized list of ten-dollar contributors costs heavily in labor, printing, stationery and postage expenses. In addition, the interplay between two humans—a fund raiser and large contributor—can be far more rewarding to both a person's ego and career than the rather mechanistic operation of mass solicitation machinery.

It is another truth that the ties between Fat Cats and officeholders work in favor of the status quo. In a sense it is inevitable since both groups have power, both need each other to preserve it, and both have the most to lose. To change anything substantial in the system that brought them to power, they argue, is needlessly risky. In many ways the point is almost too obvious to make, but it must be made again to reemphasize its importance: that no other tie so impedes the orderly process of change in America than that which binds big contributor and officeholder together.

An extension of this truth is that there is but one political party in the United States: the party of property. The Republicans and Democrats are simply feuding wings within that party vying for power. No President since Andrew Jackson has incurred the full hostility of business or, of late, labor. All Republican and Democratic candidates for President since Lincoln have been financed directly or indirectly by business or labor, or both. Every administration since Grant's has been influenced in part by very wealthy businessmen or powerful union officials, most of whom have been contributors or key men with access. The reason third parties have failed to establish themselves is that no substantial group of property owners, business or labor, has seen fit to underwrite one. "Anyone," wrote political observer Frank Kent in 1928, "who now thinks it possible to carry a national election for any candidate for whom the great New York financial forces have a strong distaste is simply deluding himself." It is still true today. When McGovern pleaded his case before Wall Street brokers during the 1972 election campaign, it was not only an acknowledgement of current political realities but an indication that he had read his history.

A further truth is that legislators are reluctant to change the law relating to campaign financing. Thus omissions and inequities are perpetuated for decades. Legislators have an interest in preserving the "fiction" of high costs to discourage competition. Like businessmen, lawmakers see competition as a necessary evil, not a foundation stone of the system. If it became easier to raise money, incumbents would have more competition, and in the eyes of many of them that is not progress. "The thought occurred to me," said Senator Russell Long during hearings in 1966, "that if we passed one of these plans to make it easier to finance senatorial and congressional campaigns, it is not going to be too popular in the [House]. The reason, I think, is that we have a lot of understanding people in the House who have to run every two years and who frequently have no opposition. One reason they do not is because it costs their opponent money to run against them. If they make it very easy to raise this money . . . it might just be that they will be guaranteed a first-class hustling opponent every time they run for office"

Incumbents benefit from any inaction in the present system. To reform campaign financing practices would increase interest in running for office, require more work by the incumbent, and expose everyone to more scrutiny. Legislators have no interest in reducing the number of advantages they have against challengers, such as the franking privilege (at the federal level), paid staff assistance, special research, radio and television facilities, and travel perquisites (at both the federal and state levels). Any increase in publicity, particularly the public accounting of their political finances, they believe, would scare away Fat Cat contributors. In fact, they argue that if it is required that contributors be named at the state level, serious money would dry up completely.

Fat Cats themselves reinforce this reluctance to disclose because most dislike publicity. During the 1972 election, for instance, Senator Muskie set a good example by voluntarily disclosing some of his early contributors. Soon thereafter, a nationally syndicated columnist wrote an article stating that some of his wealthy movie industry contributors had financed sex-oriented films. Thus Muskie, who was presenting himself as a man of integrity and virtue, was cast as a villain accepting money from "celluloid sex interests." His contributors cried foul and threatened to withhold future funds if subsequent disclosure subjected them to such unfavorable publicity.

To others, disclosure is a means of recording the chronology of their cynicism, which they would just as soon not see made public. That is to say, if a Fat Cat early in a campaign contributes a token $100 to a candidate whom the polls show is lagging behind, and then another $3,000 or so a week before the election when the polls show him ahead, it may prove embarrassing. The fact that the candidate knows that the public knows of the Fat Cat's cynicism may force the candidate after he takes office to deny any access to his benefactor, and such a prospect is not very appealing to either individual.

If there is a reluctance to change the law, there is an even stronger impulse to break what laws exist. The history of American campaign financing practices is a history of laws being broken, either willfully or with the tacit consent of those charged with enforcing the laws. In all likelihood this impulse will continue unabated into the foreseeable future, despite the flurry of prosecutions in 1969, 1970, and 1973 and the passage of the 1971 reforms.

Why is this so? In the first place, those intimately involved in campaign financing—principally key men with access and elected officials—know that the entire issue of money in American politics does not cut much ice with voters. Who gives, how much is given, what laws are being evaded, where all the money goes, and who gets what—none of these questions usually influences voting be-havior. Most people vote for more basic reasons: jobs, the cost of living, housing, prospects for the future, and so on. Witness the Watergate Affair: the fact that money was apparently sluiced through Mexican, Luxembourg, and perhaps other laundries for what appear to be less than sterling motives is no more a whistle-blowing event to an average voter than if he learns that his boss is padding his expense account. It was only after evidence had been produced indicating that there had been a cover-up of the facts that the public became aroused. Hardheaded political professionals know that money is only an issue in a campaign when it is spent in what voters consider an offensive and vulgar manner—and that takes some doing in America. As a result, they know they have more latitude in their behavior than what the law on its face allows them to do.

Second, it often pays to break the law, even in the unlikely event one is caught. Even with the passage of the 1971 reforms the risk is still worthwhile to most corporations. If the worst they can expect is a $50,000 fine, as in the case of the two West Coast shipping lines, the possibility of gaining access to, say, $500,000 worth of government contracts, through the influence an office-holder can exert, with a $5,000 or $10,000 corporate contribution is too good to ignore. Many corporations consider contributing illegally as cold-bloodedly as they would any other business invest-ment. The same would apply to labor unions. What are the risks, they ask? Minimal. What are the benefits? In many cases they are potentially enormous.

But businesses and unions do not need the enticement of pos-sible profit to encourage them to break the law. There exists a more basic urge among them to become directly involved despite the law's prohibition against such involvement. Historically, our campaign financing laws have required that a contribution origi-nate as a gift from an individual. Sometimes the gift courses its way through one or more committees and ends up being given in the name of one of them, but it originated as a gift from a single person who is, in theory, accountable for it. But individuals, by their very nature, tend to be unorganized and politically sluggish until the last days of a campaign. Businesses and unions, on the other hand, tend to be well organized and highly motivated groups which are keenly aware of the political imperatives. Often the pressures to satisfy these imperatives are sufficient to convince a business or union to play a more active financial role than the law allows.

Third, and most important of all, nearly all politicians believe (although they will seldom admit it in public) that, when it comes to the moment of truth, *the top elective offices are too important for the laws to be obeyed.* The power and prestige that have accrued over the years to the Presidency and many other offices have been so great that, for those seeking such offices, it has been worth risking everything up to and sometimes beyond the point of public tolerance, which is not necessarily the same thing as the limits of the law.

Consider, for instance, the position of a serious contender for the Presidency. If he has asked his backers to support him to the tune of $30 or $40 million or more, if he has mobilized thousands of supporters across the country on his behalf, if he has wanted the job so badly he can taste it, if he has spent two or three decades working toward the job, and if he believes his ideas and approach to problems are superior to others, is it likely that he or someone else will bring his campaign to a halt because some money was not reported, because he spent seven instead of six cents per voter on television advertising, because a few businesses and unions dipped into general funds for contributions, because he was a month late turning in a report, or because he faces the extremely remote possibility of a $1,000 fine and one year in jail? Of course not, and it is unreasonable to expect that such a situation would ever occur.

Already the Federal Election Campaign Act of 1971 is being nibbled to death by opponents of reform. The Watergate Affair, particularly the Mexican and Luxembourg laundry operations, are indicative of how far some politicians are still willing to go to hide cash sources and expenditures. The assault on the law, however, has been broadly based, coming from individual contributors, business and labor groups, elected officials and government bureaucrats. Only five months after the new law went into effect in April, 1972, the General Accounting Office reported more than 700 violations which deserved either civil or criminal action by the Justice Department.

The law prohibits an individual from contributing funds in the name of others, but before the summer was out one prominent Wall Street fund raiser, investment banker John L. Loeb, had admitted he had broken this section of the law. Other key men also managed to set up political committees which disclaimed any connection to a candidate; the money spent on partisan political advertisements was thus not applied against the candidate's media expenditure limit.

Some businesses, in direct contravention of the law, failed to disclose their corporate ties to fund-raising committees, arguing that no connection existed since the bylaws of the committees did not restrict membership or donors solely to those employed by the companies. Other firms continued to offer corporate jets free to candidates in direct violation of the prohibition against corporations providing "any service" in "connection with any election to any political office."

The law also requires that a donor list his or her occupation and company name, but some 1972 contributors hid behind donations made in the name of their respective wives, whose occupations were listed simply as "housewife." Technically, this is not against the law, but is contrary to the spirit of the law. For example, in the September 10 filings, Maude McKnight was listed as having contributed $50,000 to various Nixon committees; she was also listed as a St. Paul, Minnesota, "housewife." But more to the point, she is the wife of William L. McKnight, retired chairman of the board of the 3M Corporation and a big GOP moneybags. Likewise, Aimee Magnus Flanigan was reported to have contributed $19,720 to various Nixon committees; she was listed further as both a "Ms." and "housewife" from Palm Beach. But in reality she is the wife of New York financier Horace Flanigan and the mother of the White House's "Mr. Fixit," Peter Flanigan.

Bureaucratic rulings further nibbled away at the law. The GAO, for instance, ruled that fund-raising committees need not file until actual expenditures are made. This allows a candidate to hide the names of Fat Cat contributors until he has to spend the money, which is usually toward the end of an election period. The IRS also ruled that contributions to the same candidate in excess of $3,000 are not subject to gift taxes so long as each check does not exceed $3,000 and one third of the officers of the fund-raising committees are different. This is the manner in which Richard

Mellon Scaife avoided paying a gift tax on the million dollars he reportedly contributed to Nixon. The IRS also ruled that a contributor does not have to pay capital gains tax if he gives a block of stock to a candidate who then sells it, keeps the profit as a contribution, and returns the original purchase price to the owner. Stewart Mott, among others, used this device to contribute to McGovern in 1972, and he quotes Judge Learned Hand in justifying such a dodge: "If there are a toll bridge and a free bridge side by side," Hand was supposed to have said, "you don't take the toll bridge."

Politicians, too, have contributed their share to the nibbling. The most widespread means has been simply not to file reports, to file late or to file incorrectly, whichever appears to be most advantageous. In fact, seven weeks after the law went into effect, 91 candidates for the House of Representatives, 30 of whom were winners in their various primaries, failed to file any reports at all. Between April and November, 1972, every single major candidate for the Presidency failed to obey the reporting requirements in one manner or another.

Congressman Samuel L. Devine of Ohio sought to introduce an amendment less than two months after the new law went into effect which would have gutted Section 611 of Title 18 of the U.S. Code, a provision of the law that prohibits any business or union holding a government contract from contributing funds to any candidate for federal office. Congressman Wayne L. Hays, also of Ohio and perhaps Capitol Hill's leading opponent of reform, proposed at the same time that the number of reporting dates be reduced, that the definition of "filing date" be changed to mean the deadline day itself (rather than two days before, as previously ruled, to provide mailing time), and that the fee for campaign financing reports from the Clerk of the House be raised from ten cents to one dollar per page. All these moves were beaten back but not without a spirited fight.

The mischief, however, does not stop here. There are still many loopholes awaiting exploitation if, indeed, they have not been exploited already. For instance, earmarking is still legal and no doubt will be used increasingly in the years ahead by those who are publicity shy. Further, the law does not require the listing of contributors of $100 or less; presumably thousands of dollars will be given secretly by contributors who have the patience to sign enough checks.

A person who wishes to avoid disclosure may also buy a $100 ticket to a dozen or more fund-raising events and never see his name in print, or he might arrange to contribute to a series of political committees which contrive to take in $1,000 or less within a calendar year. The new law does not require that such committees file any disclosure reports.

Perhaps the most common tactic will be for candidates to hold off declaring their candidacy until the very last moment, which will give them some leeway in not reporting. In addition, the requirement to report all contributions of $5,000 or more received within the last five days of a campaign will be widely evaded simply by having the money contributed on the last two days (thus making the 48-hour reporting deadline for such sums meaningless) or by holding off bills until after the election.

Of course, if a person wants to evade the law with a good chance of never being caught, he can still give cash, funnel his money through nominees, give his contribution in kind, or pay bills directly out of his own pocket without the money first passing through the campaign treasury. Laws attempting to curb this type of behavior are some of the most difficult to enforce.

With these thoughts in mind, what possibly can be done to improve our campaign financing practices? The first thing we must do is to ask ourselves what kind of a political system we want. Presumably, it should be dynamic and flexible, open to all comers, competitive, capable of attracting the best minds and candidates, and provide a forum for debate, new ideas and national reconciliation. Campaign financing reforms should be molded around this ideal. We should work toward creating a broad-based financial system in which the bulk of all contributions come in sums of $500 or less. The purpose of changing the rules is not to exclude the occasional rich man who buys his way in or the incompetent who somehow stumbles in, nor to put arbitrary limits on gifts, expenditures and actions, nor to turn over the problem to another government bureaucracy, nor to weave a straitjacket of constrictive laws, but to open up the process, make it more fair to everyone, reduce the influence of and dependence upon Fat Cat contributions, explore ways in which federal and state governments might help, eliminate the clout of special interests, and explore new ways in which money can be raised and more effectively spent.

One scheme that will probably not improve matters is the one-dollar checkoff plan, a provision of the Revenue Act of 1971 which does not go into effect until the 1976 elections. A revival of an old idea previously introduced by Senator Russell Long in 1966, the plan would allow a taxpayer to earmark one dollar of his tax payment to the party of his choice. Once the party picks its Presidential nominee, the money would be turned over to him to spend as he chooses. If the candidate accepted this form of fund raising, he would have to forego other forms of financing. Indeed, if a contributor gave more than one dollar, the excess amount would be deducted from the total the candidate could receive from the checkoff fund. Tax authorities believe that over $20 million will be available for each Presidential candidate in 1976 from this scheme.

At best the plan is of dubious value. In the first place, if private funds are spent independently on behalf of a candidate, can such money be applied against the candidate's total allowable limit without a bitter fight—indeed, chaos—breaking out? Is not such a scheme an abridgement of First Amendment rights for those citizens who wish to express their support for candidates in more substantial ways?

Second, it puts a limit on Presidential campaign spending that is totally arbitrary. The amount to be spent is determined by taxpayer whim rather than the needs of the democratic process. Suppose, for instance, taxpayer interest in the scheme waned and only, say, $10 million was raised for a particular Presidential election. Is that the amount we should be spending to elect a President? Most Americans undoubtedly would say no.

Third, the money is to be contributed to parties prior to nominees being selected; thus a one-dollar donor might find himself having contributed to a party whose nominee he does not support. Furthermore, and fourth, Americans have historically supported *individuals,* not parties, with their money. This plan would enshrine the two big parties as permanent bodies on the political scene. Neither one has a particular right to permanence and should prosper or wither solely on the basis of who and what they offer the public. Were such a scheme in effect in the 1840's, no doubt we should still have a Whig party.

Fifth, such funds will tend to perpetuate the incumbents in power. The 1968 Democratic debt, in retrospect, has had a revitalizing effect on the party and, as such, is a healthy development; had its leaders been guaranteed huge sums every four years, yesterday's losers would probably still be running the party.

Sixth, such a scheme will undoubtedly wreak havoc on state and local parties because, without a fund-raising role, they will be downgraded in importance and deprived of one of their major functions. Party control will become centralized in the candidate with the money; the faithful will feel less needed, and volunteers would probably become difficult if not impossible to find.

Taken as a whole, this checkoff scheme is one of the most regressive moves made by Congress in recent years. In many respects it is a reaction on those congressional leaders who, in their heart of hearts, do not want the system to be more open, do not want competition, new ideas and fresh faces, and do not want healthy and vigorous political parties because they believe this would drain away their power.

Another frequently suggested solution to our campaign financing inequities is federal funding, in which all or part of the money needed in Presidential, House and Senate races would be simply appropriated from general tax revenues. Puerto Rico has had such a subsidy system since 1957. It allows each of the three major political parties (Popular Democratic, Statehood and Independence) to draw against a fixed allotment in off years and a larger fixed allotment in election years. A party is allowed to harbor its financial resources in off years by accumulating unspent balances of up to 50 percent of the yearly allotment. The private solicitation of additional funds is not prohibited.

The trouble with this and other similar schemes is that guaranteed money tends to entrench politicians in power; it strengthens the power of the existing parties and guarantees that they will remain on the scene for years, regardless of how spiritually and politically bankrupt they may become; it hinders the rise of new talent to the top; and it makes life difficult for splinter parties that cannot compete financially. Partial government subsidies used for specific purposes are not necessarily regressive (see below), but tend to be when they are of a general nature.

A variation on this theme involves the use of scrip for redemption by the U.S. Treasury, but the weakness here lies in the idea's ultimate complication: government printing presses would have to work overtime; a huge government distribution, redemption and compliance office would have to be established; and forgery would be a constant headache. Furthermore, the additional paperwork would be unnecessarily burdensome. Already the 1971 law requires a candidate for federal office, if he has a primary fight, to fill out eight very complicated forms a minimum of eight times a year.

From time to time it is suggested by learned observers that money could be raised in sufficient quantities if a scheme were devised which appealed to our gambling instincts. Most often suggested are either "informed citizens" contests (featuring, say, a crossword-type puzzle with historical or political themes) which would cost a contestant a dollar or so to enter, or games of chance such as raffles, which is a device widely used in Norway. The trouble here is that all these schemes are lotteries of one sort or another and are subject not only to the whims of public preference (would, for instance, the betting public ignore it if, say, the Connecticut state lottery were offering better prizes?) but to charges of forgery, theft and payoffs. Furthermore, enough thoughtful Americans recognize that democracy, itself, is such a fragile creation that to refer the political financing aspect of it exclusively to the roll of the dice would be courting national suicide.

Less worthy schemes suggested occasionally for raising money include the Primary Fee Plan, in which all voters in primaries pay one dollar to underwrite campaign costs, and the National Foundation for Political Finance Plan, in which a nonpartisan political self-improvement group composed of well-known individuals from many walks of life would be created to give the subject status. Neither scheme is likely to be beneficial, the former because it would not raise much money (since turnout in primaries tends to be light) and because it smacks of a poll tax, and the latter because the problem would be turned over to a vague, broad-based, nonpartisan group of do-gooders who in all probability would not only be ineffectual but garner very little public support.

Often the suggestion is made that the costs of campaigning could be sharply reduced if we limited the length of our campaigns. The example most widely cited is the British custom of limiting parliamentary electioneering to three weeks. Why this proposal is so seriously suggested is difficult to understand because, besides reflecting a profound ignorance of the differences between American and British political customs, it would be, short of some Draconian law, impossible to enforce.

A cursory glance at both political traditions reveals that a British government can fall at any given moment within a five-year election period. It can happen tomorrow, next week or next year; but whenever it occurs, a new election is immediately scheduled, usually no more than three weeks later. In the United States, on the other hand, Presidential administrations rise and fall every four years on predetermined dates which are known in advance. House, Senate, gubernatorial and mayoralty elections also occur on certain dates in specified years in the future, and every politician and aspiring officeholder is aware of them. Presumably an individual could set his sights on an election in, say, 1988 and campaign ceaselessly for the job from now until the first Tuesday in November of that year. To suggest that he limit his electioneering to the three weeks (or three months, or even three years) previous to election day, particularly if the job in question were the Presidency of the United States, displays considerable lack of understanding of American political traditions.

It has also been suggested that Americans imitate the British habit of limiting their spending in each parliamentary district to the equivalent of £2,000, which would be about $5,000. This suggestion is faulty on three counts: it fails to make exception for the fact that the average member of Parliament represents only about 100,000 people. This compares to the average congressman's district of over 500,000 people. Second, it fails to take into account that, except for a few areas in Scotland and Yorkshire, most British parliamentary districts are tiny in comparison to American congressional districts and thus no travel expenses need to be budgeted. Third, it ignores the fact that huge sums—millions of pounds sterling—are spent by the parties at the national level to sway public opinion. Furthermore, most of this money comes from either corporation or union treasuries and does not have to be reported publicly at all.

We would do well to avoid adopting wholesale the practices common in foreign countries. Most western European political parties are financed either by membership dues or by kickbacks from businesses and unions operative in the election district. Both are unimaginative practices that smack of coercion. Most of these countries additionally have such sketchy reporting laws that they make ours look utopian by comparison. West German law, for example, requires only that contributions over $6,250 be published.

But we could benefit from some practices that are common abroad. Many western European governments underwrite costs like election-day expenses, television time and free mailings. All these ideas could be applied beneficially to the American political process. Eliminating such partisan political expenses as pollwatching, "walking-around money," babysitting fees, and so forth, could reduce the costs of some campaigns by as much as 30 to 40 percent. The costs could be picked up by the local, state or federal governments out of general revenues. Of course, there would be stiff opposition to such a plan from local leaders whose political power derives in part from their financial clout on election day.

The British government also assigns during elections a certain number of free hours of television and radio time to the major political parties. Each can use its time as it sees fit, and the time is paid for by general tax revenues. A similar plan would be beneficial in the United States. The major television and radio networks should give a prescribed number of free hours each election year to Republican and Democratic candidates for President, Vice-President, the House and Senate, governor and mayor of cities over 200,000 in population. Minor political parties should also be given some free time, perhaps basing the amount on the number of signatures each collects. Furthermore, a bonus plan should be available to those who use their time for public debates and presentations of 15 minutes or more.

Whatever amount of time is made available should be on the generous side because it should be the viewing and listening public, not the U.S. government, which ultimately decides how much is enough. The private purchase of time should not be prohibited (to do so might be an abridgement of First Amendment rights), but the free time made available should be close enough to the saturation point so that large amounts of additional purchased time would be deemed unnecessary.

A similar scheme could be worked out for the primaries: each candidate for office would be given a small amount of free television and radio time which he could supplement with his own funds. The purpose in both instances would be to guarantee a basic access to the broadcast media, to help relieve the financial pressures of broadcast campaigning, to promote rational political discussion and to stimulate citizen participation.

The 10-, 20-, 30- and 60-second television spot often comes under fire as a regressive political expenditure since no rational discussion can be conducted in these small amounts of time. Candidates ordinarily use them only for name and party identification. The fact that they exist and, indeed, flourish should not be surprising to any alert observer of the American scene. Much of our society is made up of "60-second spots"—instant cereal, instant news, instant credit, instant gratification, and so on—and the trend is toward more of the same. There is something quite ludicrous in David Brinkley, for instance, in a 60-second spot of commentary, calling for the abolition of the 60-second political broadcast.

The answer is not to ban spots but to encourage the use of larger amounts of time to allow for more rational discussion and debate. Of course, the difficulty here is that, like those who would resist the public financing of election-day expenses, opposition would come from candidates and officeholders who have little to offer in a rational discussion or debate and who would benefit most from being marketed like soap. These people often are the very same ones who control the flow of reform legislation at the local, state and federal levels.

The British government also underwrites one free mailing for every parliamentary candidate. Such an idea should be adopted here in the United States right down to the local political level. Every announced candidate for office should be allowed one free mailing throughout his election district. The threat here is that such a plan would cause a huge paper explosion and encourage participation by self-seeking publicists who simply want to take advantage of the free postage. However, rules limiting an individual's mailing to one sheet of paper, to be sent third class, the addresses broken down by the candidate by Zip Code and street number, all of which would have to be delivered to the post office by a certain date prior to the election, would surely cut down on the postal overload. To weed out the self-seeking publicists minimal rules could also be established similar to laws designed to curb the enthusiasm of frivolous candidates. The Postal Service should not be permitted to thwart such a plan on the excuse that it does not have the manpower or facilities. If it has the capacity to distribute junk mail year round, and is willing to accept such a responsibility for a nominal fee, then it should have the capacity for short-term peak loads and be required to accept such an added responsibility for a similarly nominal fee paid out of general Treasury funds.

Adopting some of the good ideas from other countries, however, will only partially ameliorate the problem. What is needed most of all is sufficient conviction by all Americans to use the many worthy homegrown ideas already available to us.

More than anything, we must work to secure the vital centers of our campaign financing law. The fact that we do not, and probably will never have, a perfect law should not be of particular concern to us, because if we strengthen those vital centers the peripheral inadequacies, loopholes and inconsistencies will fade into insignificance.

Disclosure is the vital core of campaign finance law. The provisions of the 1971 act, as written, are quite comprehensive and only minor loopholes remain. The problem is that in time, as happened with the Corrupt Practices Act, these loopholes will become major avenues to avoid disclosure. Therefore, a constant pressure should be maintained to close off all avenues of escape.

One of the loopholes that could be closed is that which allows, through lack of clarity in the law more than anything else, foreign corporations or nationals to contribute, as happened technically in the Mexican and Luxembourg laundry operations. We have enough money and problems of our own without bringing foreign money into the equation. Another loophole that should be closed is the one that allows committees to forego reporting until money has been spent.

The loophole that permits independent political committees to escape reporting their business affiliations on the thin ice that the organization is open to anyone should also be closed. Perhaps the best way to do this would be to make a ruling requiring the listing of such affiliation if more than half the donors or members came from one business firm or union. Another loophole that should be closed is that which tacitly allows corporations and unions to lend their jet aircraft to candidates. There should be a flat ban accompanied by stiff fines for any candidate for federal office, or federal officeholder, using corporate or union transportation, or any other costly "courtesies."

Another vital area is the one that guarantees, and indeed encourages, dynamic, open and freewheeling elections. In this regard, several sections of the law are in need of revision. One is Section 315 of the Communications Act, known as the "Equal Time Provision," which hinders debate between serious candidates for a particular office because *all* candidates, no matter how frivolous, for the office are required to be given equal air time. If this section were repealed, minor party candidates would not necessarily be denied access to the media. On the contrary, the Federal Communications Commission has encouraged stations to offer free time to minor party candidates as part of their community service function. In fact, in 1972, many minor party candidates received free exposure, but at the same time there were no debates or public discussions between Nixon and McGovern, or even their surrogates.

The one-dollar checkoff scheme should also be abolished, for reasons cited previously, and the money returned to the donors.

A further provision of the law that needs eliminating is that which limits media expenditures to ten cents per voter. Although the law appears to curb profligate television and radio spending, it is in fact an invitation to break the law, despite the cost-of-living escalator clause, because of the competitive nature of American politics. There should be no laws limiting how much can be spent, but only the manner in which money can be raised. Candidates will spend every cent they can get their hands on, and to set a limit, as the old Corrupt Practices Act attempted to do, is to make constructive lawbreakers of every person running for office. Furthermore, no study has ever been made to determine how much a candidate should be spending on the media which at the same time would promote American democratic impulses. Perhaps it should be 50 cents or $3.00 per voter. Finally, such a limit, no matter what it might be, may be an abridgement of First Amendment rights by setting a maximum on the political activity in which a person may engage.

Another vital center is the one that seeks to clamp down on the power and influence of special interests. The most effective way to do this, in addition to complete disclosure, is, as has been noted, to control campaign funds at their source. While it would be distasteful, and probably unconstitutional, to legislate a monetary limit on total contributions, the influence of Fat Cats could be diminished somewhat by requiring that all cumulative gifts over $3,000 be subject to the gift tax, regardless of how many political committees the money passes through.

The ban on contributions from business and union general operating funds should also be rigidly maintained. The problem here, of course, is less with a weakness in the law and more with a weakness of government officials to prosecute violators.

The personal spending limitations in the Federal Election Campaign Act of 1971 placed on candidates for the Presidency and Vice-Presidency ($50,000), the Senate ($35,000) and House ($25,000) on their face appear unconstitutional and should be repealed. If it is legitimate for one person to contribute unlimited sums to another (even if the gift tax applied), why should a candidate not be able to spend as much on himself? Surely this abridges a man's freedom of speech. The sentiment is right: the law seeks to bar rich men from buying office. But have rich men bought their way in? History has told us, in the words of investment banker Fergus Reid, that "the graveyard of American politics is strewn with the bones of rich guys who didn't make it," and that those wealthy individuals who have succeeded in politics through the use of their own money have gone no farther than they deserve. There should be a ceiling on contributions only if large funds pose a direct and substantial danger to our political process which cannot be controlled by alternative measures, and it has never been proved that such a danger exists.

The danger of rich men in politics is not a general one, but is specifically limited to primary elections. There, a rich man whose only qualification for office is his money can do particular damage, because he does not have to compete in the political marketplace for his funds (which in itself is a winnowing process), and he forces the voter to give him attention which he might not otherwise merit. The time spent examining his qualifications, or lack of them, inevitably reduces the amount of time the voter could spend analyzing the assets of more qualified candidates. As a result, a Fat Cat candidate's money can distort the process, as John F. Kennedy's did in the 1960 Presidential primaries and as Richard Ottinger's did in the 1970 New York primary. But in the general election, a rich man's money becomes less important because traditional party sources are tapped for the bulk of the necessary campaign funds.

The problem, therefore, is to balance the influence of wealthy candidates with less wealthy ones in primary elections. One way this can be done is by offering certain free services, such as television and radio time and election-day expenses, to all comers, both rich and poor alike. Another way to equalize the imbalance without abridging individual rights (through arbitrary spending and contribution limits) would be to require an even stricter accounting of funds prior to the primary election day. For instance, the law might be expanded to require disclosure reports on the twenty-fifth and thirty-fifth, in addition to the fifteenth and fifth, days preceding the primary. In our zeal to give every break to a candidate of average financial means—a worthy goal—we do not want to end up taking away rights from others.

Yet another vital center, and perhaps the one best suited to minimize the influence of the rich and the powerful, is that body of law which encourages small, broad-based contributions. The provisions of the Revenue Act of 1971, which allow up to $100 in campaign contributions to be deducted from a joint tax return, appear to be the best means to achieve this goal. Although there are critics who argue that democracy should not be tax deductible, such a scheme has been used successfully in the past to finance many worthy causes. This provision of the law could be improved, however, by periodically increasing the limit to cover the full cost. A tax-deduction limit today of $300 per couple, for instance, would not empty the U.S. Treasury, yet it would free candidates from heavy dependence on Fat Cats and the real or implied debt that comes with their large contributions.

The federal government should also institute a Matching Fund Plan in which every dollar raised from small, broad-based solicitations such as the tax-deduction device would be matched by an additional dollar. Bonus money could also be offered in addition where expenditures are channeled toward activities that promote vigorous debate and discussion. Such a plan would further reduce both the inequities between the wealthy and the not-so-wealthy, and the power and influence of Fat Cat contributors.

The most vital element of all, of course, is American society itself. Nothing in the realm of campaign financing will change substantially unless we change some of our habits and attitudes. Adherence to our campaign financing laws will never improve until we change our attitude toward the enforcement of all our laws. It should not be surprising that our lax attitude toward enforcing many of our laws spills over into the manner in which we enforce our campaign financing laws.

Any attempt to curb the power and privileges of special interests in politics will occur only when we curb such interests throughout society. Until monopolies, polluting industries, price-fixers, closed-shop unions, lobbyists, elitist professions, and the like are brought to heel, it is unreasonable to expect them to be brought under control in our political process.

Likewise, we should require our regulatory agencies to adhere to the spirit of their original charters—to protect the public and its interests rather than those organizations it is supposed to regulate. Until we do that, can we honestly expect the GAO, IRS, FBI, FCC or any other federal agency to pursue violators of campaign financing law with the persistence they should?

It would also help if disclosure requirements throughout society were as strict as our political disclosure requirements. Undoubtedly we would all benefit if Wall Street, the legal and medical profession, lobbyists, labor unions, the churches and large corporations—of the scores of institutions and organizations that come to mind—were required to cast the cleansing light of disclosure upon their many dank financial corners.

The press could help matters by both continuing the zeal with which it examines political finance and applying it with equal vigor to all our social and political institutions. One of the reasons American political practices have not become more corrupted stems from the press's endless investigative work over the years to root out corruption. An across-the-board investigative effort throughout our society would tend to have a similarly cleansing effect, and would undoubtedly lead to a time in which the general public was not only fully informed but fully receptive to the changes that would have to be made.

The ultimate salvation of our campaign financing practices—indeed our entire society and political system as well—rests with the individual voter and his willingness (a) to inform himself and (b) to act: if he has access to the facts through disclosure, if he is exposed to the widest possible competition of ideas through a series of open debates and discussions, if he is given an opportunity to play a significant part in the political process as either a candidate or a contributor, and if the government underwrites these efforts with laws and regulations designed to expand the democratic process, then he will have the tools to do both.

As a result, our society and political system in general, and our campaign financing practices in particular, would be much healthier and in far better hands.

Sources of Information

The amount of printed material on American campaign financing practices is quite large. For reasons of space, only the more important source documents are listed below:

Adamany, David. *Financing Politics,* University of Wisconsin Press, Madison, 1969.

Alexander, Herbert E. *Financing the 1964 Election,* Citizens' Research Foundation, Princeton, New Jersey, 1966.

————. *Financing the 1968 Election,* D. C. Heath & Company, Lexington, Massachusetts, 1971.

————. *Money in Politics,* Public Affairs Press, Washington, D.C., 1972.

————, and Denny, Laura L. *Regulation of Political Finance,* Berkeley Institute of Governmental Studies, Berkeley, California, and Citizens' Research Foundation, Princeton, New Jersey, 1966.

————, ed. *Studies in Money in Politics,* Citizens' Research Foundation, Princeton, New Jersey, 1965. The book contains seven essays, one of which is entitled "Financing the 1960 Election," written by Alexander.

Belmont, Perry. *Return to Secret Party Funds,* Putnam's, New York, 1927.

Elliott, Gerald R. *Financing Congressional Campaigns.* Unpublished master's thesis, University of Minnesota, March 1968.

Heard, Alexander. *The Costs of Democracy,* University of North Carolina Press, Chapel Hill, 1960.

Overacker, Louise. *Money in Elections,* Macmillan, New York, 1932.

————. *Presidential Campaign Funds,* Boston University Press, Boston, 1946.

Pollock, James K., Jr. *Party Campaign Funds,* Knopf, New York, 1926.

Shannon, Jasper B. *Money and Politics,* Random House, New York, 1959.

Shuler, Marjorie. *Political Party Finances; Their Origin and Uses,* Stebbins & Company, Brooklyn, New York, 1922.

Twentieth Century Fund. *Electing Congress; The Financial Dilemma,* Report of the Twentieth Century Fund Task Force on Financing Congressional Campaigns, New York, 1970.

————. *Voters' Time,* Report of the Twentieth Century Fund Commission on Campaign Costs in the Electronic Era, New York, 1969.

Other books that touch on the subject include the following:

Baus, Herbert M., and Ross, William B. *Politics Battle Plan,* Macmillan, New York, 1968.

Bowden, Robert Douglas. *Boies Penrose; Symbol of an Era,* Greenberg Press, New York, 1937.

Cannon, Lou. *Ronnie & Jessie,* Doubleday, Garden City, Long Island, 1969.

Chester, Lewis; Hodgson, Godfrey; and Page, Bruce. *An American Melodrama,* Viking, New York, 1969.

Connable, Alfred, and Silberfarb, Edward. *Tigers of Tammany,* Holt, Rinehart & Winston, New York, 1967.

Croly, Herbert. *Marcus Alonzo Hanna,* Macmillan, New York, 1912.

Cunningham, Noble E., Jr. *The Making of the American Party System, 1789–1809,* Prentice-Hall, New York, 1965.

Curley, James M. *I'd Do It Again,* Prentice-Hall, New York, 1957.

Davenport, Walter. *Power and Glory; The Life of Boies Penrose,* Putnam's, New York, 1931.

Farley, James A. *Behind the Ballots; The Personal History of a Politician,* Harcourt-Brace, New York, 1938.

Flynn, Edward J. *You're the Boss,* Viking, New York, 1947.

Goodman, Walter. *A Percentage of the Take,* Farrar, Straus & Giroux, New York, 1971.

Gosnell, Harold F. *Boss Platt and His New York Machine,* University of Chicago Press, Chicago, 1933.

————. *Machine Politics, Chicago Model,* University of Chicago Press, Chicago, 1937.

Herzog, Arthur. *McCarthy for President,* Viking, New York, 1969.

Kent, Frank R. *The Great Game of Politics,* Doubleday, Garden City, Long Island, reprint, 1959.

————. *Political Behavior: Heretofore Unwritten Laws, Customs and Principles of Politics as Practiced in the United States,* Morrow, New York, 1928.

Key, V. O., Jr. *Southern Politics,* Vintage, New York, 1949.

Levin, Murray B. *Kennedy Campaigning,* Beacon Press, Boston, 1966.

Lockard, Duane. *New England State Politics,* Princeton University Press, Princeton, New Jersey, 1959.

————. *The Politics of State and Local Government,* Macmillan, New York, 1959.

Lundberg, Ferdinand. *The Rich and the Super-Rich,* Lyle Stuart, New York, 1968.

Luthin, Reinhard H. *The First Lincoln Campaign,* Harvard University Press, Cambridge, Massachusetts, 1944.

MacNeil, Robert. *The People Machine,* Harper & Row, New York, 1968.

McKean, Dayton. *The Boss,* Houghton Mifflin, New York, 1940.

Michelson, Charles. *The Ghost Talks,* Putnam's, New York, 1944.

Mintz, Morton, and Cohen, Jerry S. *America, Inc.,* Dial Press, New York, 1971.

Napolitan, Joseph. *The Election Game and How to Win It,* Doubleday, Garden City, Long Island, 1972.

Pearson, Drew, and Anderson, Jack. *The Case Against Congress,* Simon & Schuster, New York, 1968.

Peirce, Neil R. *The Megastates of America,* Norton, New York, 1972.

Pratt, Harry E. *The Personal Finances of Abraham Lincoln,* Abraham Lincoln Association, Springfield, Illinois, 1943.

Redding, Jack. *Inside the Democratic Party,* Bobbs-Merrill, New York, 1958.

Riordon, William L. *Plunkitt of Tammany Hall,* Knopf, New York, 1948.

Roseboom, Eugene H. *A History of Presidential Elections,* 3d ed., Macmillan, 1970.

Royko, Mike. *Boss: Richard J. Daley of Chicago,* Dutton, New York, 1971.

Russell, Francis. *The Shadow of Blooming Grove,* McGraw-Hill, New York, 1968.

Thomas, Lately (*pseud.* Steele, Robert V.). *A Debonair Scoundrel,* Holt, Rinehart & Winston, New York, 1962.

————. *Sam Ward: King of the Lobby,* Houghton Mifflin, New York, 1965.

Tolchin, Martin and Susan. *To the Victor . . .,* Random House, New York, 1971.

Wendt, Lloyd, and Kogan, Herman. *Lords of the Levee,* Bobbs-Merrill, New York, 1943.

Whalen, Richard J. *The Founding Father,* New American Library, New York, 1964.

White, Theodore H. *The Making of the President 1960,* Atheneum, New York, 1961.

————. *The Making of the President 1964,* Atheneum, New York, 1965.

————. *The Making of the President 1968,* Atheneum, New York, 1969.

In addition to the above books there are several hundred government publications (mostly House and Senate hearings), law journal articles and major magazine pieces devoted to the subject dating back to 1913. The Library of Congress has catalogued this material in a special bibliography. Again, for reasons of space, it is not listed here. The Citizens' Research Foundation of Princeton, New Jersey, run by Dr. Herbert E. Alexander, is also a major source of information from 1958 to the present. It is the foremost organization of its kind in the United States that concentrates its energies on studying the role money plays in our politics. *Congressional Quarterly* is also a good source as is the newer *National Journal*.

In the newspaper world, the *Washington Post, Washington Star-News* and *Wall Street Journal* consistently report developments in the world of campaign financing. Especially knowledgeable are reporters Morton Mintz, Nick Kotz and David Broder of the *Post*, Robert Walters of the *Star-News* and Jerry Landauer of the *Journal*. Walter Pincus, formerly of the old *Washington Star* and the *Washington Post* and now with the *New Republic,* is also one of the most knowledgeable individuals in the field.

Another major source of information for this book was individuals intimately involved in the political process who, if they talked at all, knew more about specific campaigns and incidents than the newspaper reporters, whose expertise tended to be more general and wide-ranging.

Index

Abplanalp, Robert H., 99, 102, 144
Acheson, Dean, 18
Action Committee for Rural Electrification, 184, 223
Adams, Henry, 37, 44
Adams, John, 26
Adams, John Quincy, 27, 28
Adams, Samuel Hopkins, 58
Adams, Sherman, 137
Addonizio, Hugh, 242
Aerojet-General Corporation, 222
Aetna Insurance Company, 53
Agnew, Spiro T., 97, 103, 195, 203, 228
Agricultural Cooperative Trust, 183, 219
Agriculture and Dairy Education Political Trust, 114, 219, 221
Ahmanson, Howard F., 98, 135, 175, 186, 209, 230
Aiken, George, 166
Ailes, Roger E., 255, 268
Albano, Vincent, 151–52
Alexander, Herbert, 162–63
Alger family, 185
Allen, Herbert A., 104
Altschul, Frank, 70, 86, 104
American Conservative Union, 107
American Dental Association, 120
American Labor party, 70
American Liberty League, 69
American Medical Political Action Committee, 88, 106, 119, 211–12
American Motors Corporation, 113
American Nursing Home Education and Political Action Committee, 223
American Petroleum Institute, 215

American President Lines, 230–31
American Trucking Association, 88
Americans for Constitutional Action, 107, 240
Americans for Democratic Action, 88, 89, 240
Ames, A. A., 40
Anderson, Cyrus T., 140
Anderson, Robert B., 85
Anderson, Robert O., 102, 148, 192
Anderson, William R., 120
Andreas, Dwayne, 104–5, 111–12, 114, 179
Anheuser-Busch, Inc., 145
Annenberg, Walter, 85, 103, 144, 147
Annunzio, Frank, 120
Anti-Saloon League, 61
Archbold, John D., 55
Arkus-Duntov, Yura, 92
Armco Steel Corporation, 149
Arvey, Jake, 168–69
Ashbrook, John, 239
Ashley, Thomas L., 200–1
Astor, John Jacob, II, 35, 39
Astor, Vincent, 68
Astor, Mrs. Vincent, 19, 103
Auchincloss, Hugh D., 70
Autry, Gene, 86, 103
Avco Corporation, 88
Avnet, Lester, 104, 135

Bache, Jules S., 52
Bagley family, 185
Bailey, Deardourff & Bowen, 257, 262–266, 268
Bailey, John, 17
Baker, George F., 70, 72